THE CHRISTMAS BOOK

The Ultimate Guide to Your
Favorite Holiday

ED DALY

ALSO BY ED DALY

Cereal: Snap, Crackle, Pop Culture
Heroes and Jerks: The Best and Worst Who Ever Lived

All profits from this book will be donated to The Human Fund.

ARTWORK by Roberto Bucci

EDITED by Meghan Stoll

FORMATTED by Muhammad Abdul Rehman

Copyright © 2021 by Ed Daly

All rights reserved. No part of this publication may be reproduced, distributed or transmitted in any form or by any means, including photocopying, recording, or other electronic or mechanical methods, without the prior written permission of the author.

For my mom and dad, who showed me the love of Christmas.
The Millennium Falcon Playset never came. But that's okay.

"It's Christmas Eve! It's... it's the one night of the year when we all act a little nicer, we smile a little easier, we... we cheer a little more. For a couple of hours out of the whole year, we are the people that we always hoped we would be"

-Frank Cross

TABLE OF CONTENTS

INTRODUCTION 1
ORIGINS OF CHRISTMAS 3
WHY WE PUT TREES IN OUR HOMES (AND OTHER ODD CUSTOMS) 17
SANTA CLAUS 27
CHRISTMAS AROUND THE WORLD 35
CHRISTMAS FOOD 65
CHRISTMAS TOYS 75
CHRISTMAS FASHION 87
CHRISTMAS BOOKS 91
CHRISTMAS MUSIC 105
CHRISTMAS MOVIES 169
CHRISTMAS ADJACENT MOVIES 201
CHRISTMAS ON TV 217
DICKENS 283
OTHER STUFF THAT HAPPENED ON CHRISTMAS 301
FINAL THOUGHTS 309
ACKNOWLEDGEMENTS 311
RANDOM TV NOTES 313
BIBLIOGRAPHY 321
INDEX 351

INTRODUCTION

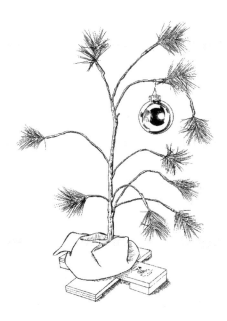

Those of us who celebrate Christmas tend to be rooted in our traditions. They may involve visiting family, decorating a tree, enjoying a special meal, watching a favorite show or movie, singing along to beloved songs, going to midnight mass, baking cookies, and so many more possibilities.

Most likely, the way you celebrate Christmas today is a slightly tweaked variation of how you did it growing up. Which is a slightly tweaked variation of how the previous generation observed the holiday, and so on. Christmas is all about nostalgia. There's comfort and beauty in tradition—as long as it doesn't involve singing along to "Grandma Got Run Over by a Reindeer," that is.

This book provides background to traditions around the world, across cultures, and over time. You may find it gives an interesting context to your own celebrations. Why do we do weird things like put trees inside our homes for a month? Why do we kiss under the mistletoe? We are about to dive into Christmas, starting with its origins, moving on to food, top Christmas toy crazes, fashion, books, songs, movies, shows, and famous December 25 anniversaries.

More than anything, the goal of this book is to celebrate the joy of the season. For as long as I can remember (which is probably around the first time I saw Big Bird try to prove Santa's existence to Oscar the Grouch), Christmas has brought me immense happiness. And so writing about it seemed like the perfect endeavor. I hope this book brings you joy and gets you geared up for this and every December 25!

Here it is—the guidebook to all things Christmas.

ORIGINS OF CHRISTMAS

Everyone knows Christmas is the day commemorating the birth of Jesus, the central figure of Christianity. But most things associated with the holiday (trees, lights, stockings, ornaments, gift giving, caroling, Santa Claus) were never mentioned in the Bible. Did you know that the origins of Christmas actually took root many years before Jesus was born? Keep in mind, these are events from thousands of years ago. People didn't write things down. There weren't local newspapers documenting specific events. Most of what we know is due to storytelling and folklore. But we do have a good idea that Christmas' earliest origins came from Northern Europe.

YULE

Centuries before Jesus, Northern Europeans held massive celebrations at the end of December. The party was filled with family, feasting, Yule logs, decorated evergreen trees, an unseeable being who judged whether people were naughty or nice, offerings left for a well-traveled magical animal to help him on his journey, and a white-bearded man bouncing from house to house. Sound familiar?

On the winter solstice, people across Scandinavia, Northern Germany, and Poland celebrated Jól— as it's known in English, Yule. The word's loose translation is "parties." It wasn't one single event, but rather a series of celebrations that kicked off right around the shortest day of the year. Why celebrate during this dark time of year? Let's take a look at life back then.

Most people who prayed to the Norse gods were farmers. Their main activity was animal breeding ("husbandry" to nomenclature snobs). Cows, importantly, provided milk, cheese, butter, and skyr (yogurt-like stuff). But in the winter, it got brutally cold, crops stopped growing for a few months, and the cows stopped producing milk. So, if you wanted to keep them alive, you needed to shelter and feed them, just like members of your family.

On top of the farming issue, these people were facing shorter daylight hours and a lot more time indoors. Homes were made of wood and had a fire pit in the middle. There was no insulation. No furnaces. No electricity. They had fire and not much else. There were no chimneys, so it was constantly smoky indoors.

So here they were, on the bleakest days of the year—entire families huddled around fires in smoke-filled rooms with little light, smelly farm animals for housemates, and the grim realization that they had better ration their food for the upcoming months. There was nowhere to go but up.

So why not throw a party? Or, better yet, a couple weeks' worth of parties?

There are three theories about the focus of their Jól celebration:

1. It was the celebration of the return of sunlight.
2. It was a midwinter party for the dead.
3. It was a fertility feast, where people sacrificed animals to the gods in the hopes that the upcoming harvest year would be productive.

There's a good chance that all three were true. And so, the people planned their year-end revelry accordingly. By late December, most of the beer and wine they had been fermenting was ready for consumption. Since there was only so much hay and indoor space each winter, lots of animals were slaughtered. A drunken meat festival was had by all. From there, some familiar traditions emerged.

Fathers and sons would bring home large logs (essentially whole trees) to burn during Yule. They burned for about ten to twelve days—the period between the solstice and the end of the year. The Norse people believed burning it would encourage the sun to return and each spark that crackled from the fire represented a new calf or pig that would soon be born. As a way to prompt tree spirits to come back with a bountiful supply next year, the Vikings would also decorate evergreen trees with food and carvings.

The most revered (and feared) god in Norse mythology was Odin. Odin played a pivotal role in just about everything that went on in this region of the world. The god meant many things to the people—from wisdom and sorcery to war, frenzy, and death. Germans believed that Odin made nocturnal flights and judged whether they'd find prosperity or death in the new year. So they stayed inside. Viking children, on the other hand, left their shoes out by the hearth on solstice eve with sugar and hay for Odin's eight-legged horse, Sleipnir.

To spread good cheer, children went from house to house giving gifts of apples and oranges spiked with cloves in evergreen-lined baskets. Many believed in the Norse tradition that Old Man Winter, a wanderer with a long white beard, would come visiting as well and join in the fun.

SATURNALIA

Winter solstice celebrations were not confined to Northern Europe. Ancient Rome had Saturnalia, a seven-day celebration that coincided with the winter sowing season (in other words, they got amped to plant seeds in the winter). Everything was in honor of Saturn, the god of agriculture. Saturnalia gave the world decorated streets and homes, wild parties with coworkers and friends, charity towards the less fortunate, and gift giving on December 24.

Romans kicked off Saturnalia week on December 17 by untying the wraps around the ivory statue of Saturn to represent his freedom to shake a tail feather. Unlike Yule, which was joyful but still slightly measured, Saturnalia parties were bonkers. It was like Mardi Gras, *The Great Gatsby*, and the house party from *Sixteen Candles* wrapped into one. And it lasted a week. Businesses and schools were closed and people ate and drank like they were headed to the electric chair. Gambling and "singing naked" were common occurrences.

The streets were joyfully festooned, houses were decked out in greenery, and people greeted each other by saying, "Io Saturnalia!" If you're not sure how to pronounce that, just think of Rocky Balboa calling, "YO SATURNALIA!" As the writer Seneca the Younger wrote, "It is now the month of December, when the greatest part of the city is in a bustle. Loose reins are given to public dissipation; everywhere you may hear the sound of great preparations…"

Raucous house parties could be found all over. On the heels of his domination of Egypt and Spain, Caesar and two thousand of his soldiers showed up at Cicero's home in 45 BC for his famous Saturnalia party. One observer noted that Caesar "ate and drank without scruple."

Even the less fortunate got their moment during Saturnalia. Slaves and their owners switched positions. Well, sort of. In rich Roman households, a slave was chosen to be the *Saturnalicius princeps* (leader of Saturnalia). This slave was tasked with organizing the celebrations and pranks that would be played in the home. They also were given the responsibility of making offerings to Penates, the god of household supplies (which is both sweet and kinda sad at the same time). Owners even had to serve their slaves dinner during Saturnalia. Mind you, the owners just had to bring the dishes up from the kitchen. The slaves still had to prepare the meal and clean up afterward.

The final days of Saturnalia were known as Sigillaria. People would make candles and wax figures and give them as gifts to each other.

JUVENALIA

Some suggest Juvenalia was also a precursor to Christmas. After all, upper-class members of Roman society celebrated it right after Saturnalia on December 25. It was said to be both a feast honoring the children of Rome and also the birthday of Mithra, the god of the rising sun.

But, upon closer examination, Juvenalia was just Nero memorializing his first shave. Seriously. The unhinged nephew of Caligula wanted to party his way into manhood, so he threw this crazy celebration where he forced members of the upper class to do humiliating acts in front of him. If they didn't follow through, he probably had them killed, as he did so many Romans under his reign.

So it's probably best to just say Yule and Saturnalia are the best starting points to Christmas as we know it.

JESUS

If you forget about all the peripheral stuff like trees, gift giving, and decorations, the actual reason Christmas is a holiday is to commemorate the birth of Jesus of Nazareth. The word itself means "mass on Christ's day." The title "Christ" comes from the Greek word *Christos*, which originally comes from Hebrew, meaning "Messiah." Messiah, in Judaism, is the name of the promised king meant to deliver the Jewish nation as prophesied in the Hebrew Bible. So, Jesus became known as Jesus Christ. And his birthday is a monumental event to a whole lot of people.

A couple thousand years ago, according to the Bible, an angel named Gabriel appeared in front of a young Jewish woman named Mary and told her that she was going to give birth to the son of God. (No pressure!) Presumably, Mary—possibly as young as twelve—shared the news with her husband-to-be, Joseph. Normally, when your virgin fiancé breaks the news that she's pregnant with a miraculously conceived baby, the wedding is off. But Joseph stayed with Mary and the two made their way from Nazareth to Bethlehem to register for a census mandated by Roman emperor Caesar Augustus.

When they got to Bethlehem, there was nowhere for Joseph and his pregnant fiancé to stay. So, the couple found a stable for animals and crashed there. That is where Mary gave birth to Jesus. The couple then took some hay and created a makeshift crib out of a manger (a feeding trough).

That night, another angel appeared to shepherds tending to their animals and broke the good news to them. The son of God was lying in a manger on the other side of town. The shepherds rushed to the stable to see the baby and quickly spread the word of the newborn king.

Then a star appeared to three wise men who were much farther away ("in the East"). This star signaled to them that a new king had been born, so they made their way towards him. The journey took about twelve days and led them to Mary, Joseph, and baby Jesus. They knelt before the son of God and gave him gifts.

The gifts from the Wise Men (also called the Magi or the Three Kings) were all pretty crazy in their own way. Gold is a bit much for a baby, wouldn't you say? Granted, the baby was the son of God, so Melchior (the sixty-year-old king of Arabia) probably wanted to make a pretty good show of it. Balthasar (the forty-year-old king of Ethiopia or Saba) was probably proud of his "land of spices," as he gave frankincense, an expensive fragrance made from trees. The twenty-year-old Gaspar (king of Tarsus, the land of merchants) gave Jesus myrrh. Myrrh is an expensive fragrance that is made from rare thorn bushes in Arabia and used as an antiseptic anointing oil and embalming fluid. Nothing like celebrating new life with a liquid that helps bodies from rapidly decomposing!

Outside of the significance of Jesus' birth, there aren't a whole lot of specifics about the setting of the Nativity that we actually *know*. The Bible documents key moments in Jesus' life, but no real details were given about the exact month or even year he was born. The New Testament wasn't written until around AD 70. Jesus was killed in his early thirties. As previously mentioned, learning ancient history means being flexible with the numbers. Most of what we know is from word of mouth passed down over generations. The birth of Christ is no different.

Even if the birth-in-a-manger account is to be accepted exactly as it was written, December 25 is an extremely unlikely date for when the Virgin Mary delivered the son of God. Shepherds wouldn't be out tending to their flocks in the middle of winter. It's doubtful a census would be taken during that time of year either. Others fixate on the "Star of Bethlehem." Some believe that the light came from the alignment of Saturn and Jupiter, which points to October a few years earlier than AD 0. Or maybe it was a comet that passed through in 5 BC, as an astronomer in the 1990s suggested. And yet other religious scholars do calculations based on John the Baptist's interaction with an angel which point to a September birthdate.

All this to say, it is far more likely that, hundreds of years after Jesus' birth, the December 25 date was *chosen*—thereby adding more significance to what were already festive year-end celebrations for Yule and Saturnalia. In any case, in AD 336, Pope Julius I made December

25 the official holiday for the Church. Over time, the lines between the various holidays were blurred and Christmas got the top billing.

By AD 432, Christmas had reached Egypt. As Christians spread their religion throughout Europe in the ensuing centuries, Christmas became more and more widely recognized. By the end of the sixth century, England was celebrating it. Haakon the Good, the tenth-century king of Norway, incorporated Christianity into Yule celebrations. He was raised a Christian in England and was looking for a way to move his people away from what he believed to be heathen behavior. Yule was the vehicle.

Over time, the pagan traditions were either marginalized or just absorbed altogether. By the Middle Ages, Christianity was the dominant religion in Europe. Naturally, as the holiday spread into new places, Christmas evolved.

THE REAL-LIFE GRINCH WHO STOLE CHRISTMAS

Christmas was humming along until the seventeenth century, when a miserable wannabe dictator named Oliver Cromwell decided to cancel it in England. Cromwell's rise was a direct result of years of misrule by the monarchy. Charles I was the king who finally stepped on the landmine that blew it all up.

With his menacing "divine right of kings" nonsense, Charles was increasingly at odds with his subjects. In short, he told everyone they needed to follow the official Anglican religious views. This didn't go over well with the Puritans in England, the Catholics in Ireland, or the Presbyterians in Scotland. When Scotland attacked, Charles expected Parliament to fall in line with his views on raising taxes and fighting new wars. Instead, they rebuked him. When he sent armed forces to arrest dissenting members of Parliament, a civil war broke out.

Eventually, the Roundheads (Parliamentarians) defeated the Cavaliers (monarchy loyalists). But, before anyone gets a sense of satisfaction knowing an oppressive monarchy was overthrown, it should be noted that the leader of the Roundheads (a nickname derived from their Puritan-style short haircuts) was an oppressive ghoul himself—Oliver Cromwell.

Cromwell was an awful leader. As soon as he defeated and executed Charles I, he turned his attention to Ireland, where he didn't just want to defeat insurrection but also commit genocide against Catholics. Instead of the divine right of kings, he believed in the divine right of Cromwell. And that's where Christmas came into play.

Cromwell and his fellow Puritans hated Christmas. They thought the singing and merrymaking throughout the Christmas season were decadent and sinful. There were no mentions in the Bible about celebrating the Nativity, so why should it be a holiday? Christmas was just a wasteful distraction from the true meaning of their faith. And so, in 1644, an Act of Parliament banned all celebration of the holiday. Oliver Cromwell cancelled Christmas.

The anti-Christmas rules lasted until Cromwell died in 1658. The "Lord Protector's" disastrous leadership was so bad that Parliament eventually asked Charles I's son, Charles II, to restore the monarchy in England. ("Sorry we beheaded your dad but would you mind taking his old job?") The new king did quickly restore the holiday and people were heard loudly caroling again soon thereafter. Across the pond, however, the anti-Christmas movement had some legs.

SADSACHUSETTS

Americans today learn that Pilgrims made their arduous journey to Plymouth Rock in 1620 to escape religious persecution. What we hear less about is how much of a total drag they were.

The Puritan separatists had a Cromwell-esque distaste for Christmas, as evidenced by their sanctimonious adage, "They for whom all days are holy can have no holiday." Any new settlers who tried to revive the festive holiday were immediately stamped out. Massachusetts Bay governor William Bradford scolded them: "My conscience cannot let you play while everybody else is out working." Thanks for the laughs, Bill.

In 1659, the Massachusetts Bay Colony officially banned it altogether. If anyone was caught celebrating Christmas, they would be fined five shillings. When the British royal governor tried to host a Christmas Day service at the Boston Town House, he feared for his life from angry Puritans and required security detail from some redcoats.

Other European settlers in different parts of the country embraced the holiday. In New York (or New Amsterdam), Dutch traditions such as leaving out shoes or hanging stockings for Sinterklaas became more commonplace. Famous wild man Ben Franklin, as you might expect, was all about the Yuletide revelry. "O blessed Season! Lov'd by Saints and Sinners / For long Devotions, or for longer Dinners," he wrote in his 1739 *Poor Richard's Almanac*.

The dull Massachusetts people held firm for more than a century, though. Despite the formation of an entirely new country with new shared cultures and traditions, the Bay State refused to budge. Even as late as 1850, government buildings and schools were still open on Christmas Day. It wasn't until Civil War times that things started to change. In 1856, Henry Wadsworth Longfellow wrote about the slight shift in attitude towards the holiday: "The old Puritan feeling prevents it from being a cheerful, hearty holiday; though every year makes it more so."

CHRISTMAS ROUNDS INTO FORM

In nineteenth-century America, a few things helped shape the way we celebrate Christmas. Since television, movies, and radio weren't yet a thing, it was mainly books and newspapers that influenced trends.

In 1819, Washington Irving (the *Sleepy Hollow* guy) wrote *The Sketchbook of Geoffrey Crayon, Gent.*, a bunch of short stories featuring Christmas celebrations and "ancient customs." Even though they were complete fabrications, people ate it up and started adopting many of them.

The nineteenth century also brought the two most influential pieces of literature on modern Christmas: the 1823 poem "A Visit from St. Nicholas" (or "'Twas the Night Before Christmas") and British author Charles Dickens' 1843 masterpiece, *A Christmas Carol*. Both were wildly successful and greatly shaped common views on Santa Claus and the spirit of Christmas (goodwill towards man and all that good stuff).

But also in the 1820s, the American economy was going through a real rough patch. Unemployment and crime numbers were through the roof. In 1828, New York City created its first police force in response to a Christmas riot. The upper class retreated somewhat on the holiday. Christmas became more of a private event spent with loved ones. Gift giving between family members became an annual tradition.

In the next decade, Alabama became the first state to declare Christmas a public holiday. The rest of the non-New England states followed shortly thereafter. Then, on June 26, 1870, President Ulysses S. Grant declared December 25 a national holiday. Take that, Beantown!

Christmas continued to explode in the next century with an influx of Christmas imagery dominating pop culture. Businesses realized that if they tied their products to Christmas giving, sales would increase. Suddenly, Christmas advertising was everywhere. Magazines like *The Saturday Evening Post* frequently tapped iconic American artist Norman Rockwell to create Christmas-themed covers. Christmas music like Irving Berlin's "White Christmas" dominated the radio. Hollywood churned out Christmas-themed television specials and movies to coincide with the season.

Christmas is now celebrated by 93 percent of Americans. While technically it is still a day dedicated to observing the birth of Jesus, it has become increasingly secular over the years. In the United States, now only 35 percent consider it a strongly religious celebration. For many, beyond religious significance, Christmas is about family and spreading good cheer. It's about "Jingle Bells" and "All I Want for Christmas Is You." It's about baking cookies. It's about trimming the tree.

WHY WE PUT TREES IN OUR HOMES
(AND OTHER ODD CHRISTMAS CUSTOMS)

CHRISTMAS TREES

A decorated tree has been the centerpiece for winter celebrations for thousands of years. Trees have been used as fertility offerings to the gods, "signifying the victory of life and light over death and darkness," or just because they look nice. While the tree has been a staple since the ancient days of Yule, several sources have tried to take credit for the first modern Christmas tree.

Both Estonia and Latvia claim to have the first Christmas tree tradition. Latvia claims 1510 and Estonia 1441 in their capital city of Tallinn. Both brag of a merchant guild called the Brotherhood of Blackheads carrying a tree through the city, decorating it, and then setting it on fire. Historians have cast doubt on that being a Christmas celebration. Considering the Brotherhood of Blackheads were a bunch of unmarried merchants, that sounds like just a typically rambunctious Friday night.

Renaissance satirist Sebastian Brant wrote in 1494 about the custom of putting fir tree branches in houses in his famous ship of fools satire, *Das Narrenschiff*. But the first modern Christmas trees probably first started popping up in the Alsace region of France (Germany at the time) during the sixteenth century. It has been documented that a tree was raised in the Strasbourg Cathedral in 1539. Soon, the tradition had become so popular that the running-short-on-trees city of Freiburg made an ordinance that forbade the people from cutting any down.

While Yule festivals featured fruit and various offerings in the trees, it was the Protestant reformer Martin Luther who is largely credited with putting lights in trees for the first time. He claimed to be inspired by the way evergreens glisten under the twinkling stars above. By 1605, fir trees in Strasbourg boasted apples *and* lights, looking very much like a modern decorated tree.

The Christmas tree has also become an international symbol of gratitude. After World War II, Norway wanted to thank the British for their support in response to the Nazi invasion. Each year since 1947, the Norwegian government has sent the United Kingdom a giant Christmas tree. The fifty-to-sixty-foot spruce is prominently displayed at Trafalgar Square every holiday season.

CHRISTMAS TREES IN AMERICA

Christmas trees began popping up in America after the Revolutionary War, thanks to Hessian troops from Germany who were hired by the British. It has been estimated that about 40 percent of the Hessians stayed in America after the war. Naturally, the German natives brought some of their traditions with them, like the decorated tree. And as more German immigrants moved throughout the United States, so did the appearance of decorated trees. Even as far west as Texas, trees were spotted decorated with cotton and popcorn.

The tree further grew in popularity in America and worldwide in the 1800s after Queen Charlotte of Germany married King George III and introduced the tree to the royal household. Then, in 1848, Queen Victoria and yet another German spouse, Prince Albert, were featured in the *Illustrated London News* with their family gathered around a decorated Christmas tree.

That feature of the royal family around the tree proved influential in America, too. Philadelphia-based magazine *Godey's Lady's Book* republished it, taking out Victoria's crown and Albert's royal sash to make them look like a normal (albeit very rich) American family. Not much later, in 1856, Franklin Pierce became the first president to display a tree in the White House.

Shortly after Thomas Edison invented the first practical light bulb, someone had the idea to make Christmas lights. In 1882, Edward H. Johnson, a partner in the Edison Illumination Company, hand-wired eighty red, white, and blue light bulbs and wound them around his Christmas tree. People were still pretty skeptical of electricity back then, so plug-in lights didn't catch on for a while. President Grover Cleveland used some indoors in 1895, but it wasn't until 1923 that the electricity lobby convinced Calvin Coolidge to light the first National Christmas Tree with three thousand lights on the White House Lawn.

In 1931, a twenty-foot-tall Christmas tree was put up at Rockefeller Center while the building was still under construction. In those days, with jobs so scarce, the Rockefeller Center site employed many. The tree there became a symbol of hope.

While there's a charm and great smell to natural Christmas trees, by the 1960s, many people began flocking to the hottest new trend—fake trees. In December 1964, *TIME* magazine published an article about the polyvinyl trees already representing 35 percent of the US Christmas tree market. By 2018, that number had climbed to 82 percent.

About thirty-five million real trees are still sold each year from about twenty-one thousand tree growers. The average tree takes about seven to ten years to grow.

WREATHS

When sixteenth century Germans brought those first Christmas trees in their homes, they trimmed them to form a perfect triangle. The three-pointed shape represented the Holy Trinity (God the Father, Son and Holy Spirit). The pruning process left them with scraps. And, since they wanted to use every part of the tree, those scraps were made into Christmas wreaths.

The origin of the wreath itself can be traced back to the ancient Greeks and Romans. When victorious Greek soldiers returned from battle, they wore horseshoe-shaped laurel wreaths in their hair. Winning athletes at the Panhellenic games were crowned with wreaths made of olives, laurel, celery, and pine.

With their great admiration for Greek culture, the Romans adopted wreaths into their literature and customs. In 8 AD, Roman poet Ovid wrote the poem *Metamorphoses*, in which the god Apollo is rejected by a nymph who turns herself into a laurel tree. The spurned deity then overcomes his pain by wearing a ring of laurels in his hair. If wreaths were good enough for the gods, they were good enough for mortals. Wreaths became a positive symbol that continued throughout the years.

So, when the Germans had these scraps of evergreen in their homes, they wove them into a wreath. And, since a wheel-like shape is a lot more convenient to hang on doors and branches than a horseshoe, they became circular symbols all to themselves. The circular shape made of evergreen came to represent eternal life. The wreath has been a prominent Christmas decoration ever since.

MISTLETOE

Mistletoe is the other greenery brought inside for the holidays. If you're standing under it, you're encouraged to kiss. The convoluted reason why involves Norse folklore.

A god named Baldur had ominous premonitions of dying. His mom, Frigg, was the goddess of motherhood and tried to get every living and nonliving thing on earth to agree to not kill her boy. After that, Baldur was known for his invincibility.

Legendary "prankster" Loki heard about it, disguised himself, and asked Frigg if she got confirmation from everything and everyone that they wouldn't kill Baldur. She said the only thing she didn't bother with was mistletoe because it was so small. So Loki, the prankster, pranked ol' Baldur by murdering him with a weapon made from mistletoe. Frigg, apparently unamused by the irony of the situation, wept. Her tears caught on the mistletoe's branches and turned into white, pearl-like berries, symbolizing her love for her boy.

In one version of this story's ending, those tear-produced berries were magical and revived Baldur. Therefore, Frigg decided that everyone who passes under mistletoe deserves a kiss. In another version, Baldur remained dead but Frigg declared mistletoe to be a symbol of peace in memory of her son.

There are other stories of Druids (ancient Celtic religious leaders) hanging mistletoe above their doorways as a peace symbol. Druids believed mistletoe was an omnipotent elixir from the oak tree. English churches weren't a big fan of this practice, so they banned the hanging of the plant. Over time, the ban lifted and somehow mistletoe became closely aligned with Christmas. In Victorian England, kissing under the mistletoe became some sort of ironbound social contract. If a girl refused to kiss a guy, she could forget about getting any marriage proposals for a least a year. Most members of society would snub said woman and she would likely die an old maid.

According to old-timey etiquette books, a proper gentleman should pluck one white berry while kissing a lady on the cheek. The slight problem with that tradition is that mistletoe is a parasitic plant that contains toxic amines. Its poisonous berries can cause drowsiness, blurred vision, vomiting, stomach pain, and even seizures. Maybe just leave the berries alone.

HOLIDAY CARDS

Former English teacher Rowland Hill set out to improve the British postal system and in 1837 published "Post Office Reform: Its

Importance and Practicability." Within three years, the British Post Office began issuing black one-penny stamps to be used for all posts, regardless of distance (the "Penny Black"). The number of letters sent rose from 76 million in 1839 to 350 million a decade later. Revenue soared and Rowland Hill was praised. His assistant was Henry Cole.

Henry Cole was a real man about town in Victorian England. Besides helping Rowland Hill design the Penny Black, he was a patron of the arts in London and had lots of fancy friends. Maintaining mail correspondence with everyone in his social circles was challenging. So Cole had one of his artist friends, J.C. Horsley, make a three-section picture that featured people helping the poor. He then had that image printed one thousand times with the salutation "TO: ____" and the greeting "A Merry Christmas and A Happy New Year to You." All Henry Cole had to do was fill in the names of his friends, and just like that, he had kept up with the Joneses and invented the Christmas card in the process.

Cole's card was not without some controversy. Horsley's drawing featured the images of young children enjoying some wine with their parents, so members of the temperance movement were not pleased. But overall, the card was a big hit. Within a few years, several prominent families were sending their own versions of the card.

The quality of the artwork kept improving. Card publishers held competitions prompting feverish growth and demand for more. People collected Christmas cards like they were rare coins or baseball cards. Newspapers reviewed them like they were the latest movie. In 1894, well-known British arts writer Gleeson White dedicated an entire issue of his magazine, *The Studio,* to the artwork of Christmas cards.

Maybe it was due to the strict moral constrictions of the Victorian era. Maybe it was just because they were bored. Whatever the reason, Christmas cards got super creepy. Their artwork started featuring dead birds, killer snowmen, ants fighting each other, pudding that has come to life, old people laughing maniacally while dumping water on carolers (actually, that one is kind of fun), and other weird stuff. The Victorian people were clearly going through something, and Christmas cards were their way to work it out.

In 1875, Prussian immigrant Louis Prang created the first Christmas card in America. Instead of dead birds and lobsters, Prang's first card was a simple painting of a flower and the words "Merry Christmas."

As people have become less religious (or more inclusive), cards have become less about Christmas itself and more about warm wishes for the whole holiday season (Christmas, Hanukkah, Kwanzaa, New Year's, or whatever the giver or recipient celebrates). The evolved tradition places much less of a premium on the artwork and is more a way to stay in touch and (in most cases) send a family picture to loved ones. Americans now send each other over 1.6 billion cards every holiday season and, quite possibly, none of them feature a dead robin.

But maybe it wouldn't be such a bad idea to sprinkle in a few fighting ants and lobsters.

ADVENT CALENDARS

The word "advent" is from the Latin word *adventus*, meaning "coming." During the fourth century in Spain, Advent was a time of preparation for the baptism of new Christians at the January Feast of the Epiphany. For forty days before the feast, the Christians would pray and fast to get ready for the big event.

In the sixth century, the Romans scrapped those plans and tied Advent to the birth of Christ. In contrast to how, currently, Christmastime is usually filled with parties, over-overeating, cookies, excessive consumption of alcohol, and the dubious substance known as eggnog, Advent was meant to be a time of fasting, abstinence, and prayer (kind of like Lent, which comes before Easter). It was a pretty intense fast from November 15 to December 19—no meat, dairy, fish, wine, or oil (actually, there were dispensations on certain days for fish, wine, and oil, but for the final few days, the only dispensations were for oil and wine). Over time, the Western world cut that number down to just three days for a "mini Lent."

In 1839, a Lutheran minister in Germany created a wreath to mark the final month of Advent. He took the wheel of a cart and put small red candles around it with four big white candles inside of it. He lit the red candles on weekdays and the white ones on Sundays. (People worked six days per week those days.) The tradition caught on and, over time, an evergreen wreath replaced the wheel. Holly, berries, and pinecones were added in certain displays. Also, because using that many candles usually leads to disaster, people started lighting just one candle for each Sunday. Often, the first and second candles were purple (for abstinence and fasting), the third candle pink (to show a shift from repentance to joy), then back to purple for the last one (because, well, there's probably still some repentance to do).

But people liked the whole countdown aspect of Advent as it built excitement for Christmas. A common tradition was to make chalk markings on one's door each day until Christmas Eve. So, in the early 1900s, Gerhard Lang produced the first Advent calendar in Germany. When he was a boy, his mom used to stick twenty-four *Wibbele* (little candies) on a piece of cardboard. Within a few years of Lang's creation, the German newspaper *Neues Tagblatt Stuttgart* gave away Advent calendars as an insert for its readers. Aside from a World War II stoppage to preserve cardboard, Advent calendars have grown in popularity ever since.

By 1958, some Advent calendars featured not only pictures but chocolate as well. Today, there are Advent calendars for nearly every type of character. They even make ones with LEGOs in them. While the calendars technically still are celebrating the coming of Jesus (even the $50,000 Harrods department store calendar in 2007), for children, these calendars are really about the countdown to Santa's visit.

SANTA CLAUS

THE ORIGINAL ST. NICK

The jolly fat guy with the rosy cheeks, red suit, and white beard didn't get his start at the North Pole. It's pretty safe to assume he didn't have a belly that jiggled, his skin wasn't very fair, and he didn't wear a whole lot of red. There's a good chance he had a beard, though.

The original St. Nick was an olive-skinned, five-foot-six, Turkish badass with a broken nose. Nicholas was born in Patara, Lycia (present-day Turkey) around AD 280 (about fifty years before Christmas was first celebrated). His parents died when he was young, so he was put under the care of his uncle and he inherited a small fortune. When he was old enough to head out on his own, instead of living rich, he used his money to help the less fortunate.

Considering it was over seventeen hundred years ago, the tales of his generosity are not exactly verified. One story said he used his wealth to pay the dowry of three poor sisters before their father was forced to sell them into prostitution. Nicholas snuck into their house at night and dropped bags of gold on several occasions before being noticed. Another story is about how he helped some falsely accused men avoid execution. But, to become a saint (as he eventually did), one has to perform miracles. According to legend, Nicholas once walked into an inn where three boys had just been murdered, dismembered, and put into barrels in the basement. Before the innkeeper was able to sell them as meat pies (like some sort of Sweeney Todd / Soylent Green situation), Nicholas was able to bring them back to life. No word on whether he was able to reattach their arms and legs. The important thing is he was generous and good to lots of people.

Later on in life, Nicholas became a bishop in a town called Myra (now known as Demre, Turkey). The bishop was known to be a bit of a rebel, so his broken nose (which was discovered by anthropologists who studied his bones many years later) could've happened in a variety of ways. The most likely culprit was goons working for Roman emperor Diocletian, who persecuted Christians. Nicholas' reputation as the protector of children and sailors continued to grow until his death on December 6, AD 343. He was buried in a church, and people claimed his grave produced a substance called manna which had healing powers.

NICK'S LEGEND CONTINUES

The buzz around the great Nicholas continued to grow until he was canonized in 1446. Around that same time, St. Nicholas took on an even more otherworldly role of bringing gifts around each year on his feast day, December 6. People started ascribing some of Norse Odin or Roman Saturn's powers to Nicholas, making him into a magical, white-bearded man who could fly. Even Christopher Columbus honored St. Nick by naming a Haitian port after him in 1492.

Then, in the sixteenth century, the Reformation movement saw the creation of Protestantism. Saints were kind of pushed to the back burner. In Holland, though, the Dutch continued to celebrate the Feast of St. Nicholas every year on December 6. The Dutch reverence for the saint eventually traveled across the Atlantic to New York, which had very strong Dutch roots. (After all, it used to be called New Amsterdam.)

Dutch families in NYC continued to honor "Sint Nikolaas" on the anniversary of his death (or "Sinter Klaas" for short). In 1804, John Pintard, the founder of the New York Historical Society, promoted St. Nicholas as the patron saint of the city. After Washington Irving joined the society in 1809, he published a satire called *Knickerbocker's History of New York*, with several mentions of a jolly St. Nick, making him less saintly and more of an elf-like, pipe-smoking Dutch burglar. The next year, when the New York Historical Society held its first Feast of St. Nicholas, Pintard commissioned an artist, Alexander Anderson, to create the first American image of St. Nick. He was shown dropping off gifts and treats in stockings hung by a fireplace.

By 1821, the story of gift-giving St. Nick had grown beyond New York City. One of the first lithographed books in America, *The Children's Friend*, mentioned a "Sante Clause" coming from the north in a sleigh with flying reindeer. Clause rewarded good children and left bad children's parents with a black rod for parents to beat them with. But in this story, Sante Clause appeared on Christmas Eve.

Two years later, an anonymously published poem called "A Visit from St. Nicholas" (or "'Twas the Night Before Christmas") essentially made a few tweaks to *The Children's Friend* and surpassed it in popularity. Santa Claus was now known as the "jolly old elf." Transition complete. Visually, the red suit-wearing Santa can be traced to the famous cartoonist Thomas Nast in 1869. Nast first drew Santa visiting the Union troops during the Civil War in 1863 for *Harper's Weekly* (because everybody knows Santa hated Jefferson Davis and Robert E. Lee). In that cartoon, Santa was wearing a stars-and-stripes fur coat in a show of support for their efforts. In 1869, Nast settled on a red suit.

In his twenty-three years drawing Santa for *Harper's Weekly*, Nast also gave him a hometown—the North Pole. There were several reasons for this. First, in the mid-nineteenth century, there had been several high-profile trips to the Arctic. Much like the Space Race having a direct influence on *Star Trek* and *Star Wars*, the expeditions to the unknown land up north captured the imagination. Plus, reindeer live up there, and Santa's use of reindeer had already been established in "A Visit from St. Nicholas." Also, the North Pole doesn't belong to any country. It's just a territory north of literally every single country. There are no preconceived notions about someone from the North Pole—no religion or politics. Santa is the only game in town up there. But maybe the most important reason Thomas Nast chose "Santa Claussville, N.P." is because it is always snowing in Santa's hometown, and snow has long been associated with Christmas.

SANTA, THE MONEYMAKER

By the end of the 1800s, Santa had become a commercial darling. He was the infallible, universally known, magical gift-giver. Brands started using the image of Santa to sell products. By 1885, for example, he was seen putting Ivory Soap in stockings (which seems more like a passive-aggressive hygiene complaint than a treat).

In 1931, Coca-Cola was struggling to change the perception that their soft drink was just a summer beverage. Who better than to hitch your wagon to than jolly ol' St. Nick? Haddon H. Sundblom, an artist for the D'Arcy Advertising Agency, was given the task of making a Santa that liked Coca-Cola. Based on his portly neighbor, Sundblom's creation was the gold standard of Santa Claus. Ever since, just about every Santa Claus seen in America has been a variation of Sundblom's vision. Eventually, Sundblom even gave Santa a wife. Mrs. Claus was based off of Sundblom's own wife—which potentially could've been a sore spot in their marriage.

THE ORIGINS OF SANTA'S ELVES

While they don't get nearly as much publicity as Santa, it is widely understood Mr. Claus couldn't pull it all off without his elves. But, unlike the beloved man in the red suit, the elves have had a mixed reputation throughout history. Way before they were aligned with Santa, elves were known throughout ancient Europe as troublemakers or, even worse, little monsters.

Like many Christmas traditions, the origin of elves can be traced back to Northern Europe. Norse mythology mentioned the *álfar* (hidden folk) as unknown beings working behind the scenes. Fairies, spirits, and elves were prevalent in Scandinavian and Celtic cultures. Germans believed in little trap-setting humanoid creatures called kobolds. Scots had household spirits called broonies or brownies. Much like ancient gods and goddesses of thunder, healing, wisdom, love, fertility, and so forth, these creatures were created to help explain the unknown. When things went well, it was because the elves were rewarding people for good behavior. Or, at the very least, the elves were leaving them alone. If the people weren't at their best, the elves would cause problems. If a kid had a nightmare, it was probably an elf sitting on her head.

Throughout the Middle Ages, elves would pop up in folklore. In the British *Beowulf*, elves were mentioned as an evil race descended from Cain (Adam and Eve's kid who murdered his brother). Later on, at the end of the 1500s, Shakespeare wrote of a mischievous elf-like creature named Puck in *A Midsummer Night's Dream*.

THE EVOLUTION OF MODERN-DAY ELVES

The perception shift from elves being associated with pranks or terror to Christmas joy can be attributed to the Icelandic people and the author of *Little Women*. Iceland, which was settled by Vikings and their Celtic slaves, really celebrated elf folklore and a whole story about thirteen Yule Lads that come each night in the thirteen days leading up to Christmas Eve. Most of them have pretty mischievous personas, but they are known for leaving gifts in the shoes of good little girls and boys.

The first time Santa's elves were specifically written about was in 1856, in Louisa May Alcott's *Christmas Elves*. Probably inspired by the famous 1823 poem, "A Visit from St. Nicholas," in which Santa is called a "right jolly old elf," Alcott wrote of elves no longer tormenting anyone but rather assisting in Christmas merriment. The following year, *Harper's Weekly* featured a poem called "The Wonders of Santa Claus," which discussed how elves were hard at work making sweets and things to put in stockings.

By the start of the twentieth century, Santa and elves were closely linked. In 1922, Norman Rockwell painted a famous image of tiny elves helping a weary Santa paint a dollhouse. Ten years later, Disney released a movie short called "Santa's Workshop" showing tiny elves building toys on an assembly line in the titular setting.

Santa's elves didn't really get their own identity until 1964's stop-motion animated special *Rudolph the Red-Nosed Reindeer*. In Rankin/Bass' first-ever animated special, a malcontent workshop elf named Hermey would rather be a dentist. It doesn't go over well for him. Then, in 2003, Will Ferrell starred in a blockbuster instant-classic Christmas movie about a human raised as an elf, called *Elf*. All was right with the world of Santa's elves.

Two years later, things took a dark turn. In 2005, a self-published author named Carol Aebersold wrote a book with an accompanying doll called *Elf on the Shelf*. Ever since, elves have turned Christmastime homes into a police state. They watch the children during the day, then report their activities back to Santa each night. And if those elves don't make their nightly flight back to the North Pole (and a different location in the home afterward), the whole operation could be in jeopardy.

CHRISTMAS AROUND THE WORLD

The celebration of Christmas varies around the world, right down to the date. In North America, most gift exchanges happen on Christmas Day. In Europe, Christmas Eve is the gift giving date, since that was the night Jesus was born. Eastern Orthodox churches honor December 25 in some ways. But, for religious observances, many use the Julian calendar, which gives primary significance to January 7.

AFRICA

The 1984 song asked about Africa, "Do they know it's Christmastime at all?" The answer is yes for just about all. But about half of Africans actually celebrate it. (The other half is mostly Muslim.) Christmas tends to be a more religious observance on this continent than in other places around the world, especially in predominantly Muslim countries like Chad, Egypt, and Gambia.

DEMOCRATIC REPUBLIC OF THE CONGO

Churchgoers on Christmas Eve in the Congo had better carve out a lot of time for services. There are big musical numbers with five or six choirs telling the story of the Bible, starting with Adam and Eve and finishing around midnight with the birth of Jesus. Some places keep the singing going until dawn. Others dismiss everyone at 1:00 A.M. so they can get some rest before the nine-in-the-morning Christmas Day service. The rest of the day is spent quietly at home (presumably sleeping).

ETHIOPIA

The Ethiopian Orthodox Tewahedo Church observes Christmas on January 7, as Coptic Christians follow the Julian calendar. On Ganna (what Ethiopians call Christmas), most wear white shawl-like clothing with colored stripes on the ends. There is no Santa or presents. Besides church services, men and boys play a game (also) called ganna, which is kind of like hockey, and the big family meal is a spicy stew with flatbread.

GHANA

Ghana has twice the reason to get excited in December: Christmas and the end of the cocoa harvest. That is why as soon as the calendar hits December, homes and streets are full of decorations and lights.

KENYA

In Kenya, Santa travels in style. Some have him arriving on a camel, but in more modern style, he rolls up in a four-wheel-drive safari Jeep.

LIBERIA

Liberia flips the script when it comes to Santa Claus at Christmastime. Instead of wishing each other a "Happy" or "Merry Christmas," Liberians greet each other during the season by saying, "My Christmas on you." This pretty much means "Please give me something nice for Christmas." Rather than having a jolly fat man who gives toys, someone named Old Man Bayka, the "devil," wanders the streets and begs you for presents every December. 'Tis the season of giving!

MADAGASCAR

Poinsettias grow all year in Madagascar, so they aren't particularly special at Christmas. On the island nation, Christmas is primarily about its religious significance. People attend big services, then usually have large community meals outside the church.

MALAWI

Malawi children go from house to house wearing skirts made of leaves and sing Christmas carols while playing handmade instruments. Church services usually involve lots of dancing.

NIGERIA

Christmas is a time for large family gatherings in Nigeria. After church services on Christmas morning, families get together for marathon parties that last all day and night. While adults eat, drink, and be merry, kids have been known to set off fireworks.

SENEGAL

Even though Senegal is almost entirely Muslim, they still get into the Christmas spirit. Even mosques are decorated with Christmas trees.

SIERRA LIONE

Christmas in this predominantly Muslim country is like a carnival. There's music and dancing and masquerade parties.

SOUTH AFRICA

South African Christmas celebrations vary by region, but for the most part, they resemble the celebrations in the United Kingdom and America with decorated streets, trees, and family gatherings. The big difference is that Christmas happens in the middle of summer. Most families gather for a cookout, called braaing, on Christmas Day. Lots of businesses close down for the entire month of December.

TANZANIA

Tanzania celebrates Christmas with church services and family gatherings. While gift giving isn't a massive focus of the holiday, it is customary to give children new outfits to wear to church or school. Food at family feasts is washed down with local beer. There are breweries seemingly in every Tanzanian village, so the brewskis are plentiful on Christmas.

UGANDA

After church services (often featuring beautiful bells and candlelit caroling), Ugandans celebrate by singing, dancing, and watching or playing football (soccer). In the evenings, they have large dinner parties where the less fortunate are also fed delicious meals.

ZAMBIA

Zambian church services take the better part of three days for Christmas and are filled with caroling, Nativity plays, and games. When mass lets out at midnight on Christmas Eve, there are lots of honking and fireworks explosions.

ANTARCTICA

Christmas has even been celebrated at the furthest possible point from Santa's village.

At Christmastime in 1946, the crew on a US Navy expedition to the South Pole tied a Canadian spruce tree to their mast to show a little spirit. But it wasn't until the early twenty-first century that a more sustainable tree was created for Antarctica. A night shift crew at the

South Pole (how's that for a bad shift?) created a tree out of scrap metal and old machine parts. Each year since then, iron crews have added ornaments made out of old tools, nuts, bolts, gears, and saw blades.

ASIA

Aside from in the Philippines and Armenia, Christianity doesn't have a huge presence in Asia. Of course, small percentages of Christians in countries like China, Indonesia, and India still mean tens of millions of people. But celebrations of the faith tend to be smaller or confined to very specific areas of non-Christian countries. And, in increasingly capitalist societies, Christmas means lots of spending, which means retailers will want to celebrate it, regardless of how religious they are.

ARMENIA

Armenia is one of the few predominantly Christian countries in Asia. In fact, it was the first country to adopt Christianity as its official religion. But the way Armenians celebrate Christmas today was largely shaped by the seven-decade Soviet occupation that ended in 1991.

During Soviet rule, religious gatherings were forbidden. Because of that, New Year's Eve and Day took on enhanced meaning to the Armenian people. Even after the Soviet Union collapse and the Armenian people were free to embrace Christmas, New Year's was still baked into all of the festivities.

Armenian churches observe the Julian calendar, making January 7 Christmas Day. So New Year's Eve is really just a kickoff of the celebrations. Instead of "Merry Christmas and Happy New Year," people in Armenia say the opposite ("Happy New Year and Christmas"). The holidays don't end until January 13.

Dzmer Pap (Winter Grandfather) shows up on New Year's Eve and places presents under children's pillows. Sometimes the presents are delivered via the ding-dong-ditch method (the doorbell rings and, when the kids go to answer it, Dzmer Pap is gone but the presents are waiting on the stoop).

CHINA

Nearly all public Christmas celebrations in China are in Hong Kong. Skyscrapers try to top each other with impressive light displays. In public squares, you can find large Christmas trees, just like any Western city.

A popular gift on Christmas Eve is a colored cellophane-wrapped apple. In Mandarin, the word for apple (*píngguǒ*) sounds a lot like the word for peace.

There is a Dongzhi Festival for the winter solstice on the twenty-first, but December 25 is just another day in the rest of the country.

INDIA

About thirty million people in the country identify as Christian. Most Christmas celebrations in India occur in either Goa, a state on the southwestern coast, or up north.

Goa was the hub of Portuguese India until 1961, so it still honors many of the traditions of the Christian country. Mango and banana trees are decorated (instead of evergreens), people attend midnight mass, and turkey is eaten at Christmas feasts.

Up north, Christians observe Badaa Din (Big Day) at Christmas. People often plant trees to celebrate.

INDONESIA

About 10 percent of Indonesia is Christian, which translates to over twenty million people who celebrate Christmas. Churches and cathedrals have big Nativity displays, sing carols like "Malam Kudus" (the Indonesian version of "Silent Night"), and perform plays depicting the birth of Jesus.

While most Christmas trees in Indonesia are fake, there is a huge tree farm on Java (its largest island) for those who want real ones. But many residents in Bali choose a third option—the feather tree. The artfully crafted chicken-feather trees can be seen in most hotels and fancy homes on the island.

Gift giving among Christians is very much like it is in the West, as Indonesia was once ruled by the Netherlands. Sinterklaas is a popular figure who can be seen in shopping malls or delivering presents to Indonesian children on Christmas Day.

Even the Indonesian government gets into the spirit with its state-run television channel broadcasting Christmas music concerts and holiday movies like *Home Alone*.

IRAN

Since practicing Christianity can either get you locked in the hoosegow or killed, Christmas celebrations among the 0.15 percent of Iranians who identify with the religion are pretty muted. There is a winter solstice celebration called Shab-e Yalda on December 21.

JAPAN

No country has embraced the secular Christmas quite like Japan. Each December, the predominantly Shintō and Buddhist country decorates with lights and trees and sings songs like "Rudolph" and "White Christmas." Instead of Santa Claus, the Japanese have Hoteiosho, an old Buddhist monk with a sackful of toys. He has eyes in the back of his head, so everyone needs to be on their best behavior at all times.

But the most uniquely Japanese Christmas tradition is its love affair with Colonel Sanders. Each year, millions of Japanese families consume Kentucky Fried Chicken as their Christmas feast. When the franchise opened in Japan in 1970, manager Takeshi Okawara overheard some foreigners wishing they could have turkey at Christmastime. He had an idea—a Christmas "party barrel." By 1974, the plan came to fruition with the tagline *"Kurisumasu ni wa kentakkii!"* ("Kentucky for Christmas!")

Over the years, fried chicken has become a staple of Japanese Christmas. Individual KFC restaurants dress up their Colonel Sanders statues with Santa costumes. Today, boxes are ordered weeks in advance or else wait in line for hours. Sales in the five days before Christmas make up one-third of KFC Japan's annual intake.

PAKISTAN

Even though only a small percentage of Pakistani citizens are Christian, Christmas has been embraced by a lot of well-off non-Christians in the country. Kiosks pop up in the capital city every year selling trees, Santa masks, and even non-alcoholic eggnog. December 25 also happens to be a holiday in Pakistan, but that is memory of Jinnah, the founder of Pakistan. Unfortunately, the Christians who do live there tend to live in ghettos, and money is stretched too thin to spend on decorations, aside from stars on their homes.

PHILIPPINES

With nearly one hundred million Christians, the Philippines are the biggest Christmas hub in Asia. And they take it seriously. Starting in late September, there are carols in shops around the country. This continues until the first Sunday of the new year, when they celebrate the Feast of the Three Kings.

In the nine days leading up to Christmas, Filipinos attend pre-dawn masses called Misa de Gallo ("Rooster Masses," because they're before dawn). Christmas Eve tends to be an all-night affair. After attending Simbang Gabi (Christmas Eve mass) Filipinos have a midnight feast, called Noche Buena.

Santa R-Kayma Klaus is a seventy-year-old Filipino citizen of Irish descent. Every year, he spreads good cheer around the Philippines, but instead of traveling in a sleigh, he does it in an air-conditioned bus. Fair enough. Even in December, the average temperature in the Philippines is in the upper eighties.

The so-called Christmas capital of the Philippines is San Fernando. Each year, San Fernando hosts Ligligan Parul (Giant Lantern Festival). Locals create *parols*, which are colored star lanterns attached to bamboo poles. These represent the Star of Bethlehem that guided the Magi towards Jesus' manger.

SINGAPORE

Thanks to the large expat community, lots of street decorations can be found in the Christmas season, especially along Orchard Road.

SOUTH KOREA

Besides the brightly lit decorations over the Han River, the thing that stands out most about Christmas in South Korea is Santa. Instead of the more typical red, Santa Haraboji's outfit is blue.

THAILAND

Despite being a Buddhist country, malls are full of Christmas decorations and people wearing Santa hats.

TURKEY

Even though it is the home country of St. Nicholas, only 0.2 percent of the Turkish population is Christian. And most of those Christians are refugees from Syria and Iran, keeping a low profile. New Year's Eve, on the other hand, is a pretty big celebration in Turkey.

VIETNAM

On Christmas Eve in Ho Chi Minh City and Hanoi, people go to city squares to enjoy light shows and throw confetti. Major hotels and department stores also usually have big light displays and decorations.

EUROPE

In most European countries, people exchange gifts on Christmas Eve, with most mass services in late afternoon. Eastern Orthodox churches honor Christmas on December 25, but they use the Julian calendar, which corresponds to January 7 on the Gregorian calendar (the one we have been using for the past four to five hundred years).

Some version of Santa delivers presents to boys and girls across the continent. It's usually a white-bearded guy who has roots that go back to St. Nicholas. But several European countries also embrace an anti-Santa figure. Two in particular stand out: Krampus and Zwarte Piet.

KRAMPUS

In the Alpine region of Europe (Austria, Germany, Hungary, Switzerland, Czech Republic, and Slovenia), there's a yang to jolly ol' St. Nick's yin—Krampus. The legend is that an insane half demon, half goat roams the streets in the weeks before Christmas, looking for naughty children to torment.

On the night before the Feast of St. Nicholas (December 6), Krampusnacht is observed. Hunting season is open for the goat-devil with an extra-long tongue, flaming coals for eyes, horns, and nasty matted fur, and wearing rags and chains. The next day, St. Nick will put presents and sweets in the good kids' shoes. But if the children have been bad? Things could get ugly. Some versions have Krampus whacking them with birch branches. Others have him stuffing the naughty kids in a sack and dragging them to hell.

Oh, and if you happen to cross paths with him, it's a good idea to offer him schnapps before he swats you with that birch branch. The cloven-hoofed fella has a hankering for fruit-flavored gin.

ZWARTE PIET

Celebrated in Belgium, the Netherlands, and parts of Germany, Zwarte Piet (Black Pete) continues to be a hot-button issue. It all comes down to one simple question—what do you do when one of your beloved Christmas traditions happens to be horribly racist?

In Belgian and Dutch folklore, instead of elves, Sinterklaas uses Zwarte Piet (or multiple Piets). Zwarte Piet carries his bag, hands out treats, and performs for the crowds at holiday parades and gatherings. As you'd expect, Sinterklaas is an older man with a white beard who wears a lot of red. Zwarte Piet, on the other hand, doesn't look anything like elves. He is a Moor from Spain. Since about 1850, Zwarte Piet has been portrayed by white people in blackface with a big, curly afro, gold hoop earrings, and bright red lips. Some argue that he's not a slave but really just someone happy to work with Sinterklaas—in other words, apparently, a contentedly subservient character who is lucky to have a white savior.

In 2013, the United Nations High Commission on Human Rights wrote to the Dutch government saying the whole thing seemed a bit racist. Many defenders of Piet argue that he isn't wearing blackface but rather soot from the chimneys he has been going down (though it miraculously doesn't soil his colorful clothing at all). In recent years, the noise has gotten loud enough that cities have drastically scaled back on the blackface stuff. Now, many of the Piets in the cities are different colors with just random streaks of soot on their cheeks, calling him

"Chimney Pete." Zwarte Piet is fading, but it's going to take a while to completely eradicate this problematic tradition.

BELGIUM

Depending on where you live in Belgium, either St. Nicholas or le Père Noël will visit the children on the night of December 5 to give them sweets and presents. Christmas Day is the time when families exchange gifts.

BULGARIA

One of the old traditions in Bulgaria is that the Christmas Eve meal has an uneven number of vegetarian dishes. Christmas Eve is also a day when each member of the family cracks a walnut for luck. If it's a good one, they're in for a good year.

CZECH REPUBLIC

To build interest in Christmas Eve dinner in the Czech Republic, everyone starves themselves during the day. Then, at night, they look for the *zlaté prasátko* (golden piglet) before they can have their traditional feast, which is usually some sort of carp preparation.

DENMARK

December 13 in Denmark is Santa Lucia Day, to commemorate a fourth-century Christian martyr. Each year, a woman dressed in white will wear a wreath adorned with candles and lead a parade of girls also in white. While it's not really a Christmas holiday, the celebration takes the place of Nativity plays and serves as a kickoff to Christmastime.

On Christmas Eve, Danish families turn it loose and do a lot of dancing around the Christmas tree.

FRANCE

The French celebrate Christmas (Noël) in the most French way imaginable: with an intricate multi-course meal on Christmas Eve, called Le Réveillon de Noël. Le Réveillon (meaning "awakening") starts with things like raw oysters and foie gras, is followed by poultry and truffles, and finishes with a rich chocolate dessert. In Provence, they lay out thirteen desserts (for Jesus and his twelve apostles).

FINLAND

Three hundred thousand people per year visit the northernmost area of Finland to see Santa's village. The first mention of Kris Kringle living in Finland was in 1927, when Finnish broadcaster Marcus Rautio announced that Santa's village had been found in Lapland, an area north of the Arctic Circle right by the Russian border. Finns saw this as a more realistic option for Mr. Claus. The North Pole didn't have reindeer.

During World War II, Lapland was destroyed by Nazis. After the war, thanks to the efforts of Eleanor Roosevelt and UNICEF, the area was revitalized. In anticipation of the former First Lady's visit, they built a cabin for her to stay. In the years after, a little village was built around the charming area and, by 1957, the *New York Times* promoted it as "Europe's Northern Wilderness."

In the '60s and '70s, there was an explosion of Christmas movies and animated specials focused on Santa and his origins. So, in 1984, the governor of Lapland capitalized on it and declared the area "Santa

Claus Land." Within a year, they had built a whole Christmas village. Eleanor's Roosevelt's cabin is still part of the village.

GERMANY

Each year, on the Friday before Advent, the Nürnberger Christkind (Christmas angel) opens the Christkindlmarkt (Christmas market) by reciting a spirited prologue. For centuries, these markets have served as a festive celebration of local delicacies, music, and crafts in the middle of a cold, dark winter. They're also great places to have some *Glühwein* (mulled wine) and party.

Besides their storied love affair with Christmas trees, the Germans also decorate their homes with colored pictures lit up by electric candles in their windows. *Sternsinger* (star singers) travel from house to house, singing and collecting money for charity. Then, while everyone is at church on Christmas Eve, der Weihnachtsmann (Santa) or Christkind delivers presents.

Not all is bright during Christmas season for many in Germany, however. A few nights before Christmas, an angry dude in fur named Belsnickel knocks on doors and asks the kids to do math problems or recite Bible verses. Then he tosses candy on the ground. If the kids act greedy or show a poor attitude, he delivers the boom with his switch. It's a way to show the kids they only have a few days left. They'd better check themselves before they wreck themselves.

GREECE

Many people still decorate boats in Greece to honor St. Nicholas, the patron saint and protector of sailors.

ICELAND

Iceland seems to have cornered the market on two of the creepiest Christmas traditions: the Yule Lads and Gryla.

Icelandic children are visited by the thirteen Yule Lads. Starting on December 12, a different lad shows up each night. They're kind of like elves but have more unsettling profiles, ranging from weird (Spoon-Licker, Sausage-Swiper, and Bowl-Licker) to the tedious (Door-Slammer and Sheep-Cote Clod, a peg-legged fella who harasses sheep). They all have a specific date for their arrival and, if the kids are good and leave out shoes, each will give them candy. But if they're bad, Sausage-Swiper and the gang will leave things like rotten potatoes in their shoes.

The mother of the thirteen lads is Gryla, a troll woman from the Icelandic mountains. Gryla is always on the prowl for kids to boil in her cauldron. If they misbehave, potatoes aren't the only negative consequence. Gryla will abduct bad kids and murder them if they don't show remorse.

Gryla and the lads also have a huge black cat for a pet. If every person doesn't get a new piece of clothing for Christmas, the cat will eat the rule-breakers.

Sweet dreams, kids!

IRELAND

Many in Ireland leave a tall red candle in their front windows on Christmas Eve, symbolizing welcome to visitors.

ITALY

Italians have been displaying the Nativity scene in preparation for Christmas since St. Francis of Assisi visited Bethlehem in 1223 and made it popular upon his return home.

The Christmas Eve Feast of the Seven Fishes (Esta dei Sette Pesci) dates back to Southern Italy, historically the poorest region of the country where fish was the most affordable food. Italians who immigrated to America in the nineteenth century brought the tradition with them. Today, the Feast of the Seven Fishes is a much bigger deal in the United States than it is in Italy.

On Christmas Day, Babbo Natale (Santa Claus) might bring a little treat, but the Epiphany (Three Kings' Day) is the big gift-giving day in Italy. On Epiphany night, an old woman named Befana puts presents in stockings by the fireplace. Some depictions have her looking like an ugly witch with a broom and a big wart on her nose. But the origin story of La Befana from back in the thirteenth century is a little more positive. On their way to see newborn Jesus, the Magi stopped at Befana's home to ask directions (even though the Star of Bethlehem was showing them the way). Befana helped them, and they asked if she wanted to join them on their journey. She turned them down because she had too much work to do but then quickly regretted it. So, she tried to find the way and dropped off treats in the stockings of every child, hoping one of them would end up being Jesus.

THE NETHERLANDS

Besides the whole slave-helper Zwarte Piet controversy, a unique Dutch tradition is the *chocoladeletters* (chocolate letters) that Sinterklaas delivers each year. When he arrives by boat on December

5, Sinterklaas puts into people's shoes giant alphabet letters that correspond to the first letter of their names. Adults also sometimes gift each other chocolate letters. Each year, the Dutch consume about thirty million of them. It's a regrettable time for people whose names begin with the letter *I*.

NORWAY

Much like the Danes and Swedes, the Feast of St. Lucia is a big celebration in mid-December in Norway. But the other big traditions during Julebord display their love of gingerbread and hearts. The Christmas tree is covered with heart-shaped paper baskets called *julekurver*. Gingerbread cookies shaped like hearts often hang in the windows. December 23 is a big gingerbread house-baking day. Norway loves gingerbread houses so much, the town of Bergen boasts of having the largest gingerbread city in the world.

Norwegians also hide their brooms around Christmas so witches can't ruin all the fun. If you leave out a broom on Christmas Day, you're asking for bad luck.

On Julaften (Christmas Eve), instead of Santa, a smaller elf-like creature with a red hat and a white beard named Julenissen goes door to door, delivering presents.

POLAND

Traditionally, the Polish leave an extra setting at the dinner table at Christmas in case anyone shows up uninvited.

PORTUGAL

A traditional Christmas dessert in Portugal is *bolo-rei* (king's cake). *Bolo-rei* is a fluffy spiced cake that is like nutty sweet bread with spices and two surprises inside: a fava bean and a small toy. The small toys are intended for the kids. If you are the unfortunate person to find a bean in your slice, you're on the hook for making *bolo-rei* next year.

RUSSIA

Even though the Soviet Union collapsed decades ago, Russia still does not have formal Christmas celebrations. Instead, they focus on New Year's traditions. These include New Year's trees (*yolka*) covered with lights and Grandfather Frost (Ded Moroz) traveling home to home bringing presents to children.

Since the Russian Orthodox Church follows the Julian calendar, any actual Christmas observance in Russia occurs on their Christmas Eve (January 6). The holiday season in Russia is also considered the best time to tell fortunes. Typically, young girls use mirrors and shadows. May not make a lot of sense but, then again, neither does their love of techno music.

SPAIN

Psychiatrists would have a field day with one of the cherished traditions in Catalonia (the Barcelona area). One of their Nativity scene characters is the Caganer, a defecating peasant. While Mary, Joseph, and the Three Kings marvel at the newborn Jesus, the Caganer is off in the corner relieving himself. Some opine that it has to do with fertilizing the earth. Others think it's a counterbalance to the wonder of the moment. Either way, it's pretty gross.

The scatological festivities of the Catalonians don't end there. Each Christmas, children nurture Tió de Nadal, a hollow log with a painted face, sticks for legs, and a *barretina* (red Catalan hat). They feed and wrap Tió de Nadal in a blanket each night. On Christmas morning, they beat it with sticks until he poops out presents and sweets! They literally try to hit the crap out of him.

In Northern Spain, children are taught about a figure named L'Home dels Nassos (the man of the noses). On New Year's Day, the mythological creature has 365 of them. By the following New Year's Eve, the man of the noses is down to one. That's probably for the best, considering all the olfactory damage Caganer and Tió de Nadal are doing during the holidays.

SWEDEN

Like its Scandinavian neighbors, St. Lucia's Day (or St. Lucy's Day) is a huge celebration in the middle of December. The one thing Swedish Christmas has that is unlike any other is their Yule goat. Ever since the ancient pagan days, the goat has been a symbol of year-end celebrations.

Starting in 1966, the whole goat thing has grown to a whole new level. The town of Gävle builds a forty-two-foot-tall goat out of straw. In most years, the 3.6-ton beast gets burned to the ground, hit by cars, or even almost stolen by a helicopter. Local officials now douse it in antiflammable liquid, but people still have a morbid fascination each year about whether the Gävlebocken will survive another holiday season.

SWITZERLAND

Swiss families make their own Advent calendars, enjoying different treats each day. Then, on Christmas Eve, the biggest gift is opened.

UNITED KINGDOM

Most Christmas traditions in the United Kingdom look pretty familiar to Americans. They have cards, trees, carols, big lights along major shopping streets, and so on. There are also a few slight differences—Santa Claus is called Father Christmas, stockings are hung at the ends of their beds instead of by the fireplace, they say "Happy Christmas" instead of "Merry," some put letters to Father Christmas into the fireplace instead of the mailbox, they leave out mince pie and brandy for Father Christmas instead of milk and cookies… But there are plenty of traditions that are uniquely British.

Before a traditional Christmas dinner, people enjoy crackers (not the food but the interactive table decoration). Crackers date back to Victorian England. In 1846, an English shop owner figured out if he rubbed two pieces of chemical-soaked paper together, it would create a popping sound. He put them in colored wrappers along with small toys, corny jokes, and, sometimes, a paper crown. Nearly two centuries later, crackers are still a hit.

One of the most common desserts is Christmas pudding. This is basically a booze-soaked fruitcake. Christmas pudding is made weeks in advance in order for all the flavors to blend. Then, on Christmas, brandy lit on fire is poured over the dessert, then topped with a buttery cream sauce.

In the British music industry, it's a big deal to be the "Christmas number one" song. That's the song at the top of the charts the week of Christmas. Sometimes it's a Christmas song. Others, it's just a chart-topper that has longevity. Every year since 1952, a big deal has been made of the number one spot. The Beatles have the most of all time with four. Scarily enough, the Spice Girls almost caught them in the mid-'90s with three in a row.

UKRAINE

Much like other Eastern Bloc countries, New Year's in Ukraine tends to be a much bigger celebration than Christmas (since it was banned during the times of the Soviet Union). But Orthodox Christians (who make up half the population) do observe Christmas on January 7 by going caroling and bringing a bundle of wheat into their homes as a nod to their agricultural ancestors.

OCEANIA

AUSTRALIA

As an eighteenth-century British settlement, many Australian traditions match those practiced in England. In the weeks leading up to Christmas, there are caroling events all over the country. These can be small local gatherings or huge star-studded events raising money for those in need.

Father Christmas shows off a lot more skin in the Southern Hemisphere since it's hot out. Instead of woolen broadcloth and fleece, he often shows up on a surfboard or lifeboat wearing red board shorts. He still rocks the beard, though.

The partying also reflects the weather. On Christmas, many Australians gather outdoors and have a barbecue. Since 80 percent of the country lives within thirty miles of a beach, those parties tend to take place on the sand. Roast turkey and Christmas pudding are often on the menu, but the big item is prawns. Ten times as many prawns are consumed around the holiday season than any other time of year.

NEW ZEALAND

Like in Australia, it is impossible to separate the British influence from Christmas celebrations in New Zealand. Regardless of the outside temperatures, songs like "White Christmas" are sung loudly and pine trees are decorated in homes with tinsel and lights. Retail shopping is busier than ever. Christmas cards aren't quite as popular, though.

Besides the pine tree, Kiwis associate the pohutukawa with Christmas. These crimson-flowered trees line most of the beaches and are celebrated, sort of like the poinsettia.

SOUTH AMERICA

Since just about every South American country is either at or below the equator, Christmas tends to be a warm-weather event. They have lots of barbecues and outdoor gatherings that tend to go late into the night. On Christmas Eve, they attend late-night church services ("Rooster Mass," as it's referred to in Spanish and Portuguese because it finishes in the early hours when the rooster is ready to crow). They follow mass with family barbecues and gift exchanges. Not all fingers make it to Christmas morning, however, as fireworks are a massive part of Christmas Eve celebrations.

While many people throughout South America have Christmas trees, they are usually fake, as fir and pine trees aren't native to the region. A popular decoration is the *nacimiento* (Nativity scene) or *pesebre* (manger). People will go from house to house or church to church to see who has the coolest Nativity scene.

Santa and Papai Noel deliver presents in Peru and Brazil, respectively. In places like Brazil, Argentina, Colombia, and Venezuela, they wait for El Niño Dios (the baby Jesus) to bring their gifts. After that, he will rest in the manger display. Three Kings' Day (Reyes Magos) is another big day for exchanging gifts. Children will leave water and hay for the Three Kings' horses outside the door in the hope they will drop a little something in their shoes by the bed.

While there are some common themes, the countries of South America have added their own cool twists to holiday celebrations.

ARGENTINA

Since most Argentine residents are of European descent, the country at the bottom of the continent takes on many European traditions, especially Italian and Spanish, at Christmastime. But the coolest part of their Christmas Eve celebration (besides partying all night) are the Chinese lantern-like paper decorations that they release into the air, called *globos*. In addition to the firework displays, Argentinians light candles into the *globos*, which float into the sky like little hot air balloons.

BRAZIL

Like Argentina, Brazil incorporates European traditions into its Christmas. For Brazilians, it's their Portuguese roots. Besides Nativity decorations, there are also plays about the birth of Jesus, called "Os Pastores." Oddly, a shepherdess tries to steal the baby during the show. Apparently the festivity of the holidays involves kidnapping.

Christmas comes with a happy gift for all Brazilian workers. Since 1962, it has been mandatory for employers to pay a thirteenth salary at the end of the year. So employees get an extra month's pay every December.

COLOMBIA

On December 7, Colombians celebrate Día de las Velitas (Day of the Little Candles), which serves as a kickoff to Christmas celebrations. Streets and houses are decorated heavily with red and white candles, lights, and lanterns. In the final nine days before Christmas (Novena de Aguinaldos), people gather to pray at each other's houses.

PERU

Chocolate is the name of the game in Peru. Peruvians celebrate a beautiful holiday tradition called La Chocolatada. Governments, businesses, and charities brew massive pots of hot chocolate (the real stuff, not some garbage powdered packet), bake *panetón* (chocolate cake or bread), and bring in truckloads of toys give to the less fortunate.

Then, a few days after Christmas, Colombians unwind on Innocents Day. Each December 28 in Colombia is like an April Fool's Day in

America. Television stations air bloopers and funny moments from over the past year.

VENEZUELA

Venezuelans take Christmas decorating to the next level: Many paint their houses about a month before the holiday (in addition to putting up trees and lights).

NORTH AMERICA

CANADA

Each year, Canada exports about 2.2 million Christmas trees to the United States and another 2.3 to the rest of the world. Besides that, Canada's Christmas looks remarkably similar to America's. After Halloween and Thanksgiving in October, you start to see lights and decorations. Christmas markets can be found all over in December. Stockings are hung by the fire in hopes that Santa will fill them when he visits on Christmas Eve. On Christmas Day, families gather and exchange gifts, then eat turkey and drink eggnog.

There are some regional quirks. Quebec taps into French roots and celebrates Réveillon, a multi-course meal on Christmas Eve. People in Nova Scotia, Labrador, and Newfoundland get into costume and go house to house, challenging neighbors to guess their identity. In Northern Canada, there's a massive taffy pull.

CUBA

Because of poverty and the fact that Fidel Castro banned it for nearly three decades, Christmas is still a pretty muted affair in Cuba. Aside from hotels catering to tourists, there aren't a ton of lights or decorations. It has mostly been just a religious observance. But, ever since the pope visited in 1998, the more secular aspects are creeping into the culture.

DOMINICAN REPUBLIC

Each Christmas, the streets of the DR are filled with wooden handcrafted Christmas trees, called Charamicos. According to legend, people started this custom of fashioning white trees so they could experience a snowy Christmas scene in the Caribbean.

GUATEMALA

Cleaning plays an important role in Guatemalan Christmas. Local legend says that the devil and his crew creep in the dirt in every home. So, early every December, people spend a lot of time cleaning and decluttering. The junk is then piled outside the home into a big model of the devil. On December 7 at 6:00 P.M., that junk devil is set on fire in an event called La Quema del Diablo (the Burning of the Devil).

HAITI

Early in December, Haitians cut pine branches and decorate them like they're whole trees. (Well, some get entire trees from the island's mountains.) Nativity scenes also play a big role in nearly all home decorations. On Christmas Eve, the children's Christmas joy gets a jump start—booze! Haitian kids are allowed to drink anisette, a cocktail made from anise leaves soaked in rum and sweetened with sugar. Later that night, the children fill their shoes up with straw and put them on the porch. Tonton Nwèl (Santa) then arrives, takes out the straw, and puts some gifts in and around the shoes.

HONDURAS

As soon as the home is decorated, Honduran children write a letter to San Nicolás (Santa) and put it under the Christmas tree for his arrival. One staple at every Noche Buena (Christmas Eve) meal is *nacatamales* (similar to Mexican tamales). Evening ritual tends to be church, then feast, then fireworks.

MEXICO

The birth of Jesus factors heavily into Mexican Christmas decorations, as the *nacimiento* (Nativity scene) is more popular than Christmas trees. Also, between December 16 and Christmas Eve each year, children perform nine *posadas*, which are kind of like Christmas plays. *Posada* is the Spanish word for "inn." The posadas are Mary and Joseph's journey to find a place to stay before she gave birth. While holding candles and painted clay figures, children visit neighbors and sing songs. Just like Mary and Joseph in the Bible, the children are turned away. Eventually, they're let inside and there's a big party with food and a piñata. After the manger is found, a baby Jesus is placed in the manger, and they all head to midnight mass.

The most festive Christmas flower in America is the red and green one from Mexico—the poinsettia. According to an old Mexican legend, a little girl named Pepita placed a handful of weeds at the bottom of the

Nativity scene and they turned into poinsettias, which is why the colors of Christmas are red and green. That is why they are called La Flor de la Nochebuena in Mexico. The Americanized name for these flowers (poinsettia) came from the United States' first diplomat to Mexico, Joel Roberts Poinsett. He returned at Christmas with the flower and introduced them to America.

UNITED STATES

Much like the country itself, the United States' Christmas traditions stem from immigrants from around the world who settled here. Our love of trees comes from Germany. Our Santa was heavily influenced by the Dutch Sinterklaas. Our tradition of sending Christmas cards comes from the Brits. The lighting of luminaries, which are small fires that show the way on Christmas Eve, comes from Mexico. The list goes on and on.

CHRISTMAS FOOD

The one common thread through every Christmas tradition around the world is food. Regardless of how religious or secular the celebration is, at some point families and friends get together on Christmas Eve or Christmas Day and eat. Food is in Christmas music ("Oh, bring us some figgy pudding," "Chestnuts roasting on an open fire," "And I've brought some corn for popping,"

and many, many more mentions). Food plays a massive role in the final act of *A Christmas Carol* ("Hallo, my fine fellow… Do you know whether they've sold the prize Turkey that was hanging up there?"). The final scene in *How the Grinch Stole Christmas* shows the Grinch completing his redemption by carving the roast beast. Even more than trees, lights, and stockings, there is no proper Christmas without food.

Here is why we eat and drink the things we do at Christmas.

CHESTNUTS

You literally can't get one word into the most performed Christmas song of all time, "The Christmas Song," without hearing about chestnuts. And since that song is synonymous with the holiday, so are the shiny brown nuts. How'd they get there? And why doesn't anyone in America eat them anymore?

Unlike most traditional Christmas foods, chestnuts were never considered special. They were everywhere, they were cheap, and they could fill you up. Chestnuts were first associated with a different holiday—St. Martin's Day. The fourth-century French saint is the patron saint of beggars, drunkards, and the poor. On his remembrance day, the poor were given chestnuts for sustenance.

In the seventeenth and eighteenth centuries, chestnuts weren't just a Christmas treat, they were in a myriad of recipes. The massive hundred-foot chestnut trees produced a ton of acorn-sized nuts and could grow all over the United States (*USA Today*: "from Maine to Alabama, and as far west as Kentucky and Ohio"). In those days, nearly half of the trees in East Coast forests were chestnut trees.

Sadly, in 1904, a gardener in New York Zoological Park noticed a tree was sick. The blight was traced back to an Asian chestnut that had been imported to Long Island. Over the next forty years, all of the chestnut trees died. Nowadays, if you want chestnuts roasting on an open fire, you're probably going to have to go to Europe.

GOOSE

In the old days when nearly everyone was a farmer, picking the prized meal for Christmas was an important choice. If you ate chicken, you were depleting the egg supply. If you opted for steak, you said farewell to that cow's milk. Geese, on the other hand, didn't lay a ton of eggs. So they were eaten when they were at their fattest—at year's end. But still, most geese were pretty small. To illustrate that point, Charles Dickens had the Ghost of Christmas Present point out the meager bird that was the Cratchit family's Christmas dinner. In the end, part of Scrooge's redemption was getting the Cratchits heartier fare—a turkey.

HAM

To honor Freyr, pagans had a boar's head at their solstice feasts. Not too long after Christmas was established as a holiday by Pope Julius I and the Catholic Church in the fourth century, those pagan traditions started getting associated with Christmas. More than one thousand years later, Tudor England still had a boar's head as the centerpiece of their Christmas feasts. But boars were expensive. So unless they were nobility, lots of people went with the cheaper ham. Ever since, many families have continued the ham tradition.

TURKEY

As family sizes grew, a Christmas goose just wasn't going to cut it. Turkeys were usually a little bigger and cheaper. They were born in the spring and reached a pretty good size by Christmas. So while the rich people still enjoyed their fancy stuff, the average Joe in nineteenth-century America and Britain ate turkeys on Christmas. At the end of *A Christmas Carol*, when Scrooge wants to make the Cratchit family's meal really special, he has a boy buy the "prize turkey hanging in the butcher's window."

EGGNOG

Eggnog almost certainly has its roots in medieval Britain. Back then, the wealthy would drink a warm, milky alcoholic beverage called "posset." It was consumed during winter months but was not necessarily a Christmas drink.

Then, over in America, the colonists started having their own warm, milky winter drink. The colonies were flush with farms that produced tons of milk and eggs. Also, rum was everywhere. Unlike brandy and wine, which came from Europe and were ridiculously over-taxed, rum came from the Caribbean. So people combined those three main ingredients and started having eggnog. Why the name? Well, the first syllable is pretty self-explanatory. But the second is up for debate. Some think it comes from "noggins," which were wooden cups. Others think it's because colonists called rum "grog" and the drink eventually went from "egg n' grog" to "eggnog."

It quickly took off. Even George Washington had his own recipe (with four types of booze in it!). In 1826, eggnog caused one of the United States' premier military academies, West Point, one of its biggest embarrassments. One of the strict rules on campus was there could be no alcohol. On Christmas Eve, a bunch of the cadets snuck several gallons of whiskey to add to their eggnog. The administration tried to put an end to the drunken revelry, and the "Eggnog Riot" erupted. Property was damaged, an officer was shot at, and about a third of the campus (including future Confederacy President Jefferson Davis) was disciplined.

CANDY CANES

The top-selling non-chocolate candy every December is the candy cane. But look for one outside that time of year, and you're probably out of luck. More than 90 percent of the 1.8 billion candy canes in America are sold between Thanksgiving and Christmas. Have you ever seen anybody sucking on a candy cane in June?

Their origins go all the way back to seventeenth-century Germany, where sugar sticks were all the rage with kids. (These were simpler times. There wasn't a whole lot to get super excited about.)

There's an apocryphal story about how a German priest gave them to kids to keep them quiet during church and had them shaped to look like shepherd staffs. There's also the possibility that candy canes originated from a local apothecary as something palatable to help with taking nasty medicine. That's why some of those old-timey cough drop brands taste like candy.

But we can trace American origins of candy canes to the same guy who helped popularize the Christmas tree in Ohio—August Imgard. In 1847, it was documented that he hung them on a prominent tree. Based on old Christmas cards, that tradition caught on shortly thereafter. But in those days, candy canes were all white. Stripes were added about fifty years later. Some think the peppermint flavor was added in the 1920s by candy maker Bob McCormack. The Wilt Chamberlain of the peppermint candy universe put peppermint into everything. Then, in 1950, a Catholic priest named Gregory Keller invented a machine that could mass produce the hooked candy sticks, and soon they were everywhere.

CHRISTMAS COOKIES

Christmas cookies probably became a thing in the Middle Ages. That's when everyone started learning about and experimenting with spices (like cinnamon, nutmeg, and ginger). And, since those spices and baking goods were expensive, people waited until there was a really special occasion—like Christmas.

Cookies lent themselves especially well to Christmas celebrations. Unlike pies and cakes, they could easily be stored for a while in case visitors showed up. Also, most people didn't have money to be buying presents. Most gifts were either crafts or baked goods, like cookies.

FIGGY PUDDING

That famous demand in the second verse of the song "We Wish You a Merry Christmas" ("So bring us some figgy pudding…") never made a ton of sense. Back in the day, carolers were expected to be fed, that's true. But why figgy pudding? And what is figgy pudding?

Figgy pudding almost never includes actual figs. Sometimes, it has been called plum pudding. And it doesn't even necessarily include plums, either. It's more like a bread pudding. The original version was disgusting—in the medieval days, the English packed spices and fruits with meat and vegetables into animal stomachs and intestines so they would stay edible longer. From there, it evolved to "plum pottage." Plum was just the word used for any dried fruit or vegetable back then, just like figs. In the sixteenth century, things shifted as they started using cloths to preserve everything (instead of animal parts) and used more fruits in the "pudding."

Over time, the pudding became more closely associated with Christmas. Oliver Cromwell banned it when he cancelled the holiday in the mid-1600s. After Cromwell died, the love of Christmas pudding came back even stronger. In *A Christmas Carol*, Charles Dickens wrote about it being the centerpiece of the Cratchits' holiday celebration:

"In half a minute Mrs. Cratchit entered—flushed, but smiling proudly—with the pudding, like a speckled cannon-ball, so hard and firm, blazing in half of half-a-quarter of ignited brandy, and bedight with Christmas holly stuck into the top."

Pudding is now one of the defining traditions of a British Christmas.

FRUITCAKE

Like a lot of sweet foods at Christmas, fruitcake was associated with the holiday because it was the only time of year when average people would splurge for things like sugar and dried fruits. Despite all the jokes from almost every sitcom over the past fifty years, fruitcake was a delicacy.

Fruitcake can be traced back to ancient Egypt, where they were placed in tombs for loved ones to take with them into the great beyond. In ancient Rome, they mixed pomegranate seeds, pine nuts, and raisins with malted barley. Since it lasted so long, Roman soldiers would take it with them when they went off to battle. This tradition continued with the Crusades in the Middle Ages.

In each century ever since, new ingredients were added to it (honey, various spices, sugar, butter, and so on). Then, in the Victorian era, they started pouring booze into it. It became so decadent that, at one point in the eighteenth century, it was banned. It worked its way back to weddings (in fact, it is still served at royal weddings) and Christmas.

In America, jokes about the cake's ability to maintain its form (because the alcohol kills bacteria) morphed into jokes about how awful it tastes. Johnny Carson once said, "The worst gift is fruitcake. There is only one fruitcake in the entire world, and people keep sending it to each other." But it's still quite popular around the world: Germany—*Stollen* (which is fruitcake with powdered sugar on top), Italy—*panettone*, Poland and Bulgaria—*keks*, Portugal— *bolo-rei*.

GINGERBREAD HOUSES

Ginger was one of the early popular items on the Silk Road. China had been using it for centuries for mostly medicinal purposes but, once it found its way to the rest of the world, its uses expanded to food. In the Middle Ages, it was used to mask the taste of preserved meats. Eventually, it was combined with molasses and formed into gingerbread. By the fifteenth century, Germany had its own gingerbread guild. The gingerbread itself had a sturdy quality which inspired the Germans to build little houses with it.

Its popularity grew until the seventeenth century, when supply became an issue. Governments restricted the usage of it to just Christmas and Easter. That is why it became more closely associated with December. The first time most of the world learned about Germany's gingerbread houses was after the Brothers Grimm fairy tale, *Hansel and Gretel*. From that point on, they became a Christmas tradition.

Queen Elizabeth I is credited with creating the first gingerbread man. As a treat to visiting dignitaries, the queen had her bakers shape and decorate the gingerbread into their likenesses.

SUGARPLUMS

Before candy manufacturers started making delicious confections, one of the few sweet treats were sugarplums. Thus, "visions of sugar-plums danced in their heads" may have been an actual thing for dreaming children at Christmastime in the early 1800s. Sugarplums, which are really candied fruit or seeds, go back at least as far back as 1609. Records show plums were boiled in sugared water to preserve them. Plums became synonymous with sweet things. In eighteenth-century England, rich people were called "plums." A good place to work was a "plum" job. Sugarplums became pretty much anything that was sugared.

CHRISTMAS TOYS

O ur love affair with Christmas usually starts at a young age when we make lists for Santa and hope we didn't end up on the "naughty" side of the ledger. If we were good over the past year, Santa will probably bring a toy we've been eyeing. For the last 120 or so years, there has always been a hot toy.

The "it" toys, over the last 120 or so years, tend to fall in one of sixteen categories:

1. **Vehicles** - Die-Cast Ford Model T (1908), Lionel Trains (1911), Matchbox Cars (1953), Tonka Pickup Truck (1955), Tonka Dump Truck (1965), Radio-Controlled Cars (1966), Hot Wheels (1968)
2. **Dolls** - Raggedy Ann (1915), Madame Alexander Collectible Dolls (1928), Shirley Temple Dolls (1934), Barbie (1959), Chatty Cathy (1960), Ken Doll (1961), Cabbage Patch Kids (1983), Bratz (2001)
3. **Stuffed Animals** - Teddy Bear (1906), Sock Monkey (1932), Beanie Babies (1995)
4. **Weapons and Military Stuff** - Buck Rogers Rocket Pistol (1934), Green Army Men (1935), Daisy's Red Ryder BB Gun (1940), Water Balloons (1950), Action Man (1964), G.I. Joe (1964)
5. **Board Games** - Monopoly (1939), Scrabble (1948), Game of Life (1959), Operation (1965), Twister (1966), Battleship (1967), Uno (1972), Connect Four (1976), Jenga (1987)
6. **Big Brain Toys** - Erector Set (1909), Chemistry Set (1920, 1969), Microscope Set (1933), Rubik's Cube (1980)
7. **Creative Toys** - Crayola Crayon (1903), Paint-by-Numbers (1952), Play-Doh (1953), Etch A Sketch (1959), LEGO (1959), Easy-Bake Oven (1962), Spirograph (1964), Lite-Brite (1966)
8. **Fisher-Price Toys** - Little People (1949), Corn Popper (1956), Rock-A-Stack (1959), Weebles *not F-P but clearly inspired by them* (1969), Chatter Telephone (1971)
9. **Sporting Goods and Active Stuff** - Yo-Yos (1928), Whiffle Ball (1953), Pogo Stick (1956, 2001), Hula Hoops (1957),

Skateboards (1958), Frisbee (1960), Superball (1963), Hippety Hoppers (1971), NERF Football (1972), BMX (1982), Laser Tag (1986), Koosh Balls (1987), Razor Scooters (2000)

10. **Interactive Animals** - Teddy Ruxpin (1986), Tamagotchi (1997), Furby (1998), FurReal Cat (2002), Robosapiens (2003), Zhu Zhu Pets (2009), Teksta the Robotic Puppy (2013), Zoomer Dino (2014)

11. **Movie- and Television-Related Merchandise** - Mickey Mouse (1923), Gumby Colorforms (1950), Smurfs (1981), Transformers (1984), Care Bears (1985), Teenage Mutant Ninja Turtles (1990), Talking Barney (1992), Talkboy (1993), Mighty Morphin Power Rangers (1994), Tickle Me Elmo (1996), Elmo Live (2008), Let's Rock Elmo (2011), Big Hugs Elmo (2013), Snow Glow Elsa Doll (2014), BB-8 (2015), Star Wars the Child Animatronic Edition *a.k.a. "Baby Yoda"* (2020)

12. **Action Figures** - Playmobil (1974), Stretch Armstrong (1977), Star Wars figures and toys (1977), Starting Lineup (1988)

13. **Electronics** - Pong (1972), Mattel Classic Football (1977), Simon (1978), Speak & Spell (1978), Atari Video Computer System (1979), Nintendo Entertainment System (1988), Game Boy (1989), Xbox 360 (2001), Nintendo DS (2004), PlayStation 3 (2006), Nintendo Wii (2006), iPod Touch (2007), Barnes & Noble Nook (2009), iPad (2010), LeapPad Explorer (2011), Wii U (2012), NES Classic (2016)

14. **Miscellaneous Classics** - Radio Flyer Wagon (1917), Pop-Up Books (1928), View Master (1939), Bubble Solution (1940), Little Golden Books (1942), Mr. Potato Head (1952), Pez Dispensers (1957), Rock 'Em Sock 'Em Robots (1964)

15. **Tough-to-Explain Things** - Pet Rock (1975), Pogs (1991), Pokémon (1999)
16. **Stuff That Got Boring by New Year's** - Joy Buzzer (1927), Magic 8-Ball (1940), Slinky (1945), Silly Putty (1952), Sea-Monkeys (1961), Barrel of Monkeys (1965), Beyblades (2002)

Here are the stories behind the biggest toys:

Teddy Bear (1906) - In 1902, President Theodore Roosevelt was on a hunting trip in Mississippi. To make the big guy feel good, a few of his handlers tied a black bear to a tree. Instead of killing the defenseless bear, Teddy set it free. Stories of the great big game hunter letting the bear go free made the news, and political cartoonist Clifford Berryman drew a picture of the incident. Brooklyn shopkeeper Morris Michtom saw that cartoon and had his wife make a stuffed fabric "Teddy's Bear" to put in his store's front window. Michtom's bear became incredibly popular, and the shopkeeper was soon running his own toy company.

Die-Cast Ford Model T (1908) - Ever since the Ford Motor Company kicked out Model Ts off their assembly lines, kids have been craving the die-cast model versions of them. Throughout the years, the cars got better, and so did the toy versions. More than a century later, there's still a good chance one or two of them will end up in the stocking of a kid near you.

Yo-Yos (1928) - The spinning-disc-on-a-string toy has been around for centuries in one form or another. There are paintings of Napoleon and Louis XVII playing with them. But the modern iteration of the toy goes back about a century, when a man named Pedro Flores began making it and calling it by its Filipino name—yo-yo. Then, in 1928, a businessman named Don Duncan saw kids marveling at Flores' yo-yo and smelled money. So Duncan teamed up with Flores and worked out some advertising deal with William Randolph Hearst, and by the end of the year, yo-yos were all the rage.

Shirley Temple Dolls (1934) - By 1934, six-year-old Shirley Temple was one of the biggest stars in America. The cute-as-a-button singer and dancer offered an escape from the Great Depression. If people were going to shell out a nickel to see any performer, it was usually Shirley Temple. So, the Ideal Toy and Novelty Company jumped on the rising star and made a doll that looked like her, pricing it at an exorbitant five dollars. Every girl had to have it. Over the next seven years, Ideal Toys raked in $45 million from Shirley Temple Dolls.

Slinky (1945) - There are some toys that, on television or when being demonstrated by a salesperson, look super cool. Then, when you take them out of the packaging, you realize they're a real bummer. No toy epitomizes that disappointment quite like the Slinky. Invented by a naval engineer named Richard James, who once accidentally knocked over a bunch of springs, the Slinky was eighty feet of wire coiled into a two-inch spiral. His wife, Betty, came up with a fun name for it. Slinky commercials had a fun theme song. And, in demonstrations, you could make it go down the stairs. Then you got it home and it maybe made it down three steps before stopping. Nonetheless, Slinky was a massive hit. James sold more than twenty thousand Slinkys by Christmas in his first year.

That was the highlight for Richard James. Lowlights included giving Slinky profits to a religious cult and abandoning his family to move to Bolivia. He wasn't the worst toy maker, though. The guy who invented Sea-Monkeys (which are really just brine shrimp) donated lots of his profits to neo-Nazi groups.

Fisher-Price Little People (1949) - In 1930, the town of East Aurora, New York was getting hammered by the Great Depression. So Mayor Irving Price asked his children's book illustrator wife, Margaret Evans Price, and a business associate, Herman Fisher, to help him come up with something special. Mr. Fisher thought little kids needed better toys. So he and Mrs. Price approached the owner of a local toy store (Helen Schelle) and the three came up with some toys (like the pull toy, a dog named Snoopy Sniffer) and started a company named Fisher-Price. For nearly a century, Fisher-Price has been the go-to toy maker for toddlers and preschoolers.

Mr. Potato Head (1952) - George Lerner figured the best way to get kids to enjoy toys was to let them create their own. So he made a bunch of limbs and facial features that could be jammed into a potato and called it Mr. Potato Head. At first, he was going to sell it to a cereal company to use as a prize in the bottom of the box, but the Hassenfeld brothers (the future founders of Hasbro) bought it instead to promote as a children's toy. To fuel the launch, the Hassenfelds made Mr. Potato Head the subject of the first-ever toy commercial on television in 1952. In the beginning, it was just a box full of body parts with the suggestion of using your own potato (but "ANY FRUIT OR VEGETABLE MAKES A FUNNY FACE MAN"). After a few years—and probably a lot of parents complaining about rotting fruits and vegetables throughout their homes— the company started supplying a plastic potato.

Barbie (1959) - The founder of the Mattel toy company, Ruth Handler, noticed her daughter liked playing with adult paper dolls and had an idea—what about adult dolls marketed to young girls? So she made a doll that seemed suspiciously like a German toy already out on the market called Bild Lilli. Lilli was a call girl gag gift that could be found in tobacco shops. Handler covered up the doll's provocative physique with clothing similar to the style of stars of the day (like Marilyn Monroe) and marketed it as Barbie. Handler sold over three hundred thousand Barbies in that first year.

In 2001, a new line of fashion dolls came out called Bratz, which were essentially just Barbies with bigger eyes. They were an instant hit. Mattel sued and was given $100 million for the theft.

LEGO (1959) - New LEGO sets dominate just about every Christmas. Nearly one hundred billion LEGO bricks are sold each year. But the company originally had nothing to do with toys. About a hundred years ago, a ladder and ironing board-maker named Ole Kirk Christiansen hit a horrible stretch of bad luck. First, his sons accidentally burned down his workshop. Then the Great Depression hit and his wife died. So he used his woodworking skills to make more affordable things that could actually sell—toys. He renamed his company Leg Godt (meaning "play well") and it eventually became LEGO. After World War II, LEGO switched to plastic bricks and patterned them after a British company called Kiddicraft (which they eventually bought). The rest is history.

G.I. Joe (1964) - Seeing the recent success of Mattel's Barbie, Hasbro came up with a male counterpart—Government-Issue Joe. Rather than call it a doll, it was dubbed an "action figure" with "twenty-one moveable parts." G.I. Joe came in four versions: Action Soldier, Pilot, Marine, and Sailor. But, as Vietnam ramped up, the appeal of having boys playing with soldiers made people feel a bit uneasy. So, in 1970, G.I. Joe became more of a man of adventure. One version was a space traveler. But, in 1978, Joe was sent packing.

By the early 1980s, G.I. Joe had a renaissance. Star Wars figures had breathed new life in the action figure world, and people began to move past Vietnam. So, in 1982, Joe figures were back. But, instead of the foot-tall soldier dolls, they returned as Darth Vader and Chewbacca-sized plastic figures (3¾-inches).

NERF Football (1972) - In 1968, Reyn Guyer (the guy who invented Twister) came up with the "world's first indoor ball." As it was made out of foam, the Parker Brothers called it "Nerf" (non-expanding recreational foam). It was pretty successful, but the NERF line didn't really take off until Minnesota Vikings kicker Fred Cox and his business partner John Mattox helped make the NERF Football in 1972. Now, NERF comes in every type of ball to go with safe ammunition for kids to shoot at each other.

Uno (1972) - After one too many arguments with his family about the changing rules of the card game crazy eights, barber Merle Robbins decided to simplify the game and write the instructions on a deck of cards. The end result was a slight departure from crazy eights and, instead, created an entirely new card game—Uno. Merle leveraged his mortgage to produce five thousand packs and toured campgrounds across the country until they were all sold. The game caught the eye of a marketer, who redesigned the cards themselves and, in 1972, released one of the more popular games in America. Eighty percent of all households have played Uno.

Star Wars Figures and Toys (1977) - In 1977, there was nothing bigger in the kids' universe than *Star Wars*. While George Lucas had been prescient enough to work a deal that would give him ownership of merchandising for the movie, the toy company Kenner was late to start production on any action figures or spaceships. Unfortunately for the parents who submitted mail orders, they were unable to produce Luke Skywalker, Princess Leia, R2-D2, and Chewbacca figures in time for Christmas. The only Star Wars items that could be tucked in stockings were vouchers for when they became available. IOUs for Christmas! Demand only increased as *Star Wars* stayed in theaters for years. By 1978, Star Wars figures were everywhere.

Simon (1978) - Technology started getting really good, and lists given to Santa started getting a whole lot more expensive. In 1978, the Studio 54 launch party for the game Simon cranked it up a notch. Developed by Ralph Baer, the man who invented the first home video game, Simon was a light-up version of Simon Says. And it cost twenty-five bucks. That's over $100 today. For an electronic Simon Says game with four colors and four sounds.

Atari Video Computer System (1979) - After the success of games like Pong and Mattel's Classic Football, it was clear there was a market for electronic games at home. In stepped the Atari Video Computer System (later called the Atari 2600). Within two years, it was in ten million homes. Over the years, popular games like Pac-Man have helped the market explode (and brought Atari fierce competition). Atari has since faded, but the home video game market is still expanding more than four decades later.

Rubik's Cube (1980) - In 1974, a Hungarian sculptor and design teacher Ernő Rubik designed a three-dimensional puzzle and called it the Magic Cube. He got a toy agent, who hooked him up with the Ideal Toy and Novelty Company, who renamed it Rubik's Cube and put it in stores in 1980. Within a couple of years, two hundred million had been sold worldwide.

Cabbage Patch Kids (1983) - All crazy Christmas shopping stories start with one doll in particular—Cabbage Patch Kids. In the late 1970s, an art student in Georgia named Xavier Roberts started hand-stitching dolls called "Little People." Each doll had its own distinctive features and name. Over time, the brand name was switched to Cabbage Patch Kids. Instead of selling them in an ordinary store, Roberts created a fake nursery out of an abandoned medical clinic in Cleveland, Georgia. All employees wore white nursing uniforms and "delivered" the babies out of a cabbage patch. Then prospective "parents" had to fill out adoption papers and pledge their eternal love for the dolls. The whole experiment worked, and soon Roberts landed a big deal with the company Coleco. By 1983, it was the most-requested toy on the market. Coleco sold more than two and a half million Cabbage Patch Kids, but demand was insatiable. Stories of rioting, injuries, and arrests over new doll deliveries were commonplace during Christmas '83. Demand dwindled as fast as it came and, by 1988, the company went bankrupt.

Teddy Ruxpin (1986) - After about eighty years, people felt the teddy bear was ready for an upgrade. Disney Imagineer Ken Forsse came up with a bear called Teddy Ruxpin that moved its eyes and mouth when you placed a cassette tape in its back. It was both terrifying and a massive hit. Demand far exceeded supply, and Teddy Ruxpin bears were fetching triple the retail price on the black market.

Talkboy (1993) - While most blockbuster movies inspire some sort of doll or action figure toy that's pretty hot by Christmas, the Talkboy from *Home Alone 2* was just a fake prop turned real. In the movie, Kevin used this sleek recording device that could replay and manipulate voices. Everyone wanted it. So they rushed out a real version of the fake prop, and it became one of the biggest toys at Christmas.

Beanie Babies (1995) - College dropout and failed actor Ty Warner got into the family business—toys—and used his inheritance to create Ty, Inc. Warner hit it big making realistic-looking cat toys in Asia. Instead of using the customary stuffing, Warner under-stuffed the toys with pellets. That way they could be posed and appear more natural. He then expanded his business to lots of different toy animals around the world and called them Beanie Babies. By pricing them at only five dollars and limiting the quantity of each animal type, Warner drove up crazy demand. By Christmas of 1995, people were going nuts trying to track down specific animals. At one point, Beanie Babies represented 10 percent of all eBay sales.

Tickle Me Elmo (1996) - Toy inventor Ron Dubren brought his tickle doll idea to Tyco, who had the rights to Sesame Street. In the '90s, Elmo kind of wrestled the popularity title belt from Big Bird and Cookie Monster. Then they turned Dubren's tickle doll into an Elmo and the toy was released in the summer of 1996. And it barely moved the needle. So, in October, Tyco's PR people got Tickle Me Elmo to be featured on the Rosie O'Donnell show. Rosie would talk about the doll and give one to everyone in the audience. By Black Friday, it was completely sold out. People were beating each other up and store employees got badly injured as they brought new boxes to the shelves. Just like Cabbage Patch Kids thirteen years earlier, black market toys and arrests became regular news stories. Now Elmo toys are a Christmas staple for preschoolers.

Furby (1998) - In the '90s, Tiger Electronics came out with the Furby, a disturbing kind of owl-hamster hybrid that spoke a fictional language called "Furbish." The hook to the Furby was that, over time, kids could teach it basic English words. When the Furby became one of the "it" Christmas toys of 1998, they didn't wait for the black market to cash in their status. Retail prices for the Furby were jacked up from $35 to $100.

iPod Touch (2007) - Steve Jobs had a massive influence on holiday wish lists in the twenty-first century with the iPod, then the iPod Touch (which Jobs called "training wheels for the iPhone"), then the iPhone, and iPad. Imitation tablets and phones soon followed. The demand was the same, but Christmas shopping was now in a whole different stratosphere in terms of pricing.

Snow Glow Elsa Doll (2014) - After the success of the movie *Frozen* at the end of 2013, little girls everywhere wanted an Elsa doll the following Christmas. After lackluster sales for previous princess movies, Disney wasn't banking on a massive success. But *Frozen* was a monster, making more than a billion at the box office. For an entire year, Snow Glow Elsa was tough to find.

CHRISTMAS FASHION

Why are red and green known as the colors of Christmas? Well, green is thought to represent evergreen trees, the Garden of Eden, and Jesus (eternal life). Red may represent Santa, or to some, the blood of Jesus. A prevailing theory is that the colors are inspired by holly, with its green leaves and red berries.

Today, red and green are symbolic of the holiday, from decorations to attire. And what is Christmas fashion? Depending on the era, the answer is wildly different.

NINETEENTH CENTURY

Victorian Britain really set the tone for Christmas wardrobe. Holiday parties became massive social events, and dressing the part was an imperative. For young unmarried women, this was a chance to present themselves. There are numerous surviving accounts of publications establishing proper etiquette and expected attire. White, delicate fabrics showed off an innocence. Married women, on the other hand, wore standout colors and materials, like lace. Throughout the nineteenth century, the dresses became fuller at Christmas balls, but the goals stayed pretty consistent—landing a husband or showing your status.

TWENTIETH CENTURY

The high-fashion Christmases trickled down into the middle class as well. By the early twentieth century, Christmas became a time for people to wear the absolute best clothing they had. Men also got into the custom, wearing fancy tuxedos to formal functions. It was understood that Christmas called for the height of fashion. From the Roaring Twenties onward, it was important that people be dressed to the nines at Christmas, whether for church or at parties.

UGLY SWEATERS

The commercial explosion of Christmas in the 1950s led to the introduction of "jingle bell sweaters." These pullovers featured snow-covered trees or reindeer. The sweaters weren't remotely considered ironic at the time, just festive. Pop culture soon made the Christmas sweater explode. Crooners like Andy Williams wore them during annual TV specials to give off a cozy, down-home vibe. By the '80s, they were fairly mainstream.

In attempts to squeeze comedy out of the Christmas sweater, sitcoms and movies like *Christmas Vacation* put their main characters in over-the-top versions of them throughout the '80s. Then, suddenly, everyone collectively decided they weren't fun or cool. And, in the '90s, they vanished. The only people who still wore them were weird uncles that you were already trying to avoid at family gatherings.

Suddenly, in the early 2000s, two events led to people collectively discovering the beauty in ironically wearing the ugly Christmas sweater: the movie *Bridget Jones's Diary*, and a certain party in Canada. In the 2001 Renée Zellweger Christmas-adjacent movie (more on that later), Colin Firth's character, Mark Darcy, is seen wearing an awful Rudolph sweater. The comic scene portrays the stuffy barrister (lawyer) as looking ridiculous. A year later, a pair of men in Vancouver fully embraced the humor of it all and hosted a Christmas sweater party, where everyone had to wear a classically bad Christmas-themed jumper. A tradition was born. Today, the ugly Christmas sweater is almost a badge of honor, with styles ranging from SpongeBob to the Wu Tang Clan.

MATCHING PAJAMAS

While ugly Christmas sweaters signaled a change from Christmas being a formal wear occasion, the rise of matching pajamas signaled the ironic trend was here to stay. For many, spending the day in matching family pajamas is now the goal. Without question, this trend emerged from social media.

As far back as the 1950s, department store catalogs advertised matching pajamas. "Mommy and me" fashion was already something pushed on consumers, so sleepwear wasn't a huge stretch. But, really, it wasn't until the dawn of social media that family matching Christmas pajamas became a staple. In 2013, a family from North Carolina posted a video, #XMASJAMMIES, in which they rapped about the past year in matching PJs. The video has gotten more than seventeen million views. Each year since, the retail market for pajamas ranging from infant to adult XXL sizes has expanded. In 2020, the retail giant Target posted sales of more than five hundred thousand matching family sets of pajamas.

Christmas has gone from evening gowns and tuxedos to the pursuit of staying cozy all day.

CHRISTMAS BOOKS

Christmas traditions used to be mostly regional. New York would have one way of celebrating, and Massachusetts or London would be vastly different. A lot of that changed in the nineteenth century, thanks to some influential books by Washington Irving, Charles Dickens, and (probably) Henry Livingston, Jr.

Through literature, people became exposed to different ways of celebrating Christmas. Also, many of history's finest writers have used the holiday season as a backdrop for their heroes' adventures. Some have given a more layered backstory to Santa Claus. Others painted vivid pictures of their childhood Christmas traditions. Popular bedtime stories at Christmas have been turned into blockbuster movies. And, once, there was a self-published short story (possibly just a pamphlet) that inspired the most famous Christmas movie of all time.

Here are some of the most famous Christmas stories:

The Sketchbook of Geoffrey Crayon, Gent. by Washington Irving (1820)

Thanks to the popularity of the Headless Horseman and Ichabod Crane, Washington Irving will always be associated with spooky Halloween tales. But his biggest cultural impact was actually on Christmas. While this collection of short stories from 1819 and 1820 does include "The Legend of Sleepy Hollow" and "Rip Van Winkle," it also has five stories in the middle ("Christmas," "The Stage Coach," "Christmas Eve," "Christmas Day," and "The Christmas Dinner") that laid the foundation for many of the Christmas traditions we have in America today. Much like his parody *A History of New York*, his Christmas stories talk of long-ago traditions that never actually were. As a result of the popularity of the stories, those traditions were adopted into annual celebrations ("good St. Nicholas came riding over the tops of the trees, in that self-same wagon wherein he brings his yearly presents to children," family dinners, singing, and more).

A Visit from St. Nicholas *probably* by Henry Livingston, Jr. (1823)

The most interesting fact about perhaps the most famous Christmas story of all time is the fact that nobody knows, for sure, who wrote it. The story now called "'Twas the Night before Christmas" first appeared in upstate New York's *Troy Sentinel* newspaper on

December 23, 1823 without any name attached to it. Twenty-one years later, a Biblical scholar named Clement Moore was given credit. Then the family of a journalist named Henry Livingston, Jr. claimed that they had been hearing that story for many years before it ever appeared in the newspaper. Who was telling the truth?

Moore was the first person to claim authorship. His family said that on Christmas Eve in 1822, Moore took his "one-horse open sleigh" to go turkey shopping. As he rode, he was inspired by thinking about Santa in his sleigh and composed the whole fifty-six-line poem in his head. When he got home, he wrote it down, then read it before everyone as they ate Christmas dinner. One family member copied it and returned to upstate New York with it. Somehow the poem got entered into the *Troy Sentinel* the following year. When the poem got famous, Moore declared it was he who was the anonymous poet and, ever since, he has been credited as the author.

Here's why that's probably garbage. The theologian seemingly hated the secular parts of Christmas. In his mind, the holiday was a time to atone for sins. When invited to join New York's St. Nicholas Society by Washington Irving and Gulian Verplanck, Clement Clarke Moore turned them down. He saw no need to join a group who collected gifts for the poor and had an annual feast in celebration. And his poetry was full of unflattering descriptions of kids, who generally deserved to be scolded. There were no "sugarplums dancing in their heads" or anything remotely celebrating the wonder of a child's imagination. Clement Clarke Moore was a real bummer.

Henry Livingston, Jr., on the other hand, was a delight. Besides writing satire and columns for New York papers and magazines under wacky pseudonyms like "Seignior Whimsicallo Pomposo," Livingston also wrote lots of lighthearted poems for his eleven kids. Moreover, his mom was Dutch. Keep in mind, this poem is one of the main works of literature credited for spreading the whole Sinterklaas thing into America from Dutch traditions. In the original poem, two of the reindeer were named "Dunder" and "Blixem." Those are the Dutch words for "Thunder" and "Lightning." Moore had no Dutch roots.

Even a neighbor of the Livingstons recalled the poem being recited each year. Vassar College English professor Don Foster did a deep dig on the two authors' writing styles, and the pronoun-adverb balance in Livingston's work very similarly matched those in *A Visit from St. Nicholas*. Moore's did not. Foster also pointed out that, even though most writers in America around that time said "Merry Christmas," it was Livingston who wrote "Happy Christmas," as St. Nick did in the last line of the poem.

A Christmas Carol by Charles Dickens (1843)

Charles Dickens wrote *A Christmas Carol* for two reasons: One, he wanted to remind the people of Victorian England to be more empathetic towards the poor, and two, he was broke. Despite all his previous success with *Oliver Twist* and *The Pickwick Papers*, supporting a large family and his 1842 American tour had emptied his wallet. So he wrote a Christmas ghost story in just six weeks to raise some funds.

A Christmas Carol was an instant success, selling all six thousand books printed in its first week. Its impact on the holiday was also instantaneous. During the Victorian era, the prevailing thought was that prisons and workhouses were taking care of those living in poverty. The average citizen needn't be concerned with their plight. But at the end of this influential book, Ebenezer Scrooge—the novella's antagonist—realized that to be a good person, he needed to share his wealth. Charitable giving around Christmas increased right away and hasn't stopped since.

The Fir-Tree by Hans Christian Andersen (1844)

This Christmas story by the Danish fairy tale legend speaks from the perspective of an insecure tree. It sees other trees in the forest get cut down and anxiously wonders when its turn will be. When it does get cut down and is decorated as a Christmas tree, again, it wonders what's next. Even if the ending takes a predictable turn, it's a pretty good tale about enjoying the moment.

Merry Christmas and Other Stories by Louisa May Alcott (1868)

This collection of Christmas short stories starts with an excerpt from Alcott's coming-of-age novel, *Little Women*. The March women receive books under their pillows on Christmas morning and talk about how they deeply cherish them during these challenging times. The other stories are more of the same—just a lot of warmth and wholesomeness without a great deal of substance.

A Letter from Santa Claus by Mark Twain (1875)

One of the perks of being the daughter of one of the greatest writers in American history is that when Santa writes you a letter, it tends to be super cool. He assures little Suzy Clemens that he had no problem reading her (and her little sister's) chicken-scratch handwriting. He is very sweet and loving (although it seems a bit odd that Santa would be kissing Twain's three-year-old daughter while she slept). He also drops some ominous warnings for the Twain's butler, George, though. "You must tell George he must walk on tiptoe and not speak—otherwise he will die someday." Yikes. The salutation at the end is interesting, because Santa ends the passage with "Your Loving Santa Claus / Whom people sometimes call "the Man in the Moon." Even though Thomas Nast had established he lived on the North Pole in the previous decade, Santa's place of residence was still up for debate in 1875.

The Adventure of the Blue Carbuncle by Arthur Conan Doyle (1892)

Arthur Conan Doyle sent the world's most famous detective on a Christmas adventure. Dr. Watson finds Sherlock Holmes trying to figure out the identity of a man who got into a scuffle on Christmas morning and dropped his hat… and his goose. Inside of that Christmas goose was a previously stolen precious jewel (the blue carbuncle). Holmes spends the rest of the story trying to figure out who stole the stone and, in the process, frees the innocent man who has already been arrested for it.

Yes, Virginia, There Is a Santa Claus by Francis Pharcellus Church (1897)

In 1897, an eight-year-old girl named Virginia O'Hanlon wrote a letter to the editor of New York's *Sun* newspaper asking if Santa Claus was real. Her friends were saying he wasn't but her father said to check with *The Sun*. (Way to pass the buck, Dad.) "Please tell me the truth, is there a Santa Claus?" That letter found its way to a seasoned newsman named Francis Church. The former Civil War correspondent and atheist could have easily ignored it or wrote some evasive what-

Christmas-is-really-about column, but instead Church directly answered the little girl. "Virginia, your little friends are wrong. They have been affected by the skepticism of a skeptical age." The column, which has been reprinted more times than any in American history, celebrates all that's innocent and possible with children. There's plenty of time in adulthood for bigger worries but, for now, a kid should just enjoy being a kid at Christmas. "Yes, Virginia, there is a Santa Claus. He exists as certainly as love and generosity and devotion exist, and you know that they abound and give to your life its highest beauty and joy." Virginia grew up to be a teacher. Church's column has been made into books, TV movies, and cartoons.

The Life and Adventures of Santa Claus by L. Frank Baum (1902)

The author of *The Wizard of Oz* made a whole origin story for Santa. The first half of the book gets a bit bogged down with discussions of how some nymphs adopted a human child and their grim view of adulthood (which plays into why Santa only visits children). "The men and women I dare not interfere with; they must bear the burdens Nature has imposed upon them. But the helpless infants, the innocent children of men, have a right to be happy until they become full-grown and able to bear the trials of humanity." It picks up about halfway through, offering a more complete picture of why Santa does the things he does (reindeer, Christmas Eve, and so on).

The Tailor of Gloucester by Beatrix Potter (1903)

Famous children's book author and illustrator Beatrix Potter wrote a Christmas story about a tailor and the mice who live in his home. The tailor is tasked with making a jacket and vest (waistcoat) for the mayor for his Christmas Day wedding. But he gets a bad fever before he can complete this make-or-break career-defining job. So the mice pitch in to help while the tailor's miserable cat, Simpkin, tries to murder them.

The Gift of the Magi by O. Henry (1905)

In December of 1905, *New York* World writer O. Henry sat down at Pete's Tavern and spent three hours kicking out an overdue column while a messenger for the paper was waiting. It turned out to be one of the most famous short stories in history—*The Gift of the Magi.*

Della and Jim are a young (and very poor) married couple who sacrifice their most prized possessions to get each other a Christmas gift. The story epitomizes the beauty of Christmas in only about twenty-two hundred words.

The Velveteen Rabbit by Margery Williams (1922)

The story opens with a stuffed rabbit resting atop a boy's Christmas stocking. From there, it's a beautiful tale of a rabbit yearning to become real, and not some worn-out old toy. It's sort of like the 1920s British version of *Toy Story*. Scarlet fever plays the role of the villain.

Rudolph the Red-Nosed Reindeer by Robert L. May (1939)

During the Great Depression, the manager at Montgomery Ward, a department store in Chicago, was looking for a way to get more families in his store. In the past, they handed out coloring books to the kids, but this year, they were hoping to do it on the cheap. So the manager asked office raconteur and funnyman Robert May to come up with something. May had dreams of becoming a great novelist but instead was writing copy for a department store. He tapped into memories of being bullied as a child and combined it with his desire to do something more substantial with his life. And he came up with one of the most successful Christmas stories of all time—*Rudolph the Red-Nosed Reindeer.*

The Greatest Gift by Philip Van Doren Stern (1943)

The self-published short story that the movie *It's a Wonderful Life* was based on follows the path of a guy named George Platt who is contemplating suicide. Unlike the movie everyone knows, there is no missing money or Old Man Potter bearing down on him. George is just a malcontent who wishes he was never born. Then an old man shows up, tells him suicide is a bad idea, and suggests George go wander around town pretending to be a brush salesman so he can see what life would be like if he was never born. It's pleasant enough but lacks a great villain like Potter and the backstory of earnest George Bailey that has you pulling for him. This original version of George Platt seems like an overly dramatic guy who had a bad day.

A Visit to the Bank by Shirley Jackson (late 1940s?)

Shirley Jackson (the twisted short story writer of *The Lottery*) tried her hand at a Christmas tale with *A Visit to the Bank*. It's about a woman who is trying to get a loan right before Christmas. She brings her daughters along to hopefully garner some sympathy from the manager. Then a Santa shows up and things get awkward for Mom.

A Child's Christmas in Wales by Dylan Thomas (1955)

Welsh poet Dylan Thomas' Christmas prose was originally performed on BBC Radio and released as a book a few years later. On one hand, it perfectly captures how people hold warm and fuzzy memories of the Christmases of their youth. On the other, Thomas paints a somewhat strange picture of Christmastime in Wales in the 1920s. Some things seem familiar (family, playing in the snow, turkey for dinner, singing Christmas songs). Others (blowing up multiple balloons until they burst, smoking as many cigarettes as possible, wondering about hippos) don't really make a ton of sense.

Christmas Day in the Morning by Pearl S. Buck (1955)

This Christmas short story by Nobel Prize winner Pearl S. Buck is about a farm boy who wants to do something special for his father. *Christmas Day in the Morning* is a sweet reminder of the value of a heartfelt gift.

A Christmas Memory by Truman Capote (1956)

After his parents got divorced, Truman Capote was sent to live with an elderly distant cousin named Nanny in Monroeville, Alabama (the town where he became friends with Harper Lee). He wrote about that time spent with Nanny (or "Sook," as he called her) and their Christmas traditions for *Mademoiselle* magazine in 1956. It's a mostly lighthearted story of charming childhood memories like making fruitcakes, mailing letters, and getting a Christmas tree. There are a few rough exceptions—when he says Nanny's face looks kind of craggy like Abraham Lincoln's, when he is sent off to military school, and when Nanny's dog, Queenie, is kicked to death by a horse.

How the Grinch Stole Christmas! by Dr. Seuss (1957)

One of the best books to get readers into the spirit of Christmas is about a grouchy creature who hates it. Every Christmas, the Whos down in Whoville party loudly and make a big spectacle of the holiday. The Grinch isn't into it. Just like Ebenezer Scrooge in *A Christmas Carol*, the Grinch's redemption is a reminder of what the magic of Christmas is truly all about. It's enough to make your heart grow three sizes. Interestingly, in the book, the Grinch is just black and white. The green part didn't come until the TV special.

The Adventure of the Christmas Pudding by Agatha Christie (1960)

Agatha Christie's famous detective Hercule Poirot gets thrown into the most British-sounding Christmas mystery of all—*The Adventure of the Christmas Pudding*. A precious ruby is stolen from an Egyptian prince, who is having a final fling before getting married. If that ruby doesn't make its way to the bride-to-be, there's going to be a huge scandal. To keep the situation from blowing up, the police aren't consulted. Instead, the Belgian detective is brought on board. Poirot attempts to discreetly solve the case while also celebrating a traditional British Christmas.

In God We Trust: All Others Pay Cash by Jean Shepherd (1966)

Shel Silverstein convinced his raconteur friend Jean Shepherd to write down his most popular radio stories. They were published in *Playboy* in the early 1960s. Then, the complete collection was put into this book. Four of those essays turned out to be some of the greatest Christmas stories ever told. Unlike other nostalgia-themed stories, Jean Shepherd's weren't told from an adult's perspective. Shepherd's every description was exactly how a kid sees things. Ralphie Parker didn't just want a toy BB gun for Christmas. He wanted a "Red Ryder carbine-action, two-hundred-shot range model air rifle!" Within a few paragraphs, Shepherd turns readers into kids again, salivating at the thought of the upcoming holiday. "Christmas was on its way. Lovely, glorious, beautiful Christmas, upon which the entire kid year revolved." The Christmas stories were so good, the movie it inspired (*A Christmas Story*) now gets twenty-four hour airings every Christmas Eve.

Oh, and Shepherd returned the favor to Silverstein, in a sense. Shepherd frequently complained about the humiliation of growing up a boy with a girl's name (Jean). This inspired Silverstein to write the song "A Boy Named Sue," which Johnny Cash turned into a hit in 1969.

Letters from Father Christmas by J.R.R. Tolkien (1976)

More than a decade before *The Lord of the Rings*, J. R. R. Tolkien wrote fantastical tales full of Christmas adventures. Tolkien's children would write their letters to Father Christmas and leave them by the fireplace (as was the custom) and, starting in 1920, Father Christmas would respond. The first letter was just a short one confirming to his three-year-old son, John, that he would, indeed, be coming on Christmas Eve. Over the next twenty-three years, the letters became much more intricate. The envelopes would be dusted with snow and bear North Pole stamps. The contents of the letters became more involved, with tales of Father Christmas' Polar Bear assistant, various elves and gnomes, and attacks by goblins. Even the handwriting would change depending on who was writing it (sometimes Polar Bear added to the letter with his unsteady paws). On the third anniversary of Tolkien's death, his estate published the entire collection of letters written between 1920 and 1943, and gave the world a peek into what childhood was like with one of the most imaginative storytellers in history as your dad.

The Polar Express by Chris Van Allsburg (1985)

Picture book legend Chris Van Allsburg (*Jumanji*) bagged his second Caldecott Medal with the tale of a boy who boards a train bound for the North Pole on Christmas Eve. The book has a realistic-looking oil painting on every page documenting the boy's journey until he meets the big man in the red suit. *The Polar Express* is all about believing and the joy that comes to those who still hear that bell ring.

Holidays on Ice by David Sedaris (1997)

David Sedaris first received national recognition when he read his essay about working as an elf for Macy's on NPR in 1992. In "SantaLand Diaries," Sedaris gave a hilarious look behind the scenes at Santa's village inside the New York City department store, complete with a breakdown of the various Santas, the side jobs of his fellow elves, frustrations with miserable parents and their poorly behaved children, and the cold businesslike nature of the whole operation. That essay, along with five other holiday tales—including a Christmas letter from a mom who is trying to put a cheerful spin on having a philandering husband and a prostitute stepdaughter—adds up to the funniest Christmas book ever written. Unlike the usual stories that focus on goodwill, nostalgia, and love, *Holidays on Ice* is a biting take on what can sometimes be phony and ridiculous during the season.

CHRISTMAS MUSIC

Unlike with every other type of music, nobody is looking for the hot new thing in the Christmas genre. December music charts are cluttered with songs that were recorded a half century earlier. The only song in last year's Billboard Holiday 100 List that was even recorded this century was a Michael Bublé cover of "It's Beginning to Look a Lot Like Christmas." That song was written in 1951! People absolutely love the old stuff. Most radio stations that switch to holiday music see a bump in ratings each December.

Christmas music hits a different part of a person's brain than regular music. It takes you back to performing in the school holiday show next to your best friend, or getting your first Nintendo Game Boy, or having a good laugh at your grandparents' dinner table. Christmas music is about nostalgia. And, because of that, anytime you leave the house in December, you are guaranteed to hear a song that was written before you were even born.

With nostalgia driving the bus, there's very little room for any new Christmas music to crack the rotation. Come December, pop stars compete with the ghosts of Bing Crosby, Dean Martin, John Lennon, and Mariah Carey. (Yes, Mariah is still with us, but "All I Want for Christmas Is You" is closer to the 1969 Moon landing than it is to today.)

Christmas songs can be broken into four categories:

1. THE CLASSICS (Before 1930) - These songs are the ones you hear a lot in commercials and TV shows or from aging musicians who just got cleaned out in a divorce. These songs are public domain. That means the copyright protections have run out. If you want to sing "Away in a Manger" or "Deck the Halls," have at it. Nobody owns the rights to them anymore.
2. THE CROONER ERA (1930 - 1954) - These are the Frank Sinatra/Dean Martin/Bing Crosby songs that everyone hears every single time they go to the supermarket in December. Many of these tunes appeared in crummy old movies with really bad sets and fake snow. They are the sound of Christmas. They're like an old, comfortable sweatshirt.
3. LATE TWENTIETH CENTURY (1955-1999) - This era contains some of the greatest Christmas songs, musically speaking, as artists were taking more chances. The studios

didn't quite have the firm grip they used to, which allowed a lot of different kinds of classics (rock, punk, new wave, rap).
4. MODERN (2000 - Present) – The newest ones aren't as recognizable as all the rest because they are fighting for airtime with our never-ending appetite for old songs. Some will break out. But most songs need a good decade in rotation before they're firmly in the holiday radio mix. Appearing in Christmas movies is their best bet to make the leap.

THE CLASSICS

—

God Rest Ye Merry Gentlemen
Year: Fifteenth Century
Writer: Unknown
Notes: As the oldest published Christmas song that is still heard today, "God Rest Ye Merry Gentlemen" gets a big bump from appearing in Dickens' *A Christmas Carol*. To illustrate just how miserable he is, Scrooge grabs the ruler out of one of the carolers' hands as they are singing this song and they run away in terror.
Who did it best? Nat King Cole. This song is often background music in movies but, if you had to pick one, you pick the guy with the best pipes. Sharon Jones & the Dap-Kings do a pretty cool funky instrumental version, too.
Who did it worst? 98°. This is four guys overdoing their parts, each in the hope he will be the breakout star of the boy band and can ditch the others like Diana Ross did to the Supremes.

We Wish You a Merry Christmas

Year: Sixteenth Century

Writer: Unknown (English)

Notes: As far back as the thirteenth century, people visited house to house, spreading well wishes during the winter months. They weren't necessarily singing but rather reaching out to friends during some dark, lonely times and receiving hot drinks and treats such as pudding. They called it wassailing. Soon after St. Francis of Assisi started using music in his Christmas church services, singing Christmas songs was incorporated into wassailing and Christmas caroling was born. Songs were passed from generation to generation but not written down until well after the writers of songs like "We Wish You a Merry Christmas" were forgotten. This song, as opposed to the dominance of religious songs of the era, is simply about spreading good cheer (and anticipating something sweet for the effort).

Who did it best? Willie Nelson. This song has been done by just about everyone. Probably the most stripped-down version is just Willie with his guitar and his soothing voice. The Muppets and John Denver do a fun rendition for the kids.

Who did it worst? Kidz Bop. There is some stiff competition for this title. Raffi, the Brady Bunch, and Pat Boone do some pretty abysmal covers. But the absolute worst—Kidz Bop—is like sitting through a school holiday concert where you have zero emotional connection to any of the singers.

Who did it weirdest? Lorne Greene. In 1963, the man who played the thrice-widowed, deep-voiced patriarch of cowboy show *Bonanza* put out a Christmas album. It sounded… like a Christmas album made by a guy who played a cowboy on TV.

O Tannenbaum (Oh Christmas Tree)

Year: 1550

Writer: Unknown (German)

Notes: Considering it was the Germans who popularized the Christmas tree, it's no surprise that there were several songs written about *die Tanne* (fir tree). Roughly translated, the song marvels about how the tree stays green all year long. Many versions exist, but the one that has endured is the 1824 one by Ernst Gebhard Salomon Anschütz. The melody is so beloved that Iowa, Maryland, Michigan, and New Jersey chose it for their official state song.

Who did it best? Vince Guaraldi Trio. The best version comes from *A Charlie Brown Christmas*. Guaraldi's jazzy piano version has a warmth to it while staying super cool. Nat King Cole does a nice version, but it's in German so it's tough to sing along to it.

Who did it worst? The Mistletoe Disco Band. Starts pretty traditional, then gets super weird. The early '80s were a very confusing time for the world.

I Saw Three Ships

Year: 1666

Writer: Unknown

Notes: This is a weird old song about three ships that are heading for Bethlehem. Some think it was inspired by the story of three ships carrying the gifts of the Magi to Cologne, Germany, in 1162. Considering Bethlehem isn't next to any body of water (the Dead Sea is twenty miles away), the song doesn't make a whole lot of sense. Musically, it sounds kind of like a poor man's sea shanty.

Who did it best? Nobody.

Joy to the World

Year: 1719

Writer: Isaac Watts

Notes: The most-published Christmas hymn in North America wasn't written to be a Christmas song nor was it even written to be a song. In 1719, Isaac Watts wrote a poetry book. He took Psalm 98 and made it a celebration about the return of Jesus. Over a century later, an influential American church music composer named Lowell Mason paired the poem with a melody called "Antioch," which was kind of a tweaked version of Handel's "Messiah."

Who did it best? Any version with a gospel choir. This is a song that needs to be belted out by a lot of people.

Who did it worst? Pentatonix. Harmonizing hell.

O Come All Ye Faithful (Adeste Fiedeles)

Year: 1743 or 1760

Writer: John Francis Wade

Notes: John Francis Wade was a refugee during the Jacobite rising of 1745. Essentially, one king got the boot and another one moved in. Some people, John Wade among them, remained loyal to the old king and his lineage. Thus, this song stayed primarily underground in the Catholic world (Protestants were in charge during that time). In 1795, the Duke of Leeds heard a performance of the song at the chapel of the Portuguese embassy in London, one of the only places in the country where Catholicism was allowed to be practiced openly. He must've really liked it and spread the word, because after that, "the Portuguese Hymn" became popular throughout England. In 1841, two men—Frederick Oakley and William Brooke—translated it to English and added a few verses, calling it "O Come All Ye Faithful."

Who did it best? Weezer. It's a pleasant song sung pretty well by a lot of people (Nat King Cole, Elvis, Carly Simon, and many others) but they all kind of sound like Carol Brady singing in church in the Christmas episode of *The Brady Bunch*. Give Weezer credit for cranking the distorted guitars and giving the song some much-needed pep.

Who did it weirdest? Bob Dylan does a version in both languages, which is kind of weird in a good way.

Hark! The Herald Angels Sing
Year: 1753
Writer: Charles Wesley, George Whitefield, and Felix Mendelssohn
Notes: The song that the Peanuts gang belts out at the end of *A Charlie Brown Christmas* isn't what its writers intended. Charles Wesley wrote a slow and somber hymn with lines like "Hark, how all the welkin [heaven] rings." Eighty-seven years later, German composer Felix Mendelssohn wrote a "soldier-like" cantata celebrating Johannes Gutenberg's printing press. Granted, the printing press had been invented nearly four hundred years earlier, but hey, it changed the world! Then, in 1855, William Cummings combined their words and music into a joyous Christmas song.

Who did it best? Ray Charles (with the Jubilation Choir). It's Ray Charles doing his magic on the keyboard as a full choir joyously sings behind him. It's impossible to be in a bad mood after hearing it.

Who did it worst? Donny Osmond. It's hard to believe someone was able to record a worse version of this song than Neil Diamond, but Donny did it with ease.

Auld Lang Syne

Year: 1788

Writer: Robert Burns

Notes: In 1788, Scotland's national poet, Robert Burns, sent the poem "Auld Lang Syne" to the Scots Musical Museum. In 1799, it was put to music by an anonymous composer. The title translates to "Old Long Since" in Scots language. It quickly became an annual tradition in Scotland on New Year's Eve. More than one hundred years later, in 1929, famous bandleader Guy Lombardo started playing the song on his popular radio show on New Year's Eve.

Who did it best? Jon Batiste and Stay Human. On the 2018 final episode of *The Late Show with Stephen Colbert*, Batiste delivered one of the great musical performances of the year with a blistering display on his Steinway piano. Sadly, it doesn't appear on any album. Look it up on YouTube. It's great.

Silent Night

Year: 1816

Writer: Joseph Mohr and Franz Xaver Gruber

Notes: From 1799 to 1815, Napoleon put Europe through a meat grinder. There were wars, occupations, and a general uneasiness. When Napoleon was defeated at Waterloo, peace was restored. The following year, a young priest in Austria, Joseph Mohr, was out on a winter stroll when he was inspired by his serene town to write "Stille Nacht, Heilige Nacht." Choir director Franz Xaver Gruber wrote the music, and the two performed the song for the first time on Christmas Eve at his church. A handyman who was working at the church took a copy of the song and brought it back to his hometown. From there, traveling singers got ahold of it and the song was quickly spread throughout Europe. It has since been translated to hundreds of languages and is the Christmas song most associated with peace.

Who did it best? Al Green. The man has a magical voice. The only challenge is keeping your clothes on while listening to him.

Angels We Have Heard on High (Gloria)

Year: 1819

Writer: Unknown (French)

Notes: This song bounced around France for a while before finally being published in 1819 in the *Nouveau recueil de cantiques* (New Hymnal) for the archdiocese of Quebec. The song is based on the Bible passage (Luke 2:6-20) where the angels celebrate the birth of Jesus. The angels sing it, then the mountains sing it back (which is supposed to represent earth rejoicing). It's just a happy song where the singer really needs to nail a complicated "Gloria" vocal run if they want to pull it off.

Who did it best? Sufjan Stevens. There are some great vocal performances by Nat King Cole and Mariah Carey, but Stevens' fifty-two-second xylophone version is kind of the best.

Who did it worst? The Monkees. They had more talent than they were given credit for, but it didn't come through in this song.

The First Noel

Year: 1823

Writer: Unknown (French)

Notes: People have been singing "The First Noel" (or "Aujourd'hui le Roi des Cieux") since the thirteenth or fourteenth century in France. The song is about an angel spreading the word about Jesus' birth in Bethlehem, as told in the Bible. *Noël* is the French word for Christmas.

The song's first official appearance in English was in Davies Gilbert's book *Some Ancient Christmas Carols* in 1823. At the time, Christmas caroling was starting to fade in England and Gilbert was hoping his collection would both preserve and, hopefully, revive it. Ten years later, a relatively unknown composer named William Sandys discovered Gilbert's book and wrote a melody to accompany "The First Nowell." In 1871, a composer named Sir John Stainer sanded a few rough edges off of Sandys' version and published it. Stainer's "First Noel" is the same song we sing and hear today.

Who did it best? Frank Sinatra. The world-famous crooner nails it alongside a choir.

Who did it worst? Anita Bryant. The former Oklahoma beauty pageant winner and orange juice spokeswoman cranks the vibrato machine up to eleven in her unsettling rendition. If she truly wanted to "save our children," she should've passed on that record deal.

Ave Maria

Year: 1825

Writer: Franz Schubert

Notes: Franz Schubert had no intention of his song being paired with the words of the Hail Mary in Latin. Schubert wrote the music to accompany Sir Walter Scott's famous narrative poem, "The Lady of the Lake." The poem is about three men trying to win the affection of a woman. There's also a part about lowland Scots battling Highland clans. Nothing Christmassy about it. But, somehow, it got linked to the prayer that, somehow, got linked to Christmas albums. And now it's regularly a part of the genre.

Who did it best? Stevie Wonder. The seventeen-year-old was already six years into his legendary career when he released his first Christmas album, *Someday at Christmas*. The whole album is fantastic, but on the third track, the teenager flawlessly pulls off probably the hardest Christmas song of all.

Who did it worst? Jim Nabors. Gomer Pyle's attempt at a difficult song is a tough listen. He kind of sounds like Adam Sandler's "Opera Man" character on *Saturday Night Live*.

O Holy Night

Year: 1847

Writer: Placide Cappeau de Roquemaure and Adolphe Charles Adam

Notes: In the most French twist possible, "O Holy Night" was a poem written for Christmas Eve mass by the commissionaire of wine. Placide Cappeau de Roquemaure used the birth of Jesus as his guide and wrote "Cantique de Noël." His friend Adolphe Charles Adam wrote music to accompany it, and it quickly became among the most popular Christmas songs in France. Following rumors that Cappeau was a socialist and Adam was a Jew, the Catholic Church banned "Cantique de Noël." But the toothpaste was already out of the tube. People still sang it outside of church services, and eventually, an American writer named John Sullivan Dwight thought it should be translated and brought to America. As an abolitionist, he loved the lyrics in the third verse that said "Chains shall he break, for the slave is our brother; and in his name all oppression shall cease." The song quickly became a hit with supporters of the Union Army.

The most significant accomplishment for "O Holy Night" came on Christmas Eve in 1906. Reginald Fessenden, the former chief chemist for Thomas Edison, was the voice ever heard over the airwaves. He recited the birth of Jesus from the Gospel of Luke. Then he played "O Holy Night" on his violin. It was the first song to ever be on the radio.

Who did it best? Mariah Carey. This song calls for power vocals in certain spots, and Mariah hits those notes. The choir backing her also brings gravitas.

Who did it worst? The Brady Bunch. The fact that the stars of the sitcom put out a Christmas album is problematic enough. Their decision to give Barry "Greg Brady" Williams the "Fall on your knees" part of this song is unforgivable.

It Came Upon a Midnight Clear

Year: 1849

Writer: Reverend Edmund Hamilton Sears

Notes: America was rapidly changing. The Industrial Revolution was dramatically altering the landscape. The California Gold Rush was in full swing. And tensions in America were ratcheting up between free states and slave states. Reverend Sears was worried and wrote a Christmas song about peace. He only wrote two songs in his life, so he made 'em count. He focused on peace and, in a rarity for religious Christmas music, didn't mention Jesus. Instead he focused on an angel. In a verse no longer included in hymnals, Sears has lines addressing the "woes of sin and strife" and "man, at war with man." That part was kind of a bummer, but overall the song has a good message of peace still relevant today.

Who did it best? Frank Sinatra. Ol' Blue Eyes was a master of the slow songs. This one moves at a snail's pace.

Who did it worst? Jimmy Swaggart. He whispers "to touch" in the creepiest way imaginable at the forty-one-second mark. At the two-minute mark, we hear noises that only his prostitutes should've heard. Not good. Anita Bryant gives another vibrato bombardment with her version.

Good King Wenceslas

Year: 1853

Writer: John Mason Neale

Notes: This song has an odd association with Christmas, given its background. Lyrics were matched with a thirteenth-century melody, the subject matter being a treacherous royal family from the tenth century. Wenceslas I, Duke of Bohemia, rose to power after his father died, his grandmother was strangled with her own veil, he banished his mother, and his jealous brother jammed a lance through his abdomen. Along the way, Vaclac the Good, as he was known, was fast-tracked to sainthood and the pope posthumously made him king. Unverified stories of his generosity grew with each century. So they made a song about him that's now associated with Christmas.

Who did it best? The Boston Pops. Nobody knows the words to this song in America. Probably best to stick to an instrumental version. Decent background music at a Christmas party.

Jingle Bells

Year: 1857

Writer: James Lord Pierpont

Notes: Despite it being one of most ubiquitous Christmas songs of all, "Jingle Bells" was never intended to be a Christmas song. There are no mentions of the holiday or Jesus. It's just about happily traveling on a snowy day. But the guy who wrote it was a real piece of garbage, so nobody should care about his intentions. He ditched his family twice, became a radicalized Confederacy supporter, and wrote gems like "Strike for the South," "We Conquer, or Die!" and "Our Battle Flag!" Fortunately, "Jingle Bells" is his most enduring song. Fun Fact: His nephew was the purple-nosed robber baron and epitome of Gilded Age greed, J.P. Morgan.

Who did it best? Bing Crosby and the Andrews Sisters. This classic version has a great tempo and the Andrews Sisters really punctuate the chorus. There are two excellent instrumental versions of the song: a twangy guitar version in 1962 by the duo Santo & Johnny (called "Twistin' Bells") and a 2007 hard rock cover by Pearl Jam.

Who did it worst? Jimmy Buffett. Buffett is trying really hard to sound relaxed. Skid Row's version will give you a headache.

Who did it weirdest? "Jingle Belz" by Bootsy Collins. The P-Funk bassist keeps it super funky on his 2006 *Christmas 4 Ever* album.

We Three Kings

Year: 1857

Writer: Reverend John Henry Hopkins

Notes: Reverend Hopkins was a renaissance man in the world of the Church: He wrote, illustrated, edited *The New York Church Journal*, and even designed stained glass windows. In 1857, he wrote this song for a Christmas pageant. It was originally called "The Quest of the Magi" but is now better known as "We Three Kings."

Who did it best? José Feliciano. The Puerto Rican's signature hybrid style of Latin and folk guitar work is on full display in his soulful instrumental version of this song.

Who did it worst? Mannheim Steamroller. This new age, over-produced Christmas album makes you feel like you're at an essential oils store in December.

Deck the Halls

Year: 1862

Writer: Thomas Oliphant

Notes: "Deck the Halls" dates back to sixteenth-century Wales. The music is from a Welsh New Year's Eve song called "Nos Galan." Originally, it was just about winter (and the love of "my fair one's bosom"). It was finally adapted to English—and Christmas—in 1862 by a Scottish songwriter named Thomas Oliphant. He kept the spirit of the song (the "fa-la-la-la-la" part) but, instead, made it about the preparation and decorating for Christmas.

Who did it best? Nat King Cole. There's a reason why the velvet-voiced singer's Christmas album is a staple for any Christmas collection. He does every song perfectly. His version of "Deck the Halls" is both joyous and smooth. Also, German guitarist Ottmar Liebert does a beautiful Spanish guitar-styled all-instrumental version.

Who did it worst? John Travolta and Olivia Newton-John. If not for *Battlefield Earth*, this would've been rock bottom for Vinnie Barbarino.

Up on the Housetop

Year: 1864

Writer: Benjamin Russell Hanby

Notes: The first Christmas song that focused on Santa was written by the son of a bishop. He was deeply involved in the abolitionist movement and helped with the Underground Railroad in Ohio. But his anti-slavery views were at odds with the conservative Church at the time. So he tried to write some alternative music for the holiday. "Up on the Housetop" was one of the results. Sadly, Hanby died of tuberculosis at just thirty-three.

Who did it best? The Jackson Five. The J-5 put their own joyous spin on the Christmas classic, complete with the brothers asking for a guitar for Tito, a basketball for Jackie, big shoes for Marlon, mistletoe for Jermaine—and Michael calling for "LOVE AND PEACE FOR EEEEEVERYONE!"

Who did it worst? Straight No Chaser. Despite MJ's plea for "love and peace for everyone!" this version makes you want to stuff these guys in a locker.

O Little Town of Bethlehem

Year: 1874

Writer: Phillips Brooks and Lewis Redner

Notes: In December of 1865, a six-foot-eight-inch Harvard-educated minister from Philadelphia traveled to Bethlehem to see the place where Jesus was born. Several years later, wanting to write a new song for the kids of his church, he thought back to the little town. The church organist, Redner, put a tune to his words.

Who did it best? Willie Nelson. One of the greatest songwriters in history, he can work magic with somebody else's words, too. Nelson's nasally voice hits the right inflection points that work perfectly with this song about the quaint little town.

Who did it worst? Jimmy Swaggart. The televangelist let his background singers do the heavy lifting while he creepily moaned out some lyrics. Nightmare fuel.

Away in a Manger

Year: 1885

Writer: Evangelical Lutheran Church (Pennsylvania)

Notes: Not a whole lot is known about this song aside from the false rumors that sixteenth-century reformer Martin Luther had something to do with it. It was actually just written by German Lutherans in Pennsylvania a few hundred years later. One concerning note about the song is in the third verse. It mentions that the baby Jesus was unable to cry. That seems like a negative on the Apgar test of newborn health.

Who did it best? Ella Fitzgerald. It's a solid Christmas song for the most famous jazz singer in history to show off her voice. Also, there must be some sort of mandate that every country music star in history must sing this one. Stick to Willie Nelson if you want to pick just one.

Who did it worst? Jimmy Swaggart. In an attempt to accentuate each and every syllable, Swaggart sounds like he is singing "Away in a Main Jar." Then a choir of kids joins in while he does nothing. Marie Osmond's over-stylized and over-produced version is also a tough pill to swallow.

Go Tell It on the Mountain
Year: 1907
Writer: John Wesley Work, Jr.
Notes: While he gets credit for the song, Work really just gathered spirituals sung by slaves and sharecroppers on plantations and put them into a book. This was the most famous of those songs that referred to Jesus Christ's birth. The title refers to the angels coming and spreading the good news.

Who did it best? Mahalia Jackson. This song requires an abundance of soul. Mahalia Jackson's version has it and it's fantastic.

Who did it worst? Hanson. This can't be happening.

Carol of the Bells

Year: 1916

Writer: Mykola Leontovich and Peter Wilhousky

Notes: The Ukrainian composer's powerful tune was just supposed to be about winter. In the original lyrics, a bird flies into someone's kitchen and tells them it's going to be a productive year. It was titled "Shchedryk," which comes from the Ukrainian word for "bountiful." The song was performed on January 13, which was New Year's Eve on the Julian calendar. Within a few years, the song was being performed all over the world and not only around the new year. An American named Peter Wilhousky heard it and created new lyrics that matched up with Christmas in 1936. It's probably the most badass Christmas song.

Who did it best? Brooklyn Tabernacle Choir. There are some good instrumental versions, but this one is best done with a choir.

Who did it worst? John Tesh. This version screams "dentist office."

THE CROONER ERA

—

Santa Claus Is Comin' to Town

Year: 1933

Writer: Haven Gillespie and J. Fred Coots

Notes: Haven Gillespie and Fred Coots were told to come up with a children's Christmas song. So they did, writing on an envelope while riding the NYC subway. Despite skepticism from record labels, Eddie Cantor sang it for his radio audience in 1934 and it was an instant hit. In the mid-1940s, it went from being just a kids' song to having a broader appeal when Perry Como released it with a swinging jazz flavor. It has been a staple ever since, taken on by just about every artist who has ever recorded a Christmas album.

Winter Wonderland

Year: 1934

Writer: Richard Smith and Felix Bernard

Notes: The carefree song about frolicking on a snowy day was actually written by a guy battling tuberculosis in a Pennsylvania sanitarium. Dick Smith wrote his joyful poem and sent it to his friend, Felix Bernard, who set it to music. Bernard got it to a guy named Richard Himber, who was not the most highly-respected bandleader but nevertheless got his version heard by Guy Lombardo, who was a massive star at the time. Lombardo rushed to record his own cover of the song, and it was an instant hit. Sadly, Dick Smith passed away soon thereafter.

Fun Fact: "Parson Brown" was never real. He was a made-up parson, which is a priest with the Church of England. The name "Brown" just helped the rhyme.

Who did it best? Darlene Love in 1963. Darlene Love brought gospel pipes to pop music. Unlike most pleasantly tame versions of "Winter Wonderland" (Dean Martin, Sinatra, Elvis, Lena Horne, the list goes on and on), Darlene Love is shot out of cannon during her rendition, and it easily makes it the most memorable.

Who did it worst? Ringo Starr in 1999. He was a Beatle. He will always have that.

White Christmas

Year: 1941

Writer: Irving Berlin

Notes: The best-selling music single of all time was written by Irving Berlin, a Russian-born Jewish immigrant. In 1941, Berlin (probably the most successful songwriter of his era) was asked to write a song about each holiday for the upcoming movie *Holiday Inn*. Writing a Christmas one was difficult. On Christmas Day in 1928, Berlin and his wife had lost their three-week-old child, and each December 25th after that brought a sadness that eventually manifested itself into this melancholy song about yearning for a happier Christmas. Bing Crosby first sang it on his radio show on Christmas Day, 1941. This was just a few weeks after Pearl Harbor was attacked. America was going through an emotional time, and the song just resonated. It built momentum with the movie the following year and became a beloved song among the soldiers in the war. In 1954, an entire movie was built around Bing's thirteen-year-old hit.

Who did it best? Otis Redding in 1968. Even though Bing's is the best-selling version, it's Otis Redding who gave the song more feeling than anyone ever has. Sadly, it was released a year after his death in a plane crash in mid-December 1967.

Who did it worst? Tiny Tim in 1994. This sounds like a ghost haunting your attic with a ukulele.

Little Drummer Boy

Year: 1941

Writer: Katherine Kennicott Davis, Jack Halloran, Harry Simeone, and Henry Onorati

Notes: The first time Katherine Davis' "Carol of the Drum" was performed was by the world-famous Trapp Family Singers (the real-life von Trapps from *The Sound of Music*). It is believed that Missouri songwriter Davis based it on an old Czech carol. But it wasn't until 1957 that the song got real traction. Keeping the "pa-rum-pum-pum-pum" drum lines, Jack Halloran reworked the song and changed it to the "Little Drummer Boy" that we know today. He then introduced it to producer Henry Onorati and recording artist Harry Simeone, who turned it into a hit in 1958.

Who did it best? The Vince Guaraldi Trio in 1965. While it's fun to say "pa-rum-pum-pum-pum" once or twice, the song is kind of repetitive and irritating in the wrong hands. Guaraldi's piano version on *A Charlie Brown Christmas* keeps it fun.

Who did it weirdest? Bing Crosby and David Bowie in 1977. It's not that this version is bad, but it is just so jarring to hear the fading crooner (he died a month later) and the Thin White Duke at the height of his powers chatting at a piano during Bing's final Christmas special. Then Bing launched into a standard take on the song while Bowie, well, David Bowied his contribution. The rock star hated the song but, since his mom was a fan of Crosby, tried to make it work. While Bing plowed ahead with it, Bowie sang "Peace on Earth" as an overlapping duet. It's completely trippy and kind of great.

Happy Holiday

Year: 1942

Writer: Irving Berlin

Notes: Despite being vilified by some in the "war on Christmas" argument, the phrase "Happy Holidays" has Christian roots. The word "holiday" is derived from the ancient word "haliday," which just stood for "holy day." The phrase "Happy Holidays" has been used in America since the mid-1800s. Christians used to use it for the collective celebration of Advent, Christmas, and the Feast of the

Epiphany. But once Christmas starting getting too secular for people, the phrase started getting divisive. Anyway, this was a song about cheerful greetings written by Irving Berlin, one of the great American songwriters of the first half of the twentieth century. He also happened to be Jewish.

Who did it best? Andy Williams in 1963. A goofy song calls for a goofy singer with a nice voice.

I'll Be Home for Christmas

Year: 1943

Writer: Kim Gannon and Walter Kent

Notes: Kim Gannon and Walter Kent wrote a song from a soldier's perspective serving in World War II. While the war certainly dictated life throughout America, many felt a song about a homesick soldier would be too depressing. But Gannon hunted down Bing Crosby on the golf course and sang part of it to him. Crosby agreed to record it and made it the B-side of his massive hit "White Christmas." Despite reservations by executives, when Crosby performed it on his USO tours, it became his most requested song. Now it is firmly entrenched in the top ten songs played each holiday season.

Who did it best? Frank Sinatra in 1957, but lots of people have done it pretty well.

Have Yourself a Merry Little Christmas

Year: 1944

Writer: Hugh Martin and Ralph Blaine

Notes: Martin and Blaine needed to come up with a song towards the end of the Judy Garland musical *Meet Me in St. Louis*. Garland and her daughter are sad about having to move to New York right after

Christmas. So Judy sings this to her daughter to console her. Then her daughter goes out and wrecks a bunch of snowmen. It was a weird time for cinema.

Who did it best? The Pretenders in 1987. Lots of people have done this charming song well, but it is fun to hear rock legend Chrissie Hynde do a soulful version.

Who did it weirdest? Twisted Sister in 2006. You have to give these guys credit for staying on brand no matter the song. They keep it noisy.

Baby It's Cold Outside

Year: 1944

Writer: Frank Loesser

Notes: In 1944, Frank Loesser and his wife, Lynn, moved into the Hotel Navarro in New York and threw themselves a housewarming party. Towards the end of the night, the songwriter and his former nightclub singer wife sang a playful duet he had just written. The back-and-forth flirty song was a big hit with partygoers and became a staple on the cocktail party circuit between New York City and Hollywood. Eventually, MGM bought "Baby, It's Cold Outside" from Frank and used it in the 1948 musical *Neptune's Daughter*, starring Esther Williams and Ricardo Montalban. The song has been a holiday favorite ever since.

Then, in the early days of social media, a different narrative about the song emerged. What started as a tongue-in-cheek column by Canada's *National Post* and a parody video on FunnyorDie.com evolved into people questioning, in earnest, whether the song was about date rape. Things got worse for the song when, in 2014, lots of women accused Bill Cosby of putting something into their drinks and molesting them. While the song still has plenty of defenders, some radio stations have banned it. The reality is that the song was and is just playful banter between a husband and wife in the mid-1940s. Language was a little different. "What's in this drink?" was a pretty well-worn comedy line which translated to, "Hey, how about giving me a stiffer drink? This is nothing." Nobody was talking about Rohypnol.

Who did it best? Ray Charles and Betty Carter in 1961. The song is meant to be both playful and seductive, and Charles and Carter seem to have the best combination of both. Dean Martin and the Andrews Sisters, Leon Redbone and Zooey Deschanel, and Willie Nelson and Norah Jones all do solid versions.

Who did it worst? John Legend and Kelly Clarkson in 2019. Legend's #MeToo-era lyrics are trying a little too hard to be proper, and just come across as lame. The changed line of "It's your body and your choice" should appear in a sex ed class, not this song.

The Christmas Song (Merry Christmas to You)

Year: 1945

Writer: Mel Torme, Bob Wells

Notes: Like a lot of Christmas songs, "The Christmas Song" was written on a sweltering day. Bob Wells wrote the first four lines just trying to think of cold-weather memories. Wells and frequent collaborator Mel Torme took it from there and, forty-five minutes later, had created one of the all-time Christmas classics.

Who did it best? Nat King Cole. If you ask anyone to think of three classic Christmas songs, Nat King Cole's "The Christmas Song" is one of them.

Let It Snow! Let It Snow! Let It Snow!

Year: 1945

Writer: Sammy Cahn and Jule Styne

Notes: While struggling to endure a brutal July heat wave in Southern California in 1945, Sammy Cahn and June Styne tried to grab onto cool memories, like snowfalls from their childhoods. Singer Vaughn Monroe made a number-one hit out of their song later that year.

Who did it best? Dean Martin in 1966. Like with just about every other song on his Christmas album, the "King of Cool" delivered a soothing hit with his cover of this song. Despite it being a frequently played holiday song, it took a little while for Dean Martin's version to finally reach the Billboard Top 100—until 2018, in fact. Twenty-three years after he died.

Who did it worst? Gloria Estefan. Her voice is fine but the synthesizer music sounds like a video game from 1986. Quite possibly the worst musical arrangement in the history of Christmas.

Merry Christmas Baby

Year: 1947

Writer: Lou Baxter, Johnny Moore, and Charles Brown

Notes: The writer of the bluesiest Christmas song had every reason to sing the blues. Despite reworking an old song to help his friend Lou Baxter pay for a throat operation, Charles Brown got no official writing credit for "Merry Christmas Baby." He also didn't get much money for it. Brown still went on to have a distinguished blues career and is said to have inspired other greats like Ray Charles. Sadly, he died less than two months before his induction into the Rock & Roll Hall of Fame in 1999.

Who did it best? Chuck Berry in 1964. There are lots of great candidates for this one (Otis Redding, Ike & Tina Turner, Elvis), but it's the "Father of Rock and Roll" that takes the top spot. Instead of the typical, high-energy Chuck Berry effort, he delivered an understated, bluesy version that still shows off his skills without turning it into a completely different song.

Here Comes Santa Claus

Year: 1947

Writer: Gene Autry and Oakley Haldeman

Notes: Gene Autry, the famous Hollywood cowboy, was riding his horse down Hollywood Boulevard in the 1946 Christmas parade when he heard kids yelling to each other, "Here comes Santa Claus!" It inspired him to write this song. He took the general idea and gave it to his partner Oakley Haldeman, who fleshed it out. And by Christmas season of 1947, he had his first Christmas hit.

Who did it best? Elvis Presley in 1957. Elvis took a pleasant little song, added his attitude, a better voice, and his backup singers, the Jordanaires, and made a version that really pops. Willie Nelson does a better country version than Autry. Bob B. Soxx & the Blue Jeans did a fun Phil Spector-y version of it.

Blue Christmas

Year: 1948

Writer: Jay W. Johnson and Billy Hayes

Notes: Around the time Bing Crosby was topping charts with songs like "White Christmas," radio jingle writer Jay Johnson wrote a sad Christmas song about unrequited love—"Blue Christmas." He had his composer buddy, Billy Hayes, write the music, and eventually, they sold the song to a country artist in Nashville, Ernest Tubb. For most of the 1950s, Tubb's song was a country Christmas music staple.

Who did it best? Elvis Presley in 1957. Once "the King" sang it, "Blue Christmas" has stayed near the top of mainstream Christmas charts ever since. The Lumineers did a cool super-depressing version in 2016.

Who did it worst? Jackie Gleason in 1967. Hold music.

Sleigh Ride

Year: 1948

Writer: Leroy Anderson and Mitchell Parish

Notes: "Sleigh Ride" is yet another wildly successful Christmas song that makes zero mention of Christmas. In fact, the original version didn't mention anything. It had no words. Shortly after being released from active duty in the army, Leroy Anderson started composing the song during a heat wave in July. It was finally first recorded by the Boston Pops in 1949. After its initial success, it was given lyrics by Mitchell Parish (a Jew) that mention wintery things and even a birthday party but no Christmas. The song also mentions "Currier and Ives," which means nothing to people in the twenty-first century. Currier and Ives were nineteenth-century painting and lithograph printers. The business was liquidated in 1907.

Who did it best? The Ronettes in 1963. Straight off the success of "Be My Baby," the teenaged pop trio gave the Christmas staple the Phil Spector treatment (the "Wall of Sound" part, not murder).

Who did it worst? The Spice Girls in 1998. This didn't have to happen.

Rudolph the Red-Nosed Reindeer

Year: 1949

Writer: Johnny Marks

Notes: Robert L. May was a Dartmouth graduate with a dying wife and a murky financial situation. Instead of writing the great American novel as he had hoped to do, he was stuck writing catalog copy for Chicago-based retail chain Montgomery Ward. Then, early in 1939, the retailer asked him if he would take a crack at writing a holiday story that they could hand out to kids. In past years, they had handed out coloring books, but this year they were hoping to save cash and have one of their employees create an in-house Christmas book. So May tapped into childhood bullying he had suffered and came up with *Rudolph the Red-Nosed Reindeer*. Despite its success (2.4 million copies were given out in the first year), the store stopped distributing it because of World War II paper shortages. May eventually got the rights to it, licensed out books and toys, and had his brother-in-law, Johnny Marks, write a Rudolph song. After Bing Crosby passed on it, Gene Autry took a shot at it, and "Rudolph the Red-Nosed Reindeer" is the second most successful Christmas song of all time.

Who did it best? The Crystals in 1963. Recorded for Phil Spector's Christmas album, the Crystals delivered strong vocals and were backed by Spector's famous "Wall of Sound" (a technique that utilized the reverberation of instruments to enhance the audio) and made a children's song into a poppy, fun holiday classic.

(Everybody's Waitin' For) The Man with the Bag

Year: 1950

Writer: Dudley Brooks, Irving Taylor, and Harold Stanley

Notes: Hal Stanley was a Hollywood nightclub owner who also managed his wife, the jazz singer Kay Starr. In 1950, Stanley collaborated with one of the musicians who played at his club, Dudley Brooks, and songwriter Irving Taylor on a Christmas song—"(Everybody's Waitin' For) The Man with the Bag." Stanley's wife recorded it, and the peppy track became one of the most popular Christmas songs of the '50s.

Who did it best? Kay Starr in 1950. Beyond the fact that she turned her husband's song into one of the only Christmas hits sung by a woman in that era, Kay Starr is probably the first Native American singer to have a hit song. The Oklahoma native's father was an Iroquois and her mother was part Choctaw, Cherokee, and Irish. Starr and Stanley's marriage didn't last long (two years), but luckily, she found love again. She had a total of six husbands in her ninety-four years.

Who did it worst? Donny Most in 2016. There's a reason Ralph Malph was never allowed to sing at Arnold's.

Silver Bells

Year: 1950

Writer: Jay Livingston and Ray Evans

Notes: Jay Livingston and Ray Evans were tasked with coming up with a Christmas song for the Bob Hope movie *The Lemon Drop Kid*. Neither wanted to do it because Christmas songs were rarely hits and their contracts were just about up. But they relented and came up with a song about Salvation Army Santas ringing their bells on street corners. The original title was "Tinkle Bells." When Livingston told his wife the title, she informed him that "tinkle" also means urinate. The title was changed to "Silver Bells." Bing Crosby and Carol Richards turned it into a hit a few months later.

Who did it best? Sharon Jones & the Dap-Kings in 2015. This funky soul version pumps new life into an old (but still lovely) holiday classic.

Frosty the Snowman

Year: 1950

Writer: Jack Rollins and Steve Nelson

Notes: After the success of Gene Autry's "Rudolph the Red-Nosed Reindeer" in 1949, the music industry was looking for another new Christmas character for him to sing about. In stepped songwriters Jack Rollins and Steve Nelson. Nelson wrote about the snowman marching through the "village square," which he based off of Armonk, New York (Nelson lived nearby in White Plains), Rollins pretty much tweaked Irving Berlin's 1932 song "Let's Have Another Cup of Coffee" to fit Nelson's words, and Autry had a second Christmas hit. Books and an animated special soon followed.

Who did it best? Fiona Apple in 2003. Despite most of her songs being filled with tension and rage, Apple delivers a mostly cheerful acoustic take on Frosty. Things do get a little tense when the traffic cop hollers "STOP!" The Ronettes also do a pretty badass version on the Phil Spector album.

Who did it worst? The Partridge Family featuring David Cassidy in 1971. As his television family was trying to cash in on their success with a Christmas album, David Cassidy seemed more interested in revving up his *Tiger Beat* fans. So he delivered an overly breathy take on a children's classic that makes you want to take a shower.

It's Beginning to Look a Lot Like Christmas

Year: 1951

Writer: Meredith Willson

Notes: Written by the same woman who wrote *The Music Man*, this is a pretty simple song about the start of the festive season.

Who did it best? Perry Como in 1951. It has been covered by every crooner. Probably the best is the one that made it famous.

Who did it worst? Michael Bublé in 2011. Bublé's cover of this song is to schmaltz as Jimi Hendrix was to the guitar.

I Saw Mommy Kissing Santa Claus

Year: 1952

Writer: Tommie Connor

Notes: A thirteen-year-old California middle schooler named Jimmy Boyd was winning the talent show circuit when he got discovered by Columbia Records. They gave him a song written by British songwriter Tommie Connor. It was a cutesy Christmas tune about a kid catching his mother kissing Santa. It was an instant pop hit, selling two and a half million copies in the first week. Despite it being pretty cheesy, it has been remade many times and consistently reappears each Christmas.

Who did it best? Amy Winehouse in 2004. The heartbreak of a talent like Winehouse, who died in 2011 at just twenty-seven, was that she was so fantastic that she could take a corny song from 1952 and turn it into gold. Her 2004 performance for BBC Radio 2 was released as a single in 2020, instantly making it the best version of the song that has ever been (or will ever be) done. The Ronettes' version on the Phil Spector album was the only thing close.

Who did it worst? Jimmy Boyd. Hard pass on thirteen-year-old boy singers not named Stevie Wonder.

Cool Yule

Year: 1953

Writer: Steve Allen

Notes: Steve Allen, the creator and first host of *The Tonight Show*, penned one of the cooler Christmas songs ever written. Allen is in the

Guinness Book of Records for being the most prolific modern songwriter (over 8,500 songs).

Who did it best? Louis Armstrong. This is one of his best.

Santa Baby

Year: 1953

Writer: Joan Javits and Phil Springer

Notes: One of the oddest Christmas songs of all was written by the niece of US Senator Jacob Javits. Essentially, it's about a woman who wants a bunch of expensive stuff (diamonds, a yacht, keys to a platinum mine) so she tries to seduce Santa Claus into giving it to her.

Who did it best? Rev Run and the Christmas All-Stars (Snoop Dogg, Onyx, Mase, Salt-N-Pepa, and Keith Murray) in 1997. It's not a great song, but at least this picks up the pace a bit and adds some Snoop.

Who did it worst? Madonna in 1987. Madonna goes with a horny Betty Boop approach to the song and leaves listeners feeling super uncomfortable.

'Zat You, Santa Claus?

Year: 1953

Writer: Jack Fox

Notes: Unlike most songs about Santa, this one almost feels like a spooky Halloween song. Armstrong openly wonders if the visitor is really coming to get him. It's a silly song made great by one of the most joyful gravelly voices in history.

Who did it best? Louis Armstrong. This is almost the perfect Satchmo song, but credit is also due to St. Paul and the Broken Bones, who did a pretty bang-up version themselves in 2018.

The Christmas Waltz

Year: 1954

Writer: Sammy Cahn and Jule Styne

Notes: Sinatra wanted his own Christmas song. He had plenty of success, sure, but he wanted his own classic hit like Crosby had with "White Christmas." So he enlisted Sammy Cahn and Jule Styne, two of the best songwriting teams of the era, and put them to work. And Sinatra got his signature Christmas song. It never reached the heights of "White Christmas," but "Christmas Waltz" is the best song on his 1957 Christmas album, widely considered one of the best Christmas albums in history.

Who did it best? Sinatra. This is his jam. But what's with that weird "Merry Christmas" at the end?

Who did it worst? Clay Aiken. The former *American Idol* contestant puts too much of a Broadway spin on a song that's supposed to be a pleasantly-flowing waltz.

Underrated songs of the era: "My Christmas Baby" (1948) – Smokey Hogg, "Mele Kalikimaka" (1949) – Bing Crosby, "Marshmallow World" (1949) – Darlene Love *covered it in 1963*, "Hey, Santa Claus" (1953) – The Moonglows

LATE TWENTIETH CENTURY

—

With the emergence of rock and roll, Christmas music stopped being about songs that dozens of singers could take a crack at interchangeably and instead became more tailored to individual styles and talents. Here are the most popular songs written over the final half of the twentieth century.

Jingle Bell Rock

Year: 1957

Writer: Joseph Carleton Beal and James Ross Boothe (and possibly Bobby Helms?)

Artist: Bobby Helms

Notes: Advertising and public relations executives tried to write a Christmas song that incorporated elements of a classic like "Jingle Bells" with the popular music at the time (like "Rock Around the Clock"). They gave it to rockabilly singer Bobby Helms, who turned it into one of the most famous Christmas songs of all time. Kind of a stretch to call it rock, though.

Santa Claus Is Back in Town

Year: 1957

Writer: Jerry Leiber and Mike Stoller

Artist: Elvis Presley

Notes: Elvis needed one more song for his first Christmas album, so he called his two best collaborators—songwriters Jerry Leiber and Mike Stoller ("Hound Dog," "Jailhouse Rock"). When they got to the studio, Elvis' meddlesome manager Colonel Tom Parker barked at the duo to write it immediately. They retreated to an office for about fifteen minutes, then came out with the most Elvis-y Christmas song possible. Their blues-rock entry, "Santa Claus Is Back in Town," was the perfect first track on a terrific album.

Run Rudolph Run

Year: 1958

Writer: Johnny Marks and Marvin Brodie

Artist: Chuck Berry

Notes: As a B-side to his also-great "Merry Christmas, Baby," Chuck Berry did a rollicking rendition of "Run Rudolph Run." Perhaps as penance for his—let's be honest—less-than-great "Rudolph the Red-Nosed Reindeer," songwriter Johnny Marks brought Rudolph back in a sequel. The song, which really celebrates the new United States intrastate highway system ("you can take the freeway down"), was very similar to Berry's "Johnny B. Goode." He deserved a writing credit. There have been many covers of the song, from Lemmy Kilmister of Motorhead to Dr. Teeth and the Electric Mayhem, but Chuck Berry's is still the absolute best.

Rockin' Around the Christmas Tree
Year: 1958
Writer: Johnny Marks
Artist: Brenda Lee
Notes: World War II Bronze Star recipient and legendary Christmas music writer Johnny Marks ("Rudolph the Red-Nosed Reindeer," "Run Rudolph Run," "A Holly, Jolly Christmas") wrote a new Christmas hit and got thirteen-year-old rockabilly singer Brenda Lee to record it. It has been a top-ten Christmas hit for the past sixty-plus years. While the diminutive (four-foot-nine) Tennesseean is still known for "Rockin' Around the Christmas Tree," Lee was a massive star back in the day, selling more than one hundred million albums in her career. In the 1960s, only Elvis, the Beatles, and Ray Charles had more top-hundred hits.

It's the Most Wonderful Time of the Year
Year: 1963
Writer: Edward Pola and George Wyle

Artist: Andy Williams

Notes: Co-written by the creator of the *Gilligan's Island* theme song, "It's the Most Wonderful Time of the Year" has the distinction of being one of the happiest and most festive Christmas songs and also the cheesiest. Hearing Andy Williams sing the saccharine song in triple time serves as both a reminder it's the "hap-happiest season of all" as well as the most neuralgia-inducing.

Pretty Paper

Year: 1963

Writer: Willie Nelson

Artist: Willie Nelson

Notes: "Pretty Paper" is a song based on a legless Texan named Frankie Brieton, who sold wrapping paper and ribbons outside a department store in the 1950s and '60s. Roy Orbison made Nelson's ballad a Christmas hit but it is Willie's version of his own song in 1979 that's the best. It also is probably the only Christmas song about wrapping paper.

Little Saint Nick

Year: 1963

Writer: Brian Wilson and Mike Love

Artist: The Beach Boys

Notes: The most Beach Boys-ish Christmas song premiered in one of the least joyous Christmas seasons in American history. One month earlier, John F. Kennedy was assassinated. "Little Saint Nick" did okay but got more traction the following year, when it was included on *The Beach Boys' Christmas Album*.

Purple Snowflakes

Year: 1964

Writer: Marvin Gaye, Dave Hamilton, and Clarence Paul

Artist: Marvin Gaye

Notes: This song took nearly three decades to see the light of day. It was originally supposed to be sung by Stevie Wonder, but Marvin Gaye took it on and recorded a version that didn't end up being released. The following year, Gaye took the backing track, gave it new lyrics, and had an R & B hit with "Pretty Little Baby." It wasn't until 1993 that his original recording of "Purple Snowflakes" finally landed on a Christmas album. The lyrics aren't anything profound (just admiring snowflakes falling), but the smooth-as-silk Marvin Gaye turned them into a chill Christmas masterpiece.

A Holly, Jolly Christmas

Year: 1965

Writer: Johnny Marks

Artist: Burl Ives

Notes: Written by the same guy who wrote "Rudolph the Red-Nosed Reindeer," "A Holly, Jolly Christmas" was supposed to be performed by the actor playing Yukon Cornelius in the television special, but since they had famous folk singer Burl Ives playing the part of Sam the Snowman, they gave it to him. Ever since, the song has been associated with Ives.

Christmas Time Is Here

Year: 1965

Writer: Vince Guaraldi and Lee Mendelson

Artist: The Vince Guaraldi Trio

Notes: Producer Lee Mendelson was looking to create a cartoon out of Charles Schulz's *Peanuts* comic strip. Needing some background music, Mendelson contacted a local jazz musician in the San Francisco Bay Area, Vince Guaraldi, to see if he would give them a song. Shortly thereafter, Coca-Cola commissioned Schultz to put out a Christmas special. Since they needed some music quick, Mendelson and Schultz went with the local guy they already knew. At the behest of Schultz, Guaraldi put out a full soundtrack with jazzy versions of old Christmas songs like "O Tannenbaum" and some new ones like "Christmas Time Is Here." The full album (made with pretty much just piano, bass, and light drums) is one of the best Christmas albums ever made.

Someday at Christmas

Year: 1966

Writer: Ronald Miller and Bryan Wells

Artist: Stevie Wonder

Notes: By 1966, the United States was fully in the throes of the Vietnam War and a generation of young Americans was struggling to process it. Unlike World War II, this war felt pointless and hopeless. "Someday at Christmas" was one of the first Christmas songs to reflect that despair and hope for a more peaceful future. It was co-written by Ronald Miller, who also wrote the great Stevie hit, "For Once in My Life."

You're a Mean One, Mr. Grinch

Year: 1966

Writer: Theodor "Dr. Seuss" Geisel and Albert Hague

Artist: Thurl Ravenscroft

Notes: The ode to the villain in the 1966 animated classic based on Dr. Seuss' book was originally supposed to be sung by the voice of the Grinch himself—Boris Karloff. But they felt that a song so important should be performed by a man with better, deeper singing pipes. So they got Thurl Ravenscroft (the voice of Frosted Flakes' Tony the Tiger). Unfortunately, when the special aired, they completely omitted him from the credits. A horrified Geisel personally wrote letters to all the major columnists of the day, begging them to give credit where credit was due.

Best cover: The rapper Tyler, the Creator did a fun update for the 2018 movie version and called it "I Am the Grinch."

What Christmas Means to Me

Year: 1967

Writer: Anna Gaye, Allen Story, and George Gordy

Artist: Stevie Wonder

Notes: The titular track was co-written by Marvin Gaye's wife. In contrast to the great yet heavy "Someday at Christmas," "What Christmas Means to Me" is just a joyous celebration of the holiday, closing with Stevie declaring, "I feel like running wild!" After hearing this song, you want to join him in celebrating "happiness in the comin' year!"

Santa Claus Go Straight to the Ghetto

Year: 1968

Writer: James Brown

Artist: James Brown

Notes: In the wake of Martin Luther King's assassination, James Brown wanted to use his platform for activism. While politicians leaned on him to help prevent cities from burning to the ground, James Brown wasn't interested in just calming everyone down. In August, he released "Say It Loud—I'm Black and I'm Proud," and in December, he released the impactful *A Soulful Christmas* album. In this highlight track, Brown points out the inequities that exist in the inner city during the holiday season.

River

Year: 1969

Writer: Joni Mitchell

Artist: Joni Mitchell

Notes: "River" opens with the chords from "Jingle Bells." The next three and a half minutes are an emotional beatdown about a woman who is heartbroken and wishes she had a river she could "skate away on." It's about loneliness around the holidays and a good song for someone who needs to step away from the festivities and have a good cry. Many argue it's not a Christmas song, but if it opens with "Jingle Bells" and the first line is about Christmas, then it's a Christmas song.

Feliz Navidad

Year: 1970

Writer: José Feliciano

Artist: José Feliciano

Notes: Blind Puerto Rican singer-songwriter Feliciano was urged by a producer to add a song of his own to his 1970 Christmas album. He had the tune in his head but realized that if the lyrics were all in Spanish, the song wouldn't get any airtime on most stations. So he made it bilingual, and the twenty-word song has been a consistent Christmas hit for more than fifty years.

Happy Christmas (War Is Over)

Year: 1971

Writer: John Lennon and Yoko Ono

Artist: John & Yoko/The Plastic Ono Band with the Harlem Community Choir

Notes: Even on their honeymoon, John Lennon and Yoko Ono actively spoke out against the Vietnam War. In December of 1969, they posted ads on billboards that said, "War Is Over! / If You Want It / Happy Christmas from John & Yoko." After the success of John's anti-war song "Imagine" in 1971, Lennon and Ono focused on turning those billboards into a song. They incorporated the Harlem Community Choir for background voices, John played the acoustic guitar and sang, and shockingly enough, they were able to overcome Yoko's creepy whispering to deliver a hit Christmas song.

Merry Xmas Everybody

Year: 1973

Writer: Noddy Holder and Jim Lea

Artist: Slade

Notes: This wildly-popular-in-the-UK Christmas hit from glam rocker Slade is a sing-along anthem celebrating the traditions of the season.

Father Christmas

Year: 1977

Writer: Ray Davies

Artist: The Kinks

Notes: In the late '70s, punk was taking off and the legendary Kinks leaned into it with a punk Christmas song about class warfare. The song is told from the teens' perspective as they rough up a department store Santa ("Father Christmas") and demand money. It's harsh, but it's a really fun tune that makes a solid point about haves and have-nots during the holiday season. Hey, they can't all be about sleigh rides.

Christmas Rappin'

Year: 1979

Writer: Denzil Miller, J.B. Moore, Kurtis Walker, Larry Smith, and Robert Ford

Artist: Kurtis Blow

Notes: *Billboard* writer Robert "Rocky" Ford's girlfriend was pregnant, and he was in bad need of money. One of his coworkers once wrote a Christmas album for Perry Como and told Ford that the genre was a gold mine. There's an appetite for the same stuff every year. So he set out to write a Christmas rap song. To this point, rap was not a commercial entity but rather a club or party thing. No radio stations were playing rap and no record stores sold rap records. Keep in mind, this was even a few months before the Sugarhill Gang had its breakout hit "Rapper's Delight." But Ford remained undeterred. He sunk his life's savings into the project, found some collaborators, and got an up-and-coming rapper who was working with twenty-one-year-old promoter Russell Simmons—Kurtis Blow. The group all got together in August and Blow rapped the entire eight-minute song in one night. After selling more than four hundred thousand copies, "Christmas Rappin'" proved to the world that rap was no fad and could be a profitable genre.

Christmas Wrapping

Year: 1981

Writer: Chris Butler

Artist: The Waitresses

Notes: ZE Records told all of its artists to record a Christmas song for a compilation. The new wave group fronted by a former waitress made one about a single woman who was a bit overwhelmed by the season. The title is a play on the popular Kurtis Blow single from a couple of years earlier.

2000 Miles

Year: 1983

Writer: Chrissie Hynde

Artist: The Pretenders

Notes: The inspiration for this song about a long-distance relationship at Christmastime is heartbreaking. Chrissie Hynde wrote it about James Honeyman-Scott, the guitarist and one of the founding members of the Pretenders, who died a year earlier. Nonetheless, it's a sweet song about wanting to be close to a loved one at Christmas.

Do They Know It's Christmas?

Year: 1984

Writer: Bob Geldof and Midge Ure

Artist: Sting, Duran Duran, Boy George, Phil Collins, Bono, George Michael, Kool & the Gang, Bananarama, Paul Young, the guy from Spandau Ballet, and others

Notes: This was the song that really kicked off a stretch of charity albums. Boomtown Rats front man Bob Geldof saw a BBC special about poverty in Ethiopia and immediately felt inspired to start a charity. It was already October, but Geldof knew that the Christmas season was the perfect time to raise money. He skipped all the middlemen (agents, record labels) and contacted everyone in the music business he could. By late November, Geldof had them all in the studio (along with copious amounts of cocaine), banging out "Do They Know It's Christmas?" Some take umbrage with the patronizing nature of the song. Nearly half of Africa is Christian. Of course they know it's Christmas. But there's no denying the song was a marvel. Just four days after that day in the studio, the song made its debut. It immediately went to the top of the charts for the next five weeks and raised over $28 million for charity.

Last Christmas

Year: 1984

Writer: George Michael

Artist: Wham!

Notes: For a group that was mainly known for such fluff as "Wake Me Up Before You Go-Go," "Last Christmas" was a surprisingly vulnerable Christmas ballad about a guy struggling to get over a breakup. Michael wrote the song in his childhood bedroom on a visit to his parents' house. For the recording, Michael played every instrument on the song. As soon as he was done with the vocals, he headed across London and joined Bob Geldof's recording of "Do They Know It's Christmas?"

Merry Christmas (I Don't Want to Fight Tonight)

Year: 1987

Writer: Joey Ramone

Artist: The Ramones

Notes: Inexplicably, this Christmas gem from punk gods the Ramones was just a B-side throwaway that never made any appearances on the charts. It's just a sweet song about keeping the peace at Christmastime, played with classic Ramones pace. It's a fun two minutes.

Fairytale of New York

Year: 1987

Writer: Jem Finer and Shane MacGowan

Artist: The Pogues (featuring Kirsty MacColl)

Notes: According to lead singer Shane MacGowan, the Pogues' producer at the time, Elvis Costello, bet him that they couldn't write a Christmas duet with bass player and future Mrs. Costello, Cait O'Riordan. After two years of attempts and retooling (and the departures of O'Riordan and Costello), the band settled on a sad song about an immigrant in a New York drunk tank reminiscing about broken dreams. And it's beautiful. From the opening piano chords, the song paints a vivid picture of a man going through a range of emotions. Kirsty MacColl proved to be the perfect foil for MacGowan as the two hash out their issues and leave the window very slightly open for optimism. The song that mixes the beauty and ugliness of the sentimental season is near perfection.

Who did it worst? Jon Bon Jovi in 2020. Nobody was asking for an update of this perfect song. In steps Bon Jovi, with watered-down lyrics and a fake Irish accent, to play both parts of the duet. Unforgivable.

Christmas in Hollis

Year: 1987

Writer: Darryl "DMC" McDaniels, Joseph "Run" Simmons, and Jason Mizell (a.k.a. Jam Master Jay)

Artist: Run-DMC

Notes: In the mid-'80s, recording engineer to the stars and future founder of Innerscope Records, Jimmy Iovine, created a Christmas album full of major artists. The most culturally important song to come out of any *A Very Special Christmas* album was "Christmas in

Hollis." At first, the group was reluctant to participate because commercialized rap, at the time, would seem "corny." Authenticity was the name of the game in rap, and Run-DMC were the unquestioned kings of the game in 1987. But, since he knew it would be good for their brand, their publicist gave DJ Jam Master Jay Clarence Carter's "Back Door Santa" to sample. Jay chopped it up and played it for McDaniels and Simmons, and they were on board. They added personal touches like a standard Christmas dinner in the McDaniels household ("chicken and collard greens"), and America suddenly had a mainstream secular Christmas song that wasn't just talking about fireplaces and snow. Plus, it gave a peek at a community that had never been in the spotlight in holiday music.

Christmas All Over Again

Year: 1992

Writer: Tom Petty

Artist: Tom Petty and the Heartbreakers

Notes: Jimmy Iovine's 1987 charity album did so well, he made another. The best song on *A Very Special Christmas 2* was Tom Petty's joyful "Christmas All Over Again." The album went double platinum, which led to yet another sequel. Over the years, Iovine's *Very Special Christmas* albums have raised more than $100 million for the Special Olympics.

All I Want for Christmas Is You

Year: 1994

Writer: Walter Afanasieff and Mariah Carey

Artist: Mariah Carey

Notes: While Bing Crosby's "White Christmas" is the best-selling single of all time, the most downloaded and streamed Christmas song (and second place isn't close) is Mariah Carey's hit song from 1994, "All I Want for Christmas Is You." While planning her Christmas album, Carey's then-husband, Sony CEO Tommy Mottola, suggested one of the tracks be a Phil Spector-y Christmas song. So songwriting collaborator Walter Afanasieff started messing around with some '60s-style piano boogying and Carey belted out, "I don't want a lot for Christmas," and, over the next few hours, they fleshed out the rest. They tweaked the song a little bit over the next two weeks, but most of the song was done in one night. When it was time to record, Afanasieff created all the music on his computer—no instruments were used. Mariah brought in some Christmas trees and lights into the studio and let her famous voice work her magic. The song's popularity has grown over the years. Every December, it shoots up the charts. In fact, it's the only song that has gone number one in four decades. It now pulls in a few million dollars in royalties every year.

Best alternate version: Aloe Blacc's funky version in 2018. It has been covered by a ton of people over the past few decades, but most are just subpar knockoffs. Polish Club's thumping rock version is also pretty cool.

Underrated songs of the era: "Santa Claus Boogie" (1955) – The Voices, "Christmas Night in Harlem" (1955) – Louis Armstrong, "Mistletoe and Holly" (1957) – Frank Sinatra, "One Little Christmas Tree" (1960) – Stevie Wonder, "Santa Claus" (1965) – The Sonics, "Presents for Christmas" (1966) – Solomon Burke, "Back Door Santa" (1968) – Clarence Carter, "Santa Claus Wants Some Lovin'" (1974) – Albert King, "Lonely This Christmas" (1974) – Lucky Soul *covered it in 2007*, "Hard Candy Christmas" (1982) – Dolly Parton, "Thank God

It's Christmas" (1984) – Queen, "The Spirit of Christmas" (1985) – Ray Charles, "Christmas Vacation" (1989) – Mavis Staples, "Millie Pulled a Pistol on Santa" (1991) – De La Soul, "All Alone on Christmas" (1992) – Darlene Love, "Just Like Christmas" (1999) – Low

MODERN ERA

—

With the abundance of classic songs, it has really been a struggle for anything new to jump on our Christmas playlists. Since "All I Want for Christmas Is You" in 1994, there have been no new songs that have come remotely close in popularity. That's not to say there aren't some deserving candidates. From joyous to melancholy, here are a handful of worthy additions to the holiday mix.

Ghostface X-mas

Year: 2008

Writer: Dennis "Ghostface Killah" Coles

Artist: Ghostface Killah

Notes: In 2008, American treasure Ghostface Killah gave the world what it has always needed—a Wu Tang Christmas song.

A Christmas Duel

Year: 2008

Writer: Randy Fitzsimmons

Artist: The Hives and Cyndi Lauper

Notes: "A Christmas Duel" features quite possibly two of the coolest voices in duet history: pop legend Cyndi Lauper and the Hives' deep-voiced Howlin' Pelle Almqvist. It also has a terrific thumping melody from the Swedish garage rock band. So why isn't this song widely known? Because it has some filthy lyrics. It's a great, great song about a dysfunctional couple who is trying to make it work at Christmas. Just be careful about playing it around Grandma.

Christmas Treat
Year: 2009
Writer: Horatio Sanz and Jimmy Fallon
Artist: Julian Casablancas
Notes: In 2000, Horatio Sanz, Jimmy Fallon, Tracy Morgan, and Chris Kattan performed a song on *Saturday Night Live* called "I Wish It Was Christmas Today." The joke was that it was childlike music with very little substance. In 2009, Julian Casablancas, the lead singer of the Strokes, took that simple song, kept the lyrics, and turned it into a thundering, head-bopping Christmas rock song.

Christmas in Harlem
Year: 2010
Writer: Kanye West, Marvin Gaye, Chauncey Hollis, Shuggie Otis, and Cydell Young
Artist: Kanye West (feat. Big Sean, Cam'ron, CyHi Da Prynce, Jim Jones, Musiq Soulchild, Pusha-T, Tenaya Taylor, Vado)
Notes: Kanye's Christmas song is a huge collaboration that samples Marvin Gaye and focuses a lot on shopping.

All I Want Is Truth (For Christmas)

Year: 2010

Writer: Laura Burhenn

Artist: The Mynabirds

Notes: Even though this Christmas song details global warming, commercialism, and war, it has a lovely, catchy melody.

It's Christmas Time (And I'm Still Alive)

Year: 2012

Writer: Jessica Dobson, Peter Mansen, Garrett Gue, and Elliot Jackson

Artist: Deep Sea Diver

Notes: This beautiful Christmas offering from the Seattle pop band is both sad and triumphant.

One More Sleep

Year: 2013

Writer: Leona Lewis, Richard "Biff" Stannard, Iain James, Jez Ashurst, and Bradford Ellis

Artist: Leona Lewis

Notes: British pop singer Leona Lewis delivered the most Mariah Christmas performance possible for someone not named Mariah.

Underneath the Tree

Year: 2013

Writer: Kelly Clarkson and Greg Kurstin

Artist: Kelly Clarkson

Notes: The pop star shows off her powerful voice in this high-energy, happy, festive song that ticks off every box on the standard Christmas checklist (snow, tree, carolers, presents, warm embraces).

Alone on Christmas Day

Year: 2015

Writer: Mike Love and Ron Altbach

Artist: Phoenix and Bill Murray

Notes: It was originally written in 1977 for a Beach Boys Christmas album that never came out. A French rock group named Phoenix and actor Bill Murray recorded it together for his Netflix special, *A Very Murray Christmas*.

Big Bulbs

Year: 2015

Writer: Saundra Williams

Artist: Sharon Jones & the Dap-Kings

Notes: You can't help but smile while listening to this double entendre track from the terrific *It's a Holiday Soul Party* album.

Everything Will Change This Christmas: The Ballad of Hans Gruber

Year: 2016

Artist: Four Eyes

Notes: Nearly three decades after *Die Hard*'s premiere, one of the great Christmas movies (more on this later) got its own Christmas song. In a fun twist, the song is somewhat sympathetic towards Hans Gruber, the bad guy. The lightly flowing song is punctuated with an R-rated profanity that shouldn't surprise any fans of the movie. Yippe-Ki-Yay!

Strangely enough, this wasn't the only 2016 Christmas ballad about Die Hard. That same year, Scottish lo-fi indie folk band eagleowl released a song from the building's perspective—"Let's Save Christmas

(The Ballad of Nakatomi Plaza)"—and Edinburgh's Jonnie Common hilariously focused on the reason the movie's hero is barefoot for most of *Die Hard*—"Yippie-Ki-Yay Father Christmas". Clearly, the *Die Hard* folk floodgates have opened.

Snowman

Year: 2017

Writer: Sia Furler and Greg Kurstin

Artist: Sia

Notes: In 2017, Australian pop star Sia released *Everyday Is Christmas*, an album full of original songs. The best of the entertaining bunch is "Snowman," about saying goodbye to a melted snowman but really a metaphor for the heartbreak at the end of a relationship.

Ribbons and Bows

Year: 2018

Writer: Kacey Musgraves, Julia Michaels, and Justin Tranter

Artist: Kacey Musgraves

Notes: The country star made her debut Christmas album with a mix of old and new songs, doing an impressive job mixing genres. This heavy clapping and saxophone track is kind of a throwback to the days of Motown and Darlene Love.

Christmas and You

Year: 2019

Writer: David Hidalgo and Louie Pérez

Artist: Los Lobos

Notes: The first-ever Christmas album from the legendary East LA quintet, Los Lobos, was full of solid covers and this beautiful song about longing for a loved one.

Christmas Butt

Year: 2019

Writer: Catherine Popper

Artist: Puss N Boots

Notes: The trio known as Puss N Boots (Norah Jones, Sasha Dobson, and Catherine Popper) finally put this live favorite on an album. "Christmas Butt" is a fun, weird song that implores everyone to "shake your Christmas butt 'til your cranky goes away" and has some salty (explicit) words for "commercial smut."

Tell Your Mama

Year: 2019

Writer: Aloe Blacc

Artist: Aloe Blacc

Notes: Aloe Blacc's Christmas album brings the funk to December. *Christmas Funk* has everything from a cool version of Mariah's "All I Want for Christmas Is You" to this song, about a kid passing along well-wishes from neighbors to his mother.

Some other underrated gems: "I Love You Like a Madman" (2008) - The Wave Pictures, "Another Christmas At Home" (2009) - Eux Autres, "These Bells Will Ring" (2016) - Bitter's Kiss & Blue Stone, "Krampus" (2017) - la-goons, "Christmas Means Nothing Without You" (2018) - Shonagh Murray, "Won't Be Alone Tonight" (2019) - Mike Krol, "Stay Away This Christmas" (2020) - Randolph's Leap,

"Christmas in July" (2020) - Alex the Astronaut, "Lonely Star (Christmas Song)" (2020) - Dream Nails

THE WORST CHRISTMAS SONGS

—

All I Want for Christmas Is My Two Front Teeth
Year: 1948
Artist: Donald Yetter Gardner
Notes: Hard to believe they were still allowed to be called the "Greatest Generation" after this novelty song.

I'm Gonna Put Some Glue 'Round the Christmas Tree (So Santa Claus Will Stick Around All Year)
Year: 1955
Artist: Joel Grey
Notes: A creepy kid has a plan of putting Santa in a *Misery*-type situation where he gets stuck in place from Christmas through Easter and the Fourth of July. The song is even more unsettling when you realize the singer was Joel Grey, a twenty-three-year-old man just trying to sound like a little boy. Joel Grey later went on to become a Broadway star and the dad of Ferris Bueller's sister.

The Chipmunk Song
Year: 1958
Artist: The Chipmunks
Notes: Some bummer named Dave has three rodents performing songs in a recording studio, and all he does is yell at them. Chipmunks are

solitary animals! They don't even pay attention to each other outside of mating season. And they're singing! In unison! Shame on you, Dave!

Please, Daddy (Don't Get Drunk This Christmas)

Year: 1973

Artist: John Denver

Notes: John Denver sings from the perspective of a seven-year-old boy trying to stage an intervention for his hard-drinking dad because "I don't want to see my mama cry." Yikes!

Step into Christmas

Year: 1973

Artist: Elton John

Notes: Elton John and Bernie Taupin, the men responsible for gems like "Rocket Man" and "Mona Lisas and Mad Hatters," decided to make a Christmas song with absolutely nothing to say. The first line of the tedious song is "Welcome to my Christmas song!" It's all downhill from there.

Grandma Got Run Over By a Reindeer

Year: 1977

Artist: Elmo & Patsy

Notes: A grandmother getting killed on Christmas Eve isn't what makes this song terrible. It's the bad singing, tedious melody, and lousy premise that solidify "Grandma Got Run Over By a Reindeer" as the worst song in Christmas history. So Grandma drinks too much eggnog and not one person in this crummy family makes sure she gets home okay? They just let her go for a walk—smashed—after midnight? Then they find hoof prints on her head and "incriminating Claus marks" on her back?!? Was this an execution? The next day, Grandpa is "watching football, drinking beer, and playing cards with cousin Mel." Seems like he murdered her and is trying to blame it on the kindest man on earth. This song stinks on ice. And if it's just all a big joke, there's a key ingredient missing—humor.

Wonderful Christmastime

Year: 1979

Artist: Paul McCartney and Wings

Notes: He wrote "Yesterday." He wrote "Blackbird." He wrote "Live and Let Die." And then he found a synthesizer and everything turned to garbage. This song is a mess.

Santa Baby

Year: 1987

Artist: Madonna

Notes: Baby talk is creepy enough. Baby talk in an attempt to seduce Santa? No bueno.

The Christmas Shoes

Year: 2000

Artist: NewSong

Notes: A Christian group put their own spin on celebrating the birth of Jesus by writing a song about a boy who wants to buy his mom a nice pair of shoes before she dies. "I want her to look beautiful if Mama meets Jesus tonight." She has mere hours left, and the boy is shopping and paying with pennies? Maybe just give her a good hug, champ. Even Jesus knows you don't wear shoes in bed.

Santa Looked a Lot Like Daddy

Year: 2013

Artist: The Robertsons

Notes: A family famous for making duck-calling whistles recorded a sing-along of a poor man's version of "I Saw Mommy Kissing Santa Claus." It went about as well as you'd think.

THE TWELVE DAYS OF CHRISTMAS, EXAMINED

The "Twelve Days of Christmas" are the days between December 25 and January 6—that is, between Christ's birth and the arrival of the three Wise Men.

The song probably originated in France, but there is no official record. The first known version of it was in a 1780 children's book called *Mirth without Mischief*. The "Twelve Days of Christmas" was most likely a memory game to see how many lyrics kids could recall. The song was played at Twelfth Night parties. If you messed up, the punishment was either kissing your opponent or doing a favor for them—kind of like a more innocent version of truth or dare.

The lyrics have changed over the years. It wasn't always "On the x-day of Christmas, my true love gave to me…." Some early reference the gift giver as "my mother" rather than "my true love." Other alternative lyrics feature "bears a-baiting" and "ships a-sailing." And the really cool gift, the gold rings, might've actually been a reference to (yup, more birds) a ring-necked pheasant.

The version and melody we all know today was written by English composer Frederic Austin in 1909. It's mostly a kids' song but has been covered by artists in different genres: Burl Ives, Perry Como, John Denver and the Muppets, and Roger Whittaker. It also has been tweaked for comedy purposes many times (the best done by Rick

Moranis and Dave Thomas as their characters Bob and Doug McKenzie on *SCTV* in 1982).

Each year since 1984, PNC Bank has put out the Total Christmas Price Index adding up the collective value of the gifts in Day Twelve of the song. Over the past thirty-seven years, that index value has pretty much doubled from about $20,000 to around $40,000. On Day Twelve, that's 78 gifts. But across all twelve days from Christmas to Three Kings' Day, that's 364 gifts total! Some are pretty terrific first-tier gifts, while others… not so much.

FIRST-TIER GIFTS (fun and valuable, but a bit much):

—

While they wouldn't provide any future value, the Twelve Drummers Drumming would be pretty cool. Anyone who doesn't enjoy a proper drumline is dead inside. If on January 5, twelve members of the Southern or Grambling State University drumline showed up and performed for you, you'd probably be pretty amped for weeks. Just thinking about it would put a pep in your step. This gift will set somebody back a few grand, but at least it's fun.

And it would be tough to knock the gift of gold. Gold is a universally valuable commodity. But eight days' worth of gold rings seems like a lot. Outside of Mr. T and Johnny Depp, not many of us would find a use for forty gold rings. You could always sell some… but then you have the issue of either: a) getting cheated at a pawn shop, or b) getting cheated by those cash-for-gold people. Still, you should be able to turn that into over six grand, whereas just about every other gift during this near-fortnight of courtship is completely worthless.

SECOND-TIER GIFTS (pricey and confusing):

—

The Nine Ladies Dancing and Ten Lords A-Leaping are interesting, at least. They're not cheap, but they're professional dancers. You rarely get to see masters at their craft perform a private show. But how long will the show be? Are they performing at the same time, or do you have to sit through two separate dance and leaping shows? Even if they do perform together, you have to think everyone is going to be low on ideas after a couple of days. The lords are going to be leaping for three days straight. The dancing ladies are there for four. And why were they picked to arrive before the musicians?

The combined few days of dancing and leaping would cost well over sixty grand. Or, you could have free gas for your car for more than two decades.

THIRD-TIER GIFTS (birds and headaches):

—

The Partridge in a Pear Tree is a charming thought. Having a fruit tree is kind of nice (even if the fruit is a subpar version of the apple). But twelve days of it means you're expected to run an orchard. You're going to have to dig a dozen holes with at least three feet of space between each hole in a sunny area of your property. Then the trees must be staked with sturdy posts. They'll need to be fertilized once per year. Then, in about five years (!), they will finally bear fruit. Actually, not really in that fifth year. Usually, the first harvest year's fruits are inedible and have to be thrown out. But in year six? Your orchard will be humming!

Two Turtle Doves are kind of cute. They're tiny and make a turr-turr sound, which is how they got their name. But they like to live on the edge of woodland areas, so if you don't live near a forest, you probably won't see them much. That's okay. They do a ton of migrating, so they'd barely be around anyway.

Three French Hens would require you to either have a lot of dinner parties (if they're already cooked) or about four standard backyard coops. For ten days, you had better learn the ins and outs of chicken farming. Because here comes thirty of them.

Four Calling Birds are a problem. You have thirty-six of them coming your way. Your neighbors will hate you and your family will never visit.

Six Geese A-Laying will turn your yard into a slippery mess. Geese are disgusting animals. They will eat all your grass and defecate everywhere. Forty-two of them will leave a lot of droppings. If you're not careful, they might even try to take down an airplane, as they did over the Hudson River in 2009.

Eight Maids A-Milking creates both a moral and logistical quandary. Milking cows is not easy work, and yet the people who do it are given minimum wages for their efforts. So here you are, a person with a pear orchard and a bunch of birds, and on the same day you receive your twentieth gold ring, here come eight minimum-wage-earning women to extract milk from cows in your yard. And what are you going to do with all that milk? It's not like you can store it all in your garage. An average dairy cow produces 7½ gallons per day. You have eight of them for five days. That's three hundred gallons of milk. Now you need to figure out how to get a distributor to help you unload it before it goes bad. It's not like you can pull up a table at the local farmer's market and sell three hundred gallons of moo juice.

Eleven Pipers Piping isn't going to be a hit with your neighbors, either. With eleven bagpipes blasting, people are going to think you're having a cop funeral in your yard. Then, the next day, you do it again! Nobody can concentrate when eleven bagpipes are going at once.

That whole bunch of gifts seems like another miss. Lots of noise, lots of destruction, and $25,000 down the drain. Maybe you can sell that milk at a premium.

FOURTH-TIER GIFTS (an awful waste of money):

—

The Seven Swans A-Swimming gift on New Year's Eve is an absolute nightmare. While they don't need a ton of water, you're going to need a pretty substantial pond with a lot of aquatic plants to keep all of them happy. Keep in mind, they start showing up on day seven. By January 5, you will need space for forty-two swans! Swans are the largest waterfowl in North America, with wingspans of around ten feet. Hope you enjoy them, because they live up to twenty years. And a few years in, each will pick a mate and they'll enter breeding season. When they're trying to procreate, swans get extremely aggressive and territorial. If you invade their space, make no mistake—you *will* get attacked. And then they will lay a half dozen eggs.

The total cost of all those swans is up around $80,000. Would you rather have forty-two swans or an around-the-world trip for two?

THE NUTCRACKER

The most ubiquitous music at Christmastime is the work of renowned nineteenth-century Russian composer Pyotr Ilyich Tchaikovsky—*The Nutcracker*. Even people who know nothing about classical music know *The Nutcracker*. Every shopping mall, pharmacy, and commercial break in December play its songs. This wasn't the case until somewhat recently, though.

In 1814, German writer E.T.A. Hoffmann wrote the story *The Nutcracker and the Mouse King*. In it, a girl named Marie receives the gift of a nutcracker, which she fears has been broken. When she goes to check on it, she finds that the nutcracker has come to life and takes her on a weird, somewhat dark, Dorothy-in-Oz-like journey to an alternate universe. Thirty years later, famous French writer Alexandre Dumas (*The Count of Monte Cristo, The Three Musketeers*) changed the girl's name to Klara and put a much lighter spin on it with his *Nutcracker of Nuremberg*. Nearly a half century after that, some men in St. Petersburg, Russia turned Dumas' version into a ballet. The music for that ballet was composed by Pyotr Ilyich Tchaikovsky (*Swan Lake, Sleeping Beauty*).

About six months before the ballet premiered in 1892, Tchaikovsky made a concert suite from the music. The St. Petersburg crowds loved it. Nearly every song received an encore. Then, in December of that year, the full ballet was performed. Concertgoers were unimpressed. All of the action was packed in the first act, while most of the second was perceived to be frivolous vignettes. Tchaikovsky died less than two years later, and the ballet was rarely performed over the next several decades.

The Nutcracker didn't leave Russia until 1934, when it was performed in London. It reached America ten years later with a Christmas Eve production by the San Francisco Ballet but still didn't get any real traction. Then, in 1954, choreographer George Balanchine revived the ballet he remembered from his youth and gave it a dazzling update for the fledgling New York City Ballet. Audiences loved it, and *The Nutcracker* became the centerpiece for the entire company. Dozens of sold-out *Nutcracker* performances allowed the ballet company to keep its doors open the other eleven months out of the year.

By the '60s, nearly every theater company throughout the country was performing *The Nutcracker* each December and a fondness for the beautiful music began to grow. Also by that point, the songs were free in the public domain. Advertisers and Hollywood started putting *Nutcracker* pieces in just about everything. From its "Overture" and "March" to the "Dance of the Sugar Plum Fairy" and "Waltz of the Flowers," everyone knows the music of *The Nutcracker*.

CHRISTMAS MOVIES

THE CLASSICS

Santa Claus (1898) - The first Christmas movie ever made was the work of British film pioneer George Albert Smith. A maid tucks two kids into bed. While they're sleeping, Smith used what Michael Brooke of BFI Screenonline called "cinema's earliest known example of parallel action" and showed Santa on the roof, climbing into the chimney. Santa then appears in the room with the kids, fills their stockings, and disappears. A simple plot, but then again, it was the nineteenth century.

Good Cheer **(1926)** - Just one year before sound was incorporated into film ("talkies"), Hal Roach's Little Rascals took a shot at a Christmas movie. After a snowball fight, the gang heads to Main Street and criticizes a Santa working at a toy store (who looks like a white-haired Hagrid from *Harry Potter*). Eventually they encounter a bunch of bootleggers dressed as Santas and knock them out with two-by-fours.

March of the Wooden Soldiers **(1934)** - The legendary comedy duo Laurel and Hardy received some of the best reviews of their careers for this update of the 1903 Mother-Goose-characters-in-a-Christmas-setting operetta (*Babes in Toyland*). In their attempts to help Bo Peep, the dimwitted Stan and his pompous friend Ollie stumble into clashes with the town villain, Barnaby. Stan's messed-up order of six hundred one-foot-tall soldiers proves to be key. There are some dreadful singing numbers to skip, but the slapstick comedy still holds up well.

Christmas in Connecticut **(1945)** - This wayyy-ahead-of-its-time comedy starring Barbara Stanwyck challenges gender roles just a few months after the end of World War II. Stanwyck plays a Martha Stewart-type author of the column "Diary of a Housewife" who really has no knack whatsoever for domestic life. For a publicity stunt, the columnist has to host a returning war hero for Christmas dinner. Comedy ensues. Randomly, Arnold Schwarzenegger directed an updated version as a TV movie in 1992.

It's a Wonderful Life **(1946)** - Nowadays, *It's a Wonderful Life* is widely considered to be one of the most popular Christmas movies ever made. But, at the time it premiered, it came and went at the box office with limited fanfare, low profits, and tepid reviews.

It did get some Oscar nominations (because Capra was pretty popular) but ultimately didn't win anything and simply disappeared. Interestingly, the film's failure gratified the United States government. You see, *It's a Wonderful Life* came out right in the middle of the Red Scare, and the government hated it. They accused the movie of "rather obvious attempts to discredit bankers by casting Lionel Barrymore as a 'Scrooge-type' so that he would be the most hated man in the picture. This, according to these sources, is a common trick used by Communists." The Red Scare faded and with it, most awareness of the movie.

Then, in 1974, thanks to a paperwork error by National Telefilm Associates (the owners of the film at the time), *It's a Wonderful Life* was no longer copyrighted and became public domain for twenty years. That meant that every local television station had a free Jimmy Stewart movie. Within a couple of years, every market in America was flooded with *It's a Wonderful Life*. It would run every day on some stations. And back then, there weren't many channels. Suddenly everyone knew about it and saw its greatness. Even though he was already considered to be one of America's finest actors, it wasn't until 1974 that most people saw Jimmy Stewart's finest work.

Shot a couple of years after he returned from World War II, Stewart harnessed the deep emotions that the war had stirred up and put them into playing a man who is coming apart at the seams. (It was also shot during a heat wave in summer, which is why Jimmy Stewart is sweating profusely during several scenes.) George Bailey is a great guy who repeatedly sacrifices his hopes and dreams to help others, and eventually, his kindness leads him to imminent disaster. (His crummy Uncle Billy should never have been employed.) George is visited by a guardian angel who hasn't yet earned his wings but is determined to help him. Donna Reed plays his fantastic, supportive wife. And Lionel Barrymore is an iconic greedy villain. It's impossible to watch *It's a Wonderful Life* and not feel at least a little bit better about humanity.

Miracle on 34th Street **(1947)** - Edmund Gwenn delivered an Oscar-winning performance as Kris Kringle in this story about how the real Santa Claus helps save Christmas for a skeptical mother (Maureen O'Hara) and daughter (Natalie Wood). Since it's rare to encounter someone sane who claims to be the real Santa, Kringle finds himself in a mental hospital, and it's up to John Payne's lawyer character to get him out. Eighties teen comedy legend John Hughes remade *Miracle on 34th Street* in 1994. It had a nice cast but just lacked the magic of Gwenn's Oscar-winning performance.

Note: The postal worker redirecting dead letters is played by Jack Albertson (a.k.a. Grandpa Joe from *Willy Wonka and the Chocolate Factory*).

The Bishop's Wife **(1947)** - Cary Grant is an angel who helps a bishop (David Niven) and his wife raise money for their church. There are a handful of Christmas references, but mostly, this mediocre movie is about Cary Grant looking terrific in a suit and doing some cool magic with his angel powers (like when he keeps filling up the wine glass with a wave of his hand to get the guy drunk). This movie was remade in 1996 (and renamed *The Preacher's Wife*).

Holiday Affair **(1949)** - "When two romantic go-gettin' guys are in love with a hard-to-get girl…" Ultimately, this was probably a studio attempt at softening Robert Mitchum's image by putting him into a rom-com. It kind of plays out how you'd think—two guys using the "I'll tell her I love her" sales pitch on a woman, and not much more of substance. It's fine. It also stars Janet Leigh and Wendell Corey (Jimmy Stewart's cop buddy in *Rear Window*).

The Lemon Drop Kid **(1951)** - Bob Hope plays a con artist who tricks people at a race track. When he happens to trick the wrong person, he has to come up with ten grand by Christmas or a mob boss will have him killed. The movie's main legacy is the introduction of the song "Silver Bells."

White Christmas **(1954)** - There are lots of parallels between this movie and *Holiday Inn*. Once again, Bing Crosby and a partner are a singing duo at a remote club around the holidays. All of the songs in both movies are written by Irving Berlin. The basic premise is that Bing Crosby and Danny Kaye are old army buddies who hit it big on Broadway. They eventually hook up with Rosemary Clooney and Vera-Ellen. The group then heads to Vermont right before Christmas, where there's a heat wave and therefore no tourists. Bing and Danny Kaye realize the inn is run by their old captain in the army. He's a real bummer because he's hemorrhaging money during this heat wave and the army won't take him back. So the guys set up a big show on Christmas Eve to honor the old dog. While not as problematic as *Holiday Inn*, the "Minstrel Number" at the fifty-four-minute mark ("I'd rather see a minstrel show than any other show I know. How those comical folks, with their riddles and jokes") is a bit tough to swallow. Not even the smooth voices of Bing Crosby and Rosemary Clooney can overcome the multitude of bad sets, bad songs (except for the titular one), and bad acting. Also, Bing looks like someone's grandfather (he was an old-looking fifty-one at the time) even though, in the beginning, he is trying to pass for an active-duty soldier.

TOP GROSSING CHRISTMAS MOVIES OF ALL TIME

Right around the time *Home Alone* was shattering box office records, studio executives got the idea that Christmas movies could make them a lot of money. So instead of putting out a Christmas movie maybe every few years or so, studios were kicking out one a year. Sometimes, multiple per year. Even if they didn't have an entirely original idea, they'd remake old ones (*Scrooged, Miracle on 34th Street, The Preacher's Wife, How the Grinch Stole Christmas, The Nativity Story, The Star, The Grinch, A Christmas Carol, The Nutcracker and the Four Realms, Black Christmas*), give them sequels (*Home Alone 2: Lost in New York, The Santa Clause 2, The Santa Clause 3: The Escape Clause, Bad Santa 2*), or take an established franchise and give it a Christmas sequel (*Ernest Saves Christmas, National Lampoon's Christmas Vacation, The Muppet Christmas Carol, The Best Man Holiday, A Madea Christmas, A Very Harold & Kumar Christmas, Daddy's Home 2, A Bad Moms Christmas*). And audiences kept coming back for more. Not all of these movies are good. Some of them are terrible. But they all made money. Because Christmas movies will always find an audience.

A Christmas Story **(1983)** - This Jean Shepherd story adaptation is really the first Christmas movie about Christmas. It's not a love story that takes place during the holiday season. There is no journey of anyone to get home to their family in time to celebrate. No jerk is finding the Christmas spirit. This movie is solely about the holiday itself, and nine-year-old Ralphie Parker's all-consuming quest to get the "official Red Ryder carbine-action, two-hundred-shot range model air rifle, with a compass in the stock and this thing that tells time." Despite the distractions of school bullies, his teacher, a nasty mall

Santa, Little Orphan Annie decoder ring disappointment, parents bickering over a leg lamp, and a bar of Lifebuoy soap, Ralphie Parker remains laser-focused on the Christmas present he wants the most. Peter Billingsley (Ralphie), Melinda Dillon (Mother Parker), and Darren McGavin (the Old Man) are terrific throughout the movie.

When *A Christmas Story* came out, it garnered mostly positive reviews without a ton of fanfare. As movie critic Roger Ebert said, "My guess is either nobody will go to see it, or millions of people will go to see it." Both guesses were kind of correct. While the Bob Clark-directed movie came and went pretty quickly at the box office, it found a new life a couple of years later on HBO and videotape. Then, in 1986, the struggling MGM studios sold a big chunk of its library to Ted Turner, including this movie. Over the years, Turner showed *A Christmas Story* on his cable channels (TBS and TNT). Then, in 1997, TBS started running it twenty-four hours straight from Christmas Eve into Christmas Day, every single year. Nearly forty years later, nobody thinks about its lackluster box office. *A Christmas Story* is now on a short list with *It's a Wonderful Life, Miracle on 34th Street, Christmas Vacation*, and *Elf*.

Santa Claus: The Movie (1985) - Fresh off of his success playing boozy billionaire Arthur in the movie of the same name, Dudley Moore took on the role of Patch, one of Santa's elves, which pretty much ruined his career. Armed with a massive budget, *Santa Claus: The Movie* was positioned to be huge. It had McDonald's Happy Meal tie-ins and a big advertising push. Ultimately, the story and the jokes just weren't very good. And the North Pole scenery looked like a Thomas Kincaid painting. Moore's Patch wants to prove to Santa (played by future Big Lebowski himself, David Huddleston) that he's a good worker, so he gets a job working for an evil industrialist in New York City, played by

John Lithgow. The candy canes the toy company was making (toy candy canes?) turn out to be an explosive hazard, so Patch has to get rid of them before they kill the children. The movie not only lost Moore's reputation but also $27 million.

Ernest Saves Christmas **(1988)** - Jim Varney's famous character Ernest, a well-intentioned moron, got his own Christmas movie in 1988. The real Santa is ready to pass along his duties to a guy in Orlando. Unfortunately, he leaves his magic toy sack in a cab driven by Ernest. That is the launching point to an unfunny mess of a movie. Ernest and a teenage runaway then have to get it back to him and save the holiday. Its heart is in the right place. The humor, on the other hand, isn't.

Prancer **(1989)** - This is a movie about, at best, the fourth most important reindeer at Christmas. Sam Elliott plays a down-on-his-luck apple farmer who seems pretty checked out as a dad. His daughter finds a wounded reindeer in the woods and thinks it's Prancer. Low-stakes drama ensues. Abe Vigoda and Cloris Leachman round out the cast in this dull Christmas story.

National Lampoon's Christmas Vacation **(1989)** - Comedy sequels tend to stink because all the jokes have been done before. Where the *Vacation* franchise succeeded was changing the kids and setting each time. Maybe the best change in this one was an entirely new director who had never seen either of the previous two *Vacation* movies. The movie is based off of John Hughes' short story that he wrote for *National Lampoon*, "Christmas '59." Clark Griswold (Chevy Chase) wants his family to host the perfect Christmas, but everything possible goes wrong: cutting the tree, lighting the house, an unwanted Cousin Eddie (Randy Quaid), condemnation from nasty neighbors (Julia

Louis-Dreyfus and Nicholas Guest), animals in the house causing serious damage, and a stingy boss. It wasn't a massive hit when it premiered, finishing second at the box office that week behind *Back to the Future Part II*, but eventually became one of the classics.

Fun Facts: 1) The day before shooting the scene where a squirrel jumps out of the tree, the trained squirrel died so they just had to use a random one. It didn't go so well. 2) The actress who played Aunt Bethany was the voice of Betty Boop. 3) Neighbors Todd and Margo lived in Roger Murtagh's house from *Lethal Weapon*.

Home Alone (1990) - Director Chris Columbus was supposed to direct *Christmas Vacation* but, after a few awful meetings with notorious jerk Chevy Chase, dropped out of the project. So, John Hughes gave Columbus a different script to work on—*Home Alone*. The highest grossing Christmas movie of all time (and highest grossing live-action comedy for more than a quarter century) was number one for twelve straight weeks! Like with his teen comedies in the '80s, John Hughes really nailed the kid mentality, as the story is mostly told through a ten-year-old's perspective. In short, Kevin McCallister (Macaulay Culkin) is left behind by his family when they go on vacation for Christmas. Meanwhile, two burglars (Daniel Stern and Joe Pesci) are systematically robbing all of the homes of people who have left town. They run into trouble when the resourceful Kevin repeatedly fights them off. Much like *The Goonies*, *Home Alone* plays out like a kid's fantasy: to be able to eat all the junk food you want and successfully fight off bad guys for a few days. There is also a sweet side story with the mysterious old man neighbor and a terrific score by John Williams (*Star Wars, Jaws, E.T., Indiana Jones*). The movie has inspired dozens of articles featuring interviews with doctors outlining the true damage Kevin's antics would've inflicted upon the Wet

Bandits (falling iron – fractured face; doorknob heated to 750 degrees – scar tissue-inducing third-degree burns; blowtorch to the head – most likely fatal but, at best, a need for complete skull replacement; paint cans to the face – more fractures and lost teeth with a likely concussion).

Home Alone 2: Lost in New York (1992) - When a movie makes the kind of money Home Alone made, it's a guarantee there will be a sequel. It followed the same basic premise. Kevin accidentally goes to New York while his less-than-attentive parents go to Florida. While it was not received quite as warmly, it's hard to imagine a sequel to this very specific premise that could be any better. Macaulay Culkin's charm and the return of Joe Pesci and Daniel Stern still make for some entertaining physical comedy.

The Santa Clause (1994) - While the accidental death of Santa in the opening few minutes of this movie doesn't seem like the setup for a runaway success, *The Santa Clause* was a massive hit. After he inadvertently causes the catastrophic injury to Claus, divorced dad Scott Calvin puts on the suit and morphs into the next Santa. It's a light, fun Christmas movie.

The Preacher's Wife (1996) - This remake of the 1947 Cary Grant-David Niven movie, *The Bishop's Wife*, follows the same framework—an inner-city pastor (Courtney B. Vance) who is struggling financially asks God for help, and down comes an angel (Denzel Washington). The acting is solid enough, but the biggest difference between the original and the remake is Whitney Houston's performance as the wife. Inevitably, Houston does some terrific gospel singing and, in the process, gives a largely forgettable story some much-needed pop.

Jingle All the Way **(1996)** - Inspired by the crazes caused by "it" toy shortages at Christmastime (like Cabbage Patch Kids and Tickle Me Elmo), Arnold Schwarzenegger stars as a dad who is doing everything he can to procure a Turbo-Man toy on Christmas Eve. Schwarzenegger tries his best but, tonally, it's all over the place. It's supposed to be for young kids but, at the same time, it kind of ruins the magic of Santa, involves attempted murder, and has Phil Hartman's character trying to seduce Schwarzenegger's wife (played by Rita Wilson).

Jack Frost **(1998)** - Michael Keaton plays a musician who dies in a car accident on Christmas Eve. The following year, he comes back to life as a snowman, then turns his son into the type of middle schooler who hangs out with a snowman. Shockingly, people think he is a weirdo. Kelly Preston plays the concerned mother but, really, all of us should be concerned with this movie.

How the Grinch Stole Christmas **(2000)** - Ron Howard's feature-length adaptation of the Dr. Seuss story was widely panned by critics but made a ton of money. Detractors felt it strayed too far from the original cartoon that they watched when they were six years old. The problem is that the 1966 special was only twenty-six minutes long. Adding an hour to it meant it had to take some turns. Also, this was a Jim Carrey movie. Carrey was in the middle of an incredible run of success, and audiences clamored for Jim Carrey to do Jim Carrey things. The Grinch delivered in a big way on that front.

The Santa Clause 2 **(2002)** - Cash grab number two (in a series of three) takes place eight years after the original. Tim Allen's movie son is now in high school and rebelling against the evil principal who hates Christmas (oooh). While this sequel has a few moments, its premise—

Santa now has to find a wife—feels pretty weak. But it made big money, so there was one more planned.

Elf (2003) - There was some excitement for the new Christmas movie starring Will Ferrell. People loved him on *Saturday Night Live* and as "Frank the Tank" in the movie *Old School*. But, for *Elf* to become something special, a lot was riding on the director. Prior to *Elf*, Jon Favreau was best known for being a teammate in the movie *Rudy* and the writer and star of the guy-getting-over-a-breakup comedy *Swingers*. This was a new challenge. And he absolutely crushed it. The stop-motion animation North Pole scenes give the movie a timeless feel (a la Rankin/Bass specials). Favreau uses New York City as both the antithesis to Buddy the Elf's hometown (traffic, used gum on subway station steps) and a magical Christmas setting (Rockefeller Center, Fifth Avenue). The tone was set even without the actors appearing. The casting was perfect, with James Caan as the man who lost his spirit and Zooey Deschanel as the woman who is eager to find it. Ed Asner has probably played Santa more times than anyone in history, so he was a good fit. Will Ferrell's innocence and energy throughout the movie never wavers. The end result is a Christmas classic. *Elf* has also been made into a Broadway show *Elf: The Musical* and a stop-motion animated special *Elf: Buddy's Musical Christmas*.

Bad Santa (2003) - Premiering only a few weeks after *Elf*, Billy Bob Thornton starred in a different kind of Christmas classic—a wildly inappropriate one. While the earnestness and charm of *Elf* wins over even the most hardened of audiences, *Bad Santa* is the perfect chaser. Billy Bob Thornton plays Willie Soke, an alcoholic mall Santa who, along with his elf partner, Marcus (played by the great Tony Cox), robs a different shopping center each year. To establish what kind of Santa Willie is going to be at the beginning of the film, a boy sits on his lap and demands Santa perform some magic. Willie tosses the kid off and says, "Let's watch you disappear." The blistering, very R-rated script (which was punched up by the Coen brothers), shows a truly nasty, seemingly unredeemable character in Willie. All that ugliness over the first two-thirds of the movie is why the final act has such a satisfying payoff. This is the funniest Christmas movie ever made. Sadly, its 2016 sequel, *Bad Santa 2*, was very comedy sequel-ish—some funny parts but mostly a rehash of the same jokes.

Love Actually **(2003)** - The third major Christmas movie from 2003 is a British rom-com that made a lot of money overseas but posted underwhelming box office numbers in America. People saw it as just another love story starring a bunch of famous British actors. Then, after word of mouth spread about how it's really a Christmas movie, it became an annual staple. Today, it's one of the more polarizing Christmas movies. Detractors call it uneven and schmalzy. Others consider it the gold standard in rom-coms. It's really somewhere in between—a fun but flawed movie with a strong, intertwining ensemble cast. The stories include an aging singer trying to have the number-one Christmas song, several workplace romances bubbling over due to Christmas spirit, and a boy trying to impress a girl at their school's Christmas show. Some of it is problematic (like Andrew Lincoln's character stalking his best friend's eighteen-year-old wife). Some of it is heartbreaking (Emma Thompson gives an acting master class in the scene when she realizes that her husband is not only probably having an affair but also thought a single compact disc was an adequate Christmas gift). Sure, it's a little corny, but then again, so is just about every Christmas movie.

The Polar Express **(2004)** - The 1985 Chris Van Allsburg book was brought to life by Robert Zemeckis using all digital capture (the first to ever do so according to the *Guinness Book of World Records*). Tom Hanks produced and starred in most of the roles—the boy, the conductor, Santa, a hobo, the boy's father. It's a visually stunning adaptation that was nominated for three Oscars.

Christmas with the Kranks (**2004**) - In 2001, famous legal-thriller author John Grisham wrote a book about a couple who decide to take a cruise instead of celebrating Christmas. This doesn't go over so well with the neighbors, and comedy (?) ensues. What should've been chalked up as a misfire actually reached number-one on *The New York Times* bestseller list and was made into a movie starring Tim Allen and Jamie Lee Curtis. Reviews weren't kind.

The Nativity Story (**2006**) - This New Line Cinemas production is a relatively straightforward yet pretty dull retelling of the biblical story. Oscar Isaac and Keisha Castle-Hughes do a solid enough job.

Deck the Halls (**2006**) - Danny DeVito and Matthew Broderick play rival neighbors who are constantly undermining each other's quest to put up the best Christmas display. It was a waste of a good cast and sits at 6 percent on Rotten Tomatoes.

The Santa Clause 3: The Escape Clause (**2006**) - The finale of the Tim Allen trilogy, which is about Santa battling with Jack Frost over Christmas supremacy, answers an important question: Is the great Martin Short great enough to lift a movie where everyone else seems to be going through the motions? No.

This Christmas (**2007**) - This movie features a really strong cast: Loretta Devine, Delroy Lindo, Regina King, Idris Elba, Mekhi Phifer, and, unfortunately, Chris Brown. It's a pleasant but not remarkable family-gets-together-for-the-holidays-and-old-dynamics-clash kind of movie.

Fred Claus **(2007)** - This Vince Vaughn movie was based on Donald Henkel's poem "A Legend of Santa and His Brother Fred." It has some humorous trademark Vaughn fast-talking scenes where he shines as Santa's ne'er-do-well brother, but the movie is kind of a mess tonally. Still, Paul Giamatti is really good as his exasperated but loving (and rather unhealthy-looking) brother, Santa. Rachel Weisz, Kathy Bates, and Kevin Spacey round out the solid supporting cast.

Four Christmases **(2008)** - Despite the Hollywood Reporter calling it "one of the most joyless Christmas movies ever," *Four Christmases* has a bunch of legitimately funny scenes. It's more of a vignette movie—Vince Vaughn and Reese Witherspoon are a couple who are on the hook for celebrating Christmas Day at their four divorced parents' houses. The first half of the movie is decidedly funnier, with scenes at the MMA-loving household of Vaughn's movie father (played by Robert Duvall) and in the randy cougar den at Witherspoon's movie mother's house (played by Mary Steenburgen).

Arthur Christmas **(2011)** - The single best feature-length animated Christmas movie is one that doesn't get a lot of play in America. It had a full theatrical release but for some reason didn't make the rotation like *The Polar Express* or the Tim Allen *Santa Clause* franchise. This movie answers a lot of the logistical questions about how Santa does it all in one night but also follows the journey of the clumsy but well-meaning son of Santa, Arthur Christmas. Arthur finds out a child has been skipped and goes on an around-the-world journey to fix Santa's mistake.

A Very Harold & Kumar 3D Christmas **(2011)** - The success of *Bad Santa* opened the door for R-rated Christmas comedies. So, in 2011, it seemed only natural that the successful stoner comedy franchise *Harold & Kumar* would enter the fray. The big selling point at the time was that it was in 3D (as a lot of big budget movies were at the time) but, really, it was a sweet turn for the twenty-first-century Cheech and Chong. There were plenty of 3D joints, smoke, and a variety of gross things popping out at viewers. But at its heart, *A Very Harold & Kumar 3D Christmas* is about two friends rekindling their dormant friendship while avoiding gangsters, getting insanely high, enjoying a waffle-making robot, and almost killing Santa Claus.

The Best Man Holiday **(2013)** - In this fourteen-years-later sequel to *The Best Man*, a lot of beautiful people from the original (Taye Diggs, Nia Long, Morris Chestnut, Regina Hall) get together for Christmas. Old issues resurface, leading to friction, romance, and heartbreak. Monica Calhoun shines as Mia Sullivan, the one who manages to get the estranged gang back together. It actually beat *Thor: The Dark World* for the top box office spot on the day it premiered.

A Madea Christmas **(2013)** - In 2013, Tyler Perry's Madea character—a loud, Yoda-like, often unintelligible ("Hallelujer!") woman—got her own Christmas movie. It's just as bad as all of the other Madea offerings. Larry the Cable Guy actually is one of the more understated parts of the movie. Essentially, it's about a couple trying to hide their secret interracial marriage from Madea's sister and some side story involving the town Christmas jubilee. Also, everyone in this town seems to be driving fifty-year-old pickup trucks.

Note: Blair from *The Facts of Life* plays the town principal.

Krampus **(2015)** - This Toni Collette-Adam Scott holiday movie focuses on one of the darker aspects of Christmas traditions—the horned European beast that punishes the naughty. Krampus plays out like many this-house-isn't-safe movies, but with a Christmas twist.

The Night Before **(2015)** - Seth Rogan, Anthony Mackie, and Joseph Gordon-Levitt are three old friends who are about to spend one last Christmas Eve together. The trio are all at different stages of their lives, and they're going out with a bang—the super exclusive party known as the Nutcracka Ball. It's a funny night-out-on-the-town movie with lots of drugs, chaos, and a strong supporting cast. Michael Shannon is terrific as the mysterious Mr. Green.

Almost Christmas **(2016)** - Danny Glover stars in this so-so dysfunctional family dramedy. In short, the dad wants the whole family to come back home and celebrate the first Christmas since their mother died. It's fine, but the audience kind of knows how every scene is going to play out.

Office Christmas Party **(2016)** - This ensemble cast (Jennifer Aniston, Jason Bateman, Kate McKinnon, Olivia Munn, T. J. Miller, and Jillian Bell) R-rated comedy is all about a company's last-ditch blowout party in order to save their company. The movie definitely has its moments and funny lines, but the overall story is largely irrelevant. It's just an out-of-control party movie.

A Bad Moms Christmas **(2017)** - The sequel to *Bad Moms* takes place at Christmas. This time, the moms (Mila Kunis, Kristen Bell, and Kathryn Hahn) are struggling with their visiting mothers (Christine Baranski, Cheryl Hines, and Susan Sarandon). All the grandmothers come across as unlikable and, therefore, not that funny.

Daddy's Home 2 **(2017)** - The 2015 Will Ferrell-Mark Wahlberg opposites-find-common ground comedy was given a Christmas sequel two years later. John Lithgow plays the super sensitive dad of Ferrell. Noted anti-Semite Mel Gibson was cast in the role of Wahlberg's gruff father. The movie's overall goal seems to want to redeem someone who isn't deserving of it. The delightful Lithgow and Ferrell can't save it.

The Star **(2017)** - This movie has the religious heavy-handedness of a *VeggieTales* episode with slightly better graphics. The only charming part of the animal retelling of the Nativity story is the pretty strong voice-over talent (Steven Yuen, Aidy Bryant, Keegan-Michael Key, and Christopher Plummer).

The Grinch **(2018)** - This third film adaptation of Dr. Seuss' legendary character makes for a fun, pleasant retelling of the story. Benedict Cumberbatch stars.

The Nutcracker and the Four Realms (2018) - This really ambitious version of Tchaikovsky's famous ballet cost a lot to make. While it had a great cast (Keira Knightley, Helen Mirren, and Morgan Freeman) and is visually impressive, the story lacks a truly memorable scene.

Last Christmas **(2019)** - This is a Christmas movie that you want to like (inspired by a great George Michael song, written by Emma Thompson, directed by *Bridesmaids* and *The Office* director Paul Feig, good cast), but just can't. Emilia Clarke plays a pretty miserable character who is swept off her feet by the charming Henry Golding. It feels like a Hallmark Channel movie with a Hollywood budget.

UNHERALDED CHRISTMAS MOVIES

Over the years, there have been many think pieces written about what is and isn't a Christmas movie. Mostly this argument centers around *Die Hard*. But what actually makes a Christmas movie? Does Christmas have to be in the title? Does there need to be Christmas music throughout the film? Does the bulk of the action have to take place on Christmas? If the answer is yes to any of those, then you have to eliminate *It's a Wonderful Life* from consideration. But, as we all know, *It's a Wonderful Life* is most certainly a Christmas movie.

Here are some major-release Christmas movies that aren't always listed as such:

The Apartment **(1960)** - Jack Lemmon stars as a guy who lets his superiors at an insurance company use his apartment for romantic hook-ups. Around Christmas, he falls for the elevator operator (Shirley MacLaine) who is having an affair with the head of the company (Fred MacMurray). While it doesn't entirely take place at Christmas, this iconic Lemmon movie centers around one of the most Christmassy movie themes of all—redemption.

Gremlins **(1984)** - A horrible inventor buys his kid a creature in a mysterious shop in Chinatown. The shop owner gives the inventor some key guidelines (never expose it to light or water and never feed it after midnight). The kid instantly breaks the rules, and chaos ensues. This Christmas horror movie is about a bad gift gone wrong.

Die Hard **(1988)** - New York police officer John McClane flies to Los Angeles to see his estranged wife and children. Just as he gets to his wife's corporate Christmas party, terrorist Hans Gruber and his henchmen take over the Nakatomi Plaza. The only person who can stop them is the tough-as-nails cop from New York.

Yes, the greatest action film of all time also happens to be a Christmas movie. As *Die Hard* writer Steven de Souza points out, it's more Christmassy than *White Christmas*. It takes place entirely at a Christmas party (as opposed to the one scene in *White Christmas*). It features four Christmas songs (versus *White Christmas*' one). *Die Hard* is about a guy trying to be with his family at Christmas. Plus, after McClane kills one of the bad guys, he writes on the guy's chest, "NOW I HAVE A MACHINE GUN HO-HO-HO." What's more Christmassy than that?

***Batman Returns* (1992)** - Tim Burton's second Batman movie takes place entirely at Christmastime. There is a key scene during a tree lighting, Batman and Catwoman kiss under the mistletoe, and part of the Penguin's origin story is getting abandoned at Christmas. If this movie were called *A Batman Christmas*, nobody would question it.

***The Ref* (1994)** - Denis Leary plays a burglar who takes a couple hostage on Christmas Eve while hiding from the police. Unfortunately for him, that couple (Kevin Spacey and Judy Davis) are in the midst of a spiraling-out-of-control marriage and can't stop fighting. More family visits, and Leary's problems only worsen. At its core it's a dysfunctional family Christmas movie. Judy Davis and (if you can separate the art from the artist) Kevin Spacey are fantastic in *The Ref*.

***Mixed Nuts* (1994)** - Steve Martin leads a solid cast running a suicide hotline on Christmas Eve. It's a comedy that's not very funny.

***The Family Stone* (2005)** - An uptight woman (Sarah Jessica Parker) spends Christmas with her boyfriend (Dermot Mulroney) and his free-spirited family. They're pretty crummy to her. She's full of foot-in-mouth moments (including a bad homophobic comment). It's a good cast, but nobody is really likable enough to care about.

***Unaccompanied Minors* (2006)** - Thanks to a snowstorm, a group of kids (who are flying without adults) are stuck at a generic Midwestern airport. Hijinks ensue. This getting-home-for-Christmas movie plays out like a lower-stakes *Home Alone*.

***In Bruges* (2008)** - A hit man makes a brutal mistake on a job and is now stuck in Bruges at Christmastime with his partner. This black-comedy Christmas movie highlights the loneliness of the season as a man takes stock of his questionable career.

HORROR

In the 1970s, a new genre emerged: Christmas horror movies. Here are a few standouts:

***Black Christmas* (1974)** - *A Christmas Story* isn't the only holiday classic directed by Bob Clark. Nine years prior to Ralphie and the leg lamp, Clark directed a slasher movie that had a big influence on its genre. At the start of their holiday break, a group of sorority sisters (including Olivia Hussey, a.k.a. Juliet from Zeffirelli's *Romeo and Juliet*, Margot Kidder, and Andrea Martin from *SCTV*) get stalked by a mysterious caller. One by one, people are killed in gruesome fashion. This movie was the first horror movie to show the view from the unknown killer's perspective and the first to employ the "the call is coming from inside the house!" trope. It was remade in 2019 with more of a #MeToo vibe, but most of the action in the new version felt forced.

Silent Night, Deadly Night **(1984)** - Following the *Psycho* template, the killer in this slasher flick is a guy who snapped after a harrowing childhood experience. From there, the department store Santa kills a lot of people and also gratuitously rips open a lot of women's shirts. What made this movie stand out was the advertising campaign launched by Tri-Star in the month leading up to the movie. Intense ads were run right in the middle of the day (including during a Green Bay Packers game), and uptight parent groups went nuts. When discussing the movie for their review show, Siskel and Ebert called any profits from it to be "blood money." Within a week, it was pulled from all theaters. A couple of years later, it found new life on video.

Rare Exports: A Christmas Tale **(2010)** - This loopy (in a good way) Finnish movie puts a Nordic spin on the Christmas horror genre. A group of scientists excavate a site in the mountains of northern Finland and find a scraggly, naked, white-bearded old man. Soon, children go missing and reindeer are murdered. This is not a jolly ol' St. Nick.

Some other solid Christmas horror movies: *Jack Frost* (1997), *A Christmas Horror Story* (2015), *Anna and the Apocalypse* (2017), *Better Watch Out* (2017)

HALLMARK AND LIFETIME CHRISTMAS MOVIES

Since 2009, the Hallmark Channel and Lifetime Network have been making variations on the same few Christmas movies. And they are huge money makers. Christmas for those networks is like St. Patrick's Day for an Irish pub. Since those channels are mostly targeting women, the main characters of nearly all these movies are women. While Lifetime is a bit more diverse, both still skew pretty white and straight. And secular. Here are some other common threads:

— Small towns are where happiness can be found. The big cities just represent headaches. Why work at an office in the city when you can just quit that job and work with your hands in a small town? Make candles! Open a bakery!
— Snow needs to be falling or already covering the ground. There's a pretty solid chance a laughter-filled snowball fight will break out at any moment.
— Even if she is not looking for it, the heroine will encounter her true love about twelve minutes into the movie.
— There's a good chance she will butt heads with that true love in the beginning. But just you wait!
— Sometime near the end of the second act, there will be some serious decorating. Whether it's cookies, a tree, or a house, there will be decorating accompanied by soft music and laughter.
— Most of the stars of these movies will be familiar faces from the 1980s and '90s. Is that Jo from *Facts of Life*? Look, it's Sabrina the Teenage Witch! Rudy Huxtable, Cliff Clavin, Winnie Cooper, Jason Seaver, Mr. and Mrs. Keaton, Andrea Zuckerman, A.C. Slater, Norm Peterson, Diane Chambers, Lorraine McFly, Blossom, D.J. Tanner, Claudia Salinger, Helen Chapel, Dawson Leery, and many, many more star in movies each and every November and December.

Here's a sampling of some Hallmark and Lifetime Christmas movies:

12 Men of Christmas **(2009)** - Kristin Chenoweth finds her boss hooking up with her boyfriend, so she flies to Montana and tries to set up a calendar starring the local fire and rescue guys. There is an unfortunate body-shaming situation where one of the firemen is called out for being pale.

A Royal Christmas **(2014)** - Lacey Chabert gets engaged to a prince, and then it's time to meet the royal family. She drinks out of the finger bowl!

Crown for Christmas **(2015)** - Danica McKellar stars as a woman who was fired by a fancy hotel but, thanks to a mysterious guest, gets a job working as a nanny and tutor in the fictitious country of Winshire (really Romania). The kid is a monster, it becomes a *Taming of the Shrew* situation, and love blossoms between McKellar and the man who would be king.

The Spirit of Christmas **(2015)** - A woman deals with a dreamy ghost who is haunting an inn for sale. He may be from a different century, but true love spans all lifetimes!

Chateau Christmas **(2020)** - A world-famous classical pianist has lost her passion for playing. On her trip to her hometown for Christmas, her ex-boyfriend convinces her to play at the local Christmas concert. As luck would have it, her ex-boyfriend is beautiful.

STREAMING

In the past few years, popular streaming services have also thrown their hats into the Christmas movie ring. The way they're churning out children's movies, comedies, musicals, Hallmark-type romance movies, and theatrical-caliber rom-coms, the streaming services clearly have every intention of being a prominent player in the Christmas movie genre.

Here are the standout streaming Christmas movies:

A Very Murray Christmas (2015) - The Murricane led his talents to Netflix for this 2015 Christmas special. In short, Bill Murray is trying to film an old-fashioned Christmas special, and an East Coast blizzard puts it in jeopardy. It's kind of a wink at the corniness of Christmas variety show specials but at the same time it *is* a Christmas variety show. George Clooney and Bill Murray do a pretty fun version of Albert King's 1974 track "Santa Claus Wants Some Lovin'." Miley Cyrus, Amy Poehler, Chris Rock, Rashida Jones, Maya Rudolph, and Jason Schwartzman also star.

A Christmas Prince (**2017**) - This is where Netflix jumped into Lifetime and Hallmark's arena. A magazine journalist named Amber is sent to write a story about a playboy prince right before Christmas. While trying to get her scoop, Amber poses as an English tutor for a young princess with spina bifida. The playboy prince takes notice, and a Christmas romance begins.

The Christmas Chronicles (**2018**) - Kurt Russell stars as a badass Santa in this family adventure movie. In short, a brother and sister try to capture Santa and, in the process, cause such a disruption that the holiday might be ruined for everyone. The movie hits on a lot of the usual tropes, but Russell really takes Santa in a different direction and makes it fun. In 2020, they made a slightly worse but still pretty fun sequel.

The Princess Switch (**2018**) - After the success of *A Christmas Prince*, Netflix dipped their toes in the fictional royalty Christmas romance pool once again. This time, a Chicago baker goes to Europe and runs into a doppelgänger duchess. They *Parent Trap* the situation, and Christmas romance follows.

Klaus (**2019**) - Santa is given an alternate origin story in this spectacularly animated Netflix movie. In it, a self-absorbed postman is given the most remote location possible (above the Arctic Circle) and befriends a hermit-like toy maker named Klaus. While there have been many great CGI-animated movies in recent years (e.g. from Pixar), there is something special about this hand-drawn throwback.

Noelle **(2019)** - One of Disney's first movies on their new streaming service was a Christmas movie starring Anna Kendrick. Her brother just inherited the role of Santa and isn't ready for it. So he leaves town, and it's up to Noelle to find him and save Christmas.

Jingle Jangle: A Christmas Journey **(2020)** - Forest Whitaker and Keegan-Michael Key star in a fantasy musical about the rebirth of a down-and-out toy maker. *Jingle Jangle* is filled with soulful and joyous songs, fantastical inventions, and a stellar cast.

Happiest Season **(2020)** - Hulu produced the first-ever wide-release LGBTQ Christmas romance movie. Kristin Stewart stars as a woman who is about to propose to her girlfriend, Harper, over the Christmas break. When she gets to her girlfriend's parents' house, she realizes that none of them know Harper is gay.

UNDERRATED CHRISTMAS MOVIES

Just like with Christmas music, it's difficult for independent and foreign movies to break into the public consciousness. Between old classics that are re-aired every year (like *It's a Wonderful Life* and *Elf*) and the one or two major releases from big studios, there just isn't a lot of room for the little guy.

Tokyo Godfathers **(2003)** - This anime film follows three homeless people who find a baby in a dumpster on Christmas Eve. Their crazy journey to find the baby's parents leads them to all kinds of drama, including attempted suicide and the Yakuza. Ultimately, it's a movie about the Christmas spirit—kindness and being there for one another in times of need.

Joyeux Noel **(2005)** - This fictionalized depiction of the World War I Christmas truce is told through the eyes of German, French, and Scottish soldiers. The movie shows how the three sides got there, how they overcame fears and agreed to the truce, and what happened when the truce ended. It was nominated for a Foreign Language Oscar in 2006.

Feast of the Seven Fishes **(2018)** - This charming comedy is like a snapshot of an Italian-American Christmas in 1983. The story has a *Dazed and Confused*-like feel of a day in the life of a working-class boy on Christmas Eve. He hits it off with a WASP-y Ivy League girl and brings her to his traditional family gathering, where she's indoctrinated into the wonderful world of the "Feast of the Seven Fishes." Plus, it has Joe Pantoliano. Everything is better with Joey Pants.

A few other solid ones: *Un Conte de Noel* (2008), *White Reindeer* (2013), *Get Santa* (2014)

THE WORST CHRISTMAS MOVIES

All these movies get coal in their stockings.

Santa Claus Conquers the Martians **(1964)** - Based on the title, you kind of know what you're getting. Martian children are apparently really lazy, so the adults kidnap Santa in hopes he can turn their behavior around. To add to that horrible plot, the sets, costumes, and acting are horrendous. The movie is so far out of touch with what is entertaining that it makes you think maybe it was written by a Martian.

The Christmas That Almost Wasn't (**1966**) - In the mid-'60s, lots of Westerns were made in Italy to lower production costs (spaghetti Westerns). In the same year as *The Good, the Bad and the Ugly*, another cheaply made Italian-American movie was released. This wasn't quite as beloved. It's about a rich guy who buys the North Pole and wants to foreclose on Santa. Santa gets a lawyer who helps him raise cash. Santa, Mrs. Claus, and the lawyer then head out on Santa's sleigh while singing the questionable song, "We've Got a Date with Children." Oh no.

One Magic Christmas (**1985**) - Imagine wishing upon a star and waking up to a bleak Harry Dean Stanton hovering over your bed. It turns out he is this family's guardian angel. And things for this sad family just keep getting sadder. On Christmas Eve, the mom (Mary Steenburgen) gets fired from her supermarket job and the dad gets murdered in a bank robbery. The children get kidnapped by the bank robber, who then drives the car off a bridge into a river. But, since the title includes the word "magic," you assume this is Harry Dean Stanton's time to shine. And he does… sort of. He saves the kids, which is great, but then Steenburgen has to break the news to the kids that Dad is never coming home. Then Stanton eventually brings the dad back to life but doesn't get the mom her job back. So, the Christmas lesson this movie teaches is to be thankful nobody was murdered.

The Christmas Gift (**1986**) - This TV movie was John Denver's first acting role since turning down (according to him) the role of Zack Mayo in *An Officer and a Gentleman*. And that's not the craziest thing you'll read about this movie. John Denver was cast as the city slicker who just moved to a small town. Mr. "Take Me Home, Country Roads" is the big city guy! Anyway, the whole town is really into Santa and Christmas magic, and his construction firm wants to destroy it.

The Kid Who Loved Christmas **(1990)** - Sammy Davis, Jr.'s final role was in a pretty crummy TV movie about a boy who is about to be adopted but then his future mother is killed in a car accident. Her husband is a musician and deemed unfit to adopt on his own. The kid goes to a mall Santa to see if he can help sort it out and gets this response: "I'm better at mending toys than broken hearts." Thanks for the wisdom, pal.

Santa With Muscles **(1996)** - Hulk Hogan stars as an arrogant rich guy who hits his head, gets amnesia, and is led to believe he is a mall Santa Claus. There's an evil scientist who is trying to destroy an orphanage and the Santa who inexplicably wears wrestling tights steps up to save them.

Note: One of the orphans is played by a young (and probably hoping everybody forgets this movie that lasted only two weeks in theaters) Mila Kunis.

I'll Be Home for Christmas **(1998)** - After leaving the sitcom *Home Improvement*, 1990s teen heartthrob Jonathan Taylor Thomas got his own movie. Too bad it was this one. He plays an obnoxious college kid (kind of like a less funny Ferris Bueller) who is bribed by his dad to go home for Christmas. Before he leaves, some guys who hate him drive him to the desert and glue a Santa outfit to him. The rest of the movie is his quest to get home and get in touch with his girlfriend (Jessica Biel), who thinks he ditched her. Thomas was never asked to carry a movie again.

The Christmas Shoes **(2002)** - In 2000, a group called NewSong released a horrible song called "The Christmas Shoes" about a boy who wants to buy his dying mother shoes. CBS decided to make it into a TV movie. Rob Lowe plays a surly guy who lacks the Christmas spirit.

When he sees the kid scrounging up money for his dying mom's shoes, he chips in and feels great about himself and Christmas. The boy runs home and gives his mom the red shoes. She says they're beautiful, then dies. Robe Lowe's character lives happily ever after.

Surviving Christmas (2004) - A rich guy pays a family to spend Christmas with him in his childhood home. Even though it stars Ben Affleck, James Gandolfini, Catherine O'Hara, and Christina Applegate, this movie is a mess from start to finish. Affleck delivers a career-worst performance as an over-the-top rich guy. It's supposed to be funny but should only be watched if you want to be filled with intense disappointment.

Noel (2004) - Chazz Palminteri directed this movie about five New Yorkers coming together at Christmas. It had an impressive cast (Susan Sarandon, Alan Arkin, Penélope Cruz, Robin Williams, Paul Walker) but it's just a soul-crushing slog of a movie set to sad piano music. By the time you get to the cloying third act, you just want it to be over.

Thomas Kinkade's Christmas Cottage (2008) - Thomas Kinkade was a wildly successful artist. His adequate paintings were sold at mall "art galleries" across America. According to his company, at one point, a Thomas Kinkade painting was hanging in one out of every twenty American homes. So, some producer thought they would make a lot of money on a movie inspired by Kinkade. The story is about a young artist who returns to his failing hometown around Christmas and rescues it with his super cool artwork. They got real stars (Peter O'Toole, Marcia Gay Harden) to be in it. And it made $41,000 in the theaters. That's to say it was a colossal flop. A realistic movie about Kinkade's final years would have provided a lot more interesting content. Kinkade racked up nearly a million dollars in penalties for defrauding people, got kicked out of a Siegfried and Roy show in Vegas for screaming, "Codpiece!" at the top of his lungs, and was caught urinating on a Winnie the Pooh figure at a Disneyland hotel claiming "ritual territory marking."

Saving Christmas **(2010)** - Tired of hearing about the pagan roots of Christmas traditions, Kirk Cameron goes through lots of mental gymnastics to prove all things Christmas actually took place in the Bible. Everyone in the movie holds empty mugs and pretends they're drinking hot chocolate. Meanwhile, Kirk and his brother-in-law sit in a parked car talking for an hour. At the end, viewers are treated to about ten minutes of unfunny outtakes. This might be the worst thing ever made.

CHRISTMAS ADJACENT MOVIES

For those who love Christmas but have seen George Bailey and Buddy the Elf one too many times, there is yet another type of Christmas movie to enjoy during the season—Christmas Adjacent. These are films that might have a Christmas scene or two but have little to do with the holiday itself. Some get thrown into Christmas movie programming and are just assumed to be Christmas movies (*Holiday Inn*, *The Nightmare Before Christmas*). Others are beloved films that have a forgotten Christmas hook (*GoodFellas*, *Castaway*).

Here they are, the Christmas Adjacent:

Bright Eyes **(1934)** - During the Great Depression, people were disproportionately excited to see a six-year-old girl sing and dance. Shirley Temple even won an Oscar for this role in which she sings "Good Ship Lollypop" to a group of military guys. Temple plays an orphan who really loves her godfather but is forced to live with her rich, angry uncle. After an unpleasant Christmas in her new home, Temple runs away and starts an adventure that ultimately ends up with an insane custody decision. The movie concludes with a woman slapping her daughter.

The Thin Man **(1934)** - A former detective and his rich wife investigate a murder at Christmastime for fun. "The next person that says 'Merry Christmas' to me, I'll kill him." The bad guy from a beloved Christmas movie plays a big role in the mystery.

Holiday **(1938)** - On Christmas, Cary Grant's character finds out the woman he intends to marry is from an incredibly wealthy family.

Remember the Night **(1940)** - Fred MacMurray plays a prosecutor who feels bad for a witness awaiting trial. Rather than let her sit in jail over the Christmas break, he invites her to come home with him. Predictable romance ensues.

The Shop Around the Corner **(1940)** - Jimmy Stewart and Margaret Sullivan star as coworkers at a leather goods store (randomly set in Budapest). Both have pen pal romances without knowing it is each other. The romance builds in the weeks leading to Christmas. The guy who plays the Wizard of Oz is their boss.

Meet John Doe **(1941)** - A woman is fired by a newspaper but is asked to write one final column. She makes up a story about a guy who's going to kill himself on Christmas Eve and, in the process, starts a political movement.

Holiday Inn **(1942)** - The movie that gave the world the song "White Christmas" is full of problems. Bing Crosby and Fred Astaire are part of a trio with a woman. When the woman chooses to be with the dancer (Astaire), the singer (Bing) decides to move to a farm in Connecticut. Then he turns that farm into a club. But not just any club. It's a club that is only open on holidays. "Honey, pack your bags! It's the sixteenth president's birthday! Time to go clubbing!" Oh, and on Lincoln's birthday celebration, Bing gets in blackface and sings about "Abraham" freeing the slaves. In the middle of the song, it cuts to a black woman in the kitchen named Mamie who then sings to her kids about freeing the "darkies." It's jarring. But, even if you chalk that up to being from a different time, you can't ignore that the movie is trash. The old partners return and there's a new woman in the mix, but ultimately, it's a terrible movie about a terrible business venture with terrible songs (except for "White Christmas").

Meet Me in St. Louis **(1944)** - Much like "Holiday Inn," this Judy Garland movie launches one of the most iconic Christmas songs ("Have Yourself a Merry Little Christmas") during the Christmas part of the movie but most of it really isn't at or about Christmas. There's some drama about Judy Garland's husband getting transferred to New York from St. Louis. The family is leaving right after Christmas, so Judy sings the famous song to her daughter. Then the daughter has a psychotic break and smashes a haunting group of snow people set up in her yard. It's one of the more bizarre sequences in movie history.

The Bells of St. Mary's **(1945)** - Bing Crosby stars in this movie about a "cool" priest who butts heads with a stubborn nun about ways to save an inner-city school. There's a Christmas pageant in the movie, but maybe its best connection to Christmas is in that it appeared in two separate Christmas scenes from other movies. In *The Godfather*, Michael Corleone and Kay go see this movie at Radio City on the December night his father gets shot. Also, this movie is on the marquee as George Bailey sprints through Bedford Falls at the end of *It's a Wonderful Life*. "MERRY CHRISTMAS, MOVIE HOUSE!"

It Happened on 5th Avenue **(1947)** - A homeless guy moves into a mansion while the owner is south for the winter. Then he starts taking in more down-on-their-luck people, including a young Skipper from *Gilligan's Island*. Both Christmas and New Year's appear in the movie.

Cover Up **(1949)** - This murder mystery takes place at Christmastime. Someone killed the most hated man in town.

We're No Angels **(1955)** - Three escaped convicts (Humphrey Bogart, Aldo Ray, and Peter Ustinov) spend Christmas with a family in French Guyana and, in the process, help them get back on their feet.

Blast of Silence **(1961)** - A gravelly-voiced narrator tells the tale of a sullen hit man who comes to New York City to kill a middle manager in the mob. Even though it's more than sixty years ago, what stands out is how similar 1961 Christmas in New York is to today (Rockefeller Center, lights).

Robin and the 7 Hoods **(1964)** - The "Rat Pack" stars of this Prohibition-era version of *Robin Hood* end up as charity Santas on the street in the end.

The Lion in Winter (1968) - Anthony Hopkins stars as twelfth-century Henry II, who is looking for his successor on Christmas Eve.

On Her Majesty's Secret Service (1969) - To help execute the evil Blofeld's plans of bacteriological warfare, henchman Irma Bunt talks about a "Holy Night celebration" as she drugs a group of women in the Swiss Alps so they can be his "Angels of Death." Even James Bond villains have a Christmas tree. This movie also features a pretty lousy Christmas song called "Do You Know How Christmas Trees Are Grown?"

The French Connection (1971) - The Gene Hackman cop-chasing-down-an-international-drug-smuggling-operation movie begins around Christmas. Undercover Popeye Doyle attempts to bust a dealer while dressed as Santa.

The Godfather (1972) - Michael and Kay go Christmas shopping on Fifth Avenue. Also, Don Corleone gets set up around Christmas. When Michael has to switch his father's hospital room so he doesn't get killed, you see a few Christmas lights and a small tree.

Three Days of the Condor (1975) - This Robert Redford-Faye Dunaway post-Watergate paranoia movie takes place at Christmastime. You see some decorations and Salvation Army Santas in the background in certain scenes.

Diner (1982) - Barry Levinson's movie about young guys navigating their early twenties in 1959 Baltimore opens at a Christmas dance. Holiday decorations are seen throughout.

Fast Times at Ridgemont High (1982) - The drudgery of working in a mall at Christmastime is on full display as we see a kid peeing on Santa's leg, and Santa then taking out his misery on pizza parlor server

Stacy Hamilton. Across the way, she is being ogled by Mark "the Rat" Ratner and Mike Damone.

Trading Places **(1983)** - This modernized telling of Mark Twain's *The Prince and the Pauper* takes place between Thanksgiving and early January. Two mean, rich brothers have a nature-versus-nurture bet that involves switching the lives of Louis Winthorpe (Dan Aykroyd), a rich, white commodities trader, and Billy Ray Valentine (Eddie Murphy), a black con artist. Louis crashing the Duke & Duke Christmas party in a disgusting Santa suit is a key scene, but the New Year's Eve train ride plays an even bigger role. One of the great comedies.

Rocky IV **(1985)** - Rocky and Adrian ditch their son at Christmas so he can fight Ivan Drago in Moscow on December 25.

Better Off Dead **(1985)** - This black comedy is about a high school student named Lane (John Cusack) who is suicidal after his girlfriend dumps him. Lane's mom gives everyone frozen TV dinners for Christmas. Meanwhile, across the street, Lane's gross neighbor gives a picture of himself to their French exchange student.

The Sure Thing **(1985)** - This road trip comedy is about a couple of college students who are sharing a ride to California for the Christmas break.

Die Hard 2 **(1990)** - It's Christmas Eve two years later and John McClane is at Dulles airport to pick up his wife. Immediately he notices skulduggery is afoot. Terrorists are about to cause mass mayhem and crash Holly McClane's airplane. The rest of the movie is supercop John McClane once again battling terrorists. Although there are lots of Christmassy things at the airport and it does take place on

Christmas Eve, this movie is more Christmas adjacent. There are no Christmas parties like the last one, and there's less relationship drama that John has to overcome.

GoodFellas **(1990)** - Fresh off the $6 million Lufthansa heist, the gang celebrates Christmas at a bar while *A Christmas Gift for You from Phil Spector* plays in the background. When other members of the crew show up with expensive new purchases (new car, mink coat), Jimmy demands they return them.

Edward Scissorhands **(1990)** - There are lots of Christmas moments in this weird Tim Burton movie about a man with scissors for hands. Edward's creator died while giving him a Christmas present. Edward makes an ice sculpture in the backyard during a Christmas party. The violent conclusion takes place at Christmas.

Grumpy Old Men **(1993)** - John's daughter (Daryl Hannah) visits on Christmas and tries to get him (Jack Lemmon) to reconcile with his old friend and neighbor (Walter Matthau). The feud continues into spring.

Sleepless in Seattle **(1993)** - On Christmas, Tom Hanks' character's son calls a radio show saying his dad has been sad and lonely ever since his wife died—thus kick-starting an iconic romantic comedy.

Cronos **(1993)** - Guillermo del Toro's first movie about a sixteenth-century vampire in Mexico takes place at Christmastime.

Look Who's Talking Now **(1993)** - The horrendous talking-baby movie got an even more pathetic sequel. This time it's with a talking dog and it takes place at Christmas. The baby is now a boy who is struggling with his spirit after seeing a crummy mall Santa.

The Nightmare Before Christmas **(1993)** - This popular stop-motion animated movie that gets played every December is about the king of Halloween Town stumbling into Christmas Town and getting jealous. So he kidnaps Santa and tries to take his place. Just because Christmas is in the title, it's not part of the genre. The whole movie has a spooky vibe and it's all about how the people of Halloween Town react to some Christmas stuff.

Little Women (1994) - The ailing Beth receives a piano at Christmas in this coming-of-age drama.

Star Trek Generations **(1994)** - The only movie in the *Star Trek* universe that features Christmas shows Captain Picard celebrating while mourning the death of his brother and nephew.

Nobody's Fool **(1994)** - Paul Newman plays a prickly old man who is trying to reconnect with his son and grandson at Christmastime in snowy upstate New York.

Money Train **(1995)** - This movie about two transit cop foster brothers who decide to rob a train begins at Christmas.

While You Were Sleeping **(1995)** - Sandra Bullock stars as a transit worker forced to work on Christmas. She saves a guy's life, but he's in a coma. At the hospital, a misinterpreted statement makes everyone think he's her fiancé. Over time, she starts to fall for the guy's brother. A good chunk of the movie takes place at Christmastime but, ultimately, the movie bleeds into the next year.

L.A. Confidential **(1997)** - This dirty cop neo noir opens with Russell Crowe's character breaking up a domestic violence situation by ripping down a guy's Christmas lights.

CHRISTMAS ADJACENT MOVIES

You've Got Mail (**1998**) - Tom Hanks and Meg Ryan are delightful in this remake of 1940's *Shop Around the Corner*. Hanks runs a Barnes & Noble-type store moving into the same neighborhood as Ryan's little bookstore. The middle part of the movie takes place at Christmas.

Stepmom (**1998**) - A grim dying-mom movie does everything it can to make the audience cry, including a "this is her final Christmas" scene.

Go (**1999**) - Katie Holmes' character opens this Tarantino-inspired crime-comedy movie by talking about what she likes about Christmas presents. A drug dealer (Timothy Olyphant) wears a Santa hat (and has a great critical take on the comic *Family Circus*).

Eyes Wide Shut (**1999**) - A bored couple participates in orgies at Christmastime.

Cast Away (**2000**) - After Christmas dinner, FedEx employee Chuck Nolan (Tom Hanks) gets on a plane that ends up crashing into the ocean.

The Royal Tenenbaums (**2001**) - While Margo leaves Raleigh, the *Charlie Brown Christmas* song "Christmas Time Is Here" plays.

Serendipity (**2001**) - John Cusack and Kate Beckinsale play two people who meet and have an incredible date at Christmastime in New York, then lose touch with each other. Most of the movie doesn't involve Christmas. It does end back at Christmas, though.

Behind Enemy Lines (**2001**) - On Christmas Day, navy flight officer Lieutenant Chris Burnett (Owen Wilson) gets shot down while doing some reconnaissance work during the Bosnian War.

Bridget Jones's Diary **(2001)** - While the movie begins at New Year's (with decorations still up), the story of the thirty-two-year-old struggling through relationships concludes at the following Christmas.

Catch Me If You Can **(2002)** - Key interactions between con man Frank Abignale (Leonardo Dicaprio) and the man trying to catch him (Tom Hanks) take place at Christmas.

About a Boy **(2002)** - A forty-year-old bachelor (Hugh Grant) has been living off the royalties of a Christmas song his dad wrote in 1958 ("Santa's Super Sleigh"). His story also concludes at Christmas.

Mean Girls **(2004)** - The Plastics (the popular clique in school) do a seductive dance interpretation of "Jingle Bell Rock" during the school's Christmas show.

Just Friends **(2005)** - Ryan Reynolds stars in this rom-com about a former high school misfit-turned-womanizer who returns to his hometown years later for Christmas.

The Ice Harvest **(2005)** - A lawyer tries to steal money from the mob on Christmas Eve.

The Holiday **(2006)** - After some relationship issues, a British writer (Kate Winslet) and a Los Angeles producer (Cameron Diaz) execute a house swap in late December. In their new locales, the two women stumble into new relationships. Christmas always lurks in the background in this movie, but it continues until New Year's and the holiday is never a focal point. Yes, new relationships blossom but kind of accidentally.

Note: "The Ugly" from *The Good, the Bad and the Ugly* (Eli Wallach) plays the charming older man whom Winslet befriends when she gets to Los Angeles.

Step Brothers **(2008)** - Will Ferrell and John C. Reilly play forty-year-old men who live at home. When their parents get married, they are forced to live together. On Christmas Eve, the dysfunctional marriage comes to a head.

The Girl with the Dragon Tattoo **(2011)** - The intense hacker (Rooney Mara) buys a Christmas present for the journalist (Daniel Craig) she is working with.

Prometheus **(2012)** - There's a small Christmas scene in which Idris Elba sets up a little tree on the spaceship. But HBO took it one step further by calling this *Alien* prequel the "perfect Christmas movie" because it involves faith, an unknown source of pregnancy, and wise men following a star.

Silver Linings Playbook **(2012)** - The charming Bradley Cooper-Jennifer Lawrence movie about a mentally ill man trying to piece his life back together features a Christmas scene before the big dance contest. Robert De Niro also delivers the most nonsensical sports line in movie history: "We gotta beat the Giants if we wanna have any chance of getting into the division." That's not how the NFL works, buddy.

Tangerine **(2015)** - This low-budget indie film follows a transgender prostitute as she tries to find her ex-boyfriend on Christmas Eve.

Love the Coopers **(2015)** - This poor man's *Love Actually* features a strong ensemble cast (Diane Keaton, John Goodman, Marisa Tomei,

Anthony Mackie, and others) and a pretty weak bunch of intertwining stories taking place on Christmas Eve.

Carol **(2015)** - Rooney Mara plays a woman who gets into a relationship with an older woman (Cate Blanchett) at Christmastime in the 1950s.

Spotlight **(2015)** - It's Christmastime when Michael Keaton's character breaks the news to the Catholic Church's counsel that they are going to publish the story about the Boston priest sex scandal.

Pottersville **(2017)** - Michael Shannon plays a shop owner in a small town who finds his wife with another man, gets drunk, puts on a gorilla suit, and wanders around town at Christmastime. Rumors that it was Bigfoot turns the small town into a media sensation.

Little Women (2019) - Father returns from the Civil War at Christmas in this update of the coming-of-age drama.

WW84 **(2020)** - This subpar Wonder Woman sequel set in 1984 ends at a Christmas market. Wonder Woman opts to not use lethal force against a kid who pelts her with a snowball.

Godmothered **(2020)** - An unskilled fairy godmother attempts to save a little girl who has since grown up at Christmastime.

The Green Knight **(2021)** - A mysterious Green Knight shows up at Camelot and challenges the Round Table to a "Christmas game." King Arthur's impulsive nephew takes the emerald-skinned stranger's bait.

SHANE BLACK

One of the most successful Hollywood screenwriters of the '80s had a common thread throughout most of his films—Christmas. As Shane Black told *Den of Geek* in 2013, "Christmas is fun. It's unifying, and all your characters are involved in this event that stays within the larger story. It roots it, I think, it grounds everything. At Christmas, lonely people are lonelier, seeing friends and families go by. People take reckoning, they take stock of where their lives are at Christmas. It just provides a backdrop against which different things can play out, but with one unifying, global heading."

Shane Black is the king of Christmas adjacent. Here are some of his movies:

Lethal Weapon **(1987)** - Two very different cops (Danny Glover and Mel Gibson) are paired together to catch a gang of drug smugglers. Christmas plays throughout. This movie inspired producer Joel Silver to set *Die Hard* at Christmas. This is a Christmas movie.

Note: The "too old for this" Danny Glover was only forty when this movie came out.

The Last Boy Scout **(1991)** - Bruce Willis' character's kid draws a demented Santa holding a severed head—Satan Claus.

Last Action Hero **(1993)** - In the film-within-this-film (*Jack Slater III*), a bad guy takes kids hostage at Christmas.

The Long Kiss Goodnight **(1996)** - A schoolteacher's (Geena Davis) past life of violence catches up to her. The movie opens at Christmas.

***Kiss Kiss Bang Bang* (2005)** - This Christmastime neo noir stars Val Kilmer and Robert Downey. Michelle Monaghan wears a pretty revealing Santa outfit in a key scene.

***Iron Man 3* (2013)** - This is Marvel's most Christmassy movie. Tony Stark has let his alter ego (Iron Man) take over his life, and it is affecting his relationships. It's a Very Iron Man Christmas.

***The Nice Guys* (2016)** - A pair of private investigators search for a missing girl. The last scene of the movie takes place at Christmas.

HARRY POTTER

Since each book and movie takes place over the course of one school year, the Harry Potter universe has a lot of Christmas scenes. In fact, the only movie that makes no mention of the holiday is the final one, 2011's *Harry Potter and the Deathly Hallows: Part 2*.

***Harry Potter and the Sorcerer's Stone* (2001)** - Harry gets an invisibility cloak as his first-ever Christmas gift.

***Harry Potter and the Chamber of Secrets* (2002)** - Harry, Hermione, and Ron celebrate Christmas together for the first time and take Polyjuice Potion.

***Harry Potter and the Prisoner of Azkaban* (2004)** - The gang goes to snowy Hogsmeade.

***Harry Potter and the Goblet of Fire* (2005)** - The students attend the Yule Ball, where snow falls from the ceiling.

Harry Potter and the Order of the Phoenix **(2007)** - Santa rides a broomstick. Harry and Cho kiss under the mistletoe. And there's a big Christmas celebration at the Weasleys'.

Harry Potter and the Half-Blood Prince **(2009)** - There's a Christmas dinner at the Weasleys' and a party at Hogwarts.

***Harry Potter and the Deathly Hallows: Part* 1 (2010)** - Harry and Hermione visit his parents' graves at Christmas.

CHRISTMAS ON TV

MUSIC AND VARIETY SHOWS

From the early days of television, variety shows were a major part of the December television landscape. Each year, the biggest performers of the day would host a Christmas special and invite their famous "friends" to join them. In this age before social media, Christmas specials offered a rare platform for stars to be seen and heard.

Audiences loved these Christmas specials. Despite very mixed performances, ratings were always solid. So they kept producing more. They tended to fall into two categories: sincere singing or goofy comedy. There were some ongoing shows, like that of "champagne music" bandleader Lawrence Welk (and the orchestra he barely paid), whose annual Christmas specials started airing in the late '50s. Julie Andrews had multiple Christmas specials in the '70s and '80s (including filming her 1987 show from the Austrian town where they shot some of *The Sound of Music*). From 1976 to 1985, Johnny Cash and his talented family and friends held Christmas shows that contained a mix of hits ("I Walk the Line"), Christmas medleys, and religious stories. From 1976 to 1986, the Osmond family had Christmas sing-alongs (while all looking frighteningly similar to each other).

Lots of other stars got a crack at Christmas specials as well. Comedians Bud Abbott and Lou Costello hosted a Christmas special for the *Colgate Comedy Hour* in 1952. Judy Garland hosted a special in 1963. As did Mitzi Gaynor (1967), John Denver (1975), Sonny and Cher (1975), Captain & Tennille (1976), Paul Lynde (1977), the Carpenters (1978), George Burns (1981), Dolly Parton (1990), Luther Vandross (1996) and many, many more. But without question, the big hitters, when it came to Christmas variety shows, were Bob Hope, Perry Como, Andy Williams, Dean Martin, and Bing Crosby.

Bob Hope - From the mid-'50s to the early '90s, Bob Hope hosted specials around the world, usually near some sort of global conflict or war. During Vietnam, he did shows in Southeast Asia. In the early 1980s, he hosted in Beirut. In the early '90s, it was the Persian Gulf.

Most of it doesn't hold up today. Bob would make a few corny dad jokes (e.g. complaining about mosquitoes in Thailand), bring out some beautiful young woman (Brooke Shields or that year's reigning Miss USA), then tell some more local jokes for the troops. And they loved it. Christmas can be a lonely time when separated from your family. Bob Hope helped spread some holiday cheer to servicemen and women around the world.

Perry Como and Andy Williams - These two did more straightforward singing shows. Between 1959 and 1994, Como held specials in various locations around the world (Austria, Bethlehem, Paris, colonial Williamsburg, Virginia, and many more). He would croon right from the start and maybe touch on some of the local customs and religious traditions. The saccharine Williams would do more of the same, but usually on wintry-looking studio sets, and often brought out his crooning brothers as well.

Dean Martin - The charming Martin applied his boozy Vegas act through some really broad sketches with friends like Dom DeLuise, Jonathan Winters, Rodney Dangerfield, Bob Hope, Nipsey Russell, and Bob Newhart. He sprinkled in some beautiful women and Christmas standards, and called it a night.

Bing Crosby - The famous crooner was all over the place with his Christmas specials from 1957 to 1977. Some years, it was a pretty standard-looking production on a stage. One year he did a courtroom scene where Santa was on trial. Others, he was riding an open sleigh through the woods with his family. And then, in 1977, Bing recorded the strangest moment in television history (*Bing Crosby's Merry Olde Christmas*), a duet with David Bowie. Keep in mind, Bing Crosby was born in 1903. By the time television became a major part of entertainment, Bing was already pretty seasoned. But, since family Christmas specials ruled the day, Bing caked on the makeup and did his best to seem like a youthful dad and, to connect with younger demographics, attempted to mix it up with rock stars like David Bowie.

Modern Variety Shows - Maybe the best Christmas variety show of all was a children's show—1988's *Christmas at Pee-wee's Playhouse*. The show thrived on nonsense and bizarre interactions, so a visit from Magic Johnson, Oprah, Cher, Little Richard, or Charo didn't feel forced or implausible. It just felt like another contribution to the madness. The show already had a talking chair and a genie. Why not add Grace Jones singing "The Little Drummer Boy"?

The tradition of specials featuring fake holiday parties that promoted recently-released Christmas albums continued well into the 1990s, but at some point, the specials became more of a punch line than a cherished tradition. Aside from Kathie Lee Gifford (who plowed ahead with outdated Christmas shows from 1994 to 1998), everyone kind of sensed the game was over.

There started to be more comedy shows about the corniness of the genre than actual Christmas variety shows. In 2002, Canadian comedian and *Kids in the Hall* co-founder Dave Foley released *Dave Foley's The True Meaning of Christmas Specials* for the CBC. It featured surf guitar legend Dick Dale, Andy Richter, Jason Priestley, Joe Flaherty, Dave Thomas, Mike Myers, and the Ghost of Christmas Specials Past. Three years later, comedian Denis Leary's 2005 *Merry F#%$in' Christmas* poked fun at holiday specials with the help of William Shatner, Charlie Murphy, and Carmen Electra. In 2008, Stephen Colbert's *A Colbert Christmas: The Greatest Gift of All* was a wink-at-the-camera old-fashioned Christmas special featuring Willie

Nelson, John Legend, Elvis Costello, a ravenous bear, and Jon Stewart, who sings a lovely duet with Colbert about Hanukkah. And, in 2010, the intentionally absurd sketch show *Tim and Eric Awesome Show, Great Job!* had their own take on these programs ("Chrimbus Special"). It certainly seemed as if the Christmas music and variety show was done.

And then Mariah Carey got involved. Considering the never-ending support for her Christmas hit, "All I Want for Christmas Is You," networks were quick to recreate the old-fashioned Christmas music and variety show for her. Starting in 2010, Carey has released several Christmas specials (2010's *Merry Christmas to You*, 2015's *Merriest Christmas*, 2020's *Magical Christmas Special*). Lady Gaga and Kelly Clarkson followed Carey with their own shows in 2013. In 2019, Kacey Musgraves combined old and new by making a fun, campy Christmas special while also letting the audience know she knows it's all pretty silly. The end result actually worked.

The most bizarre moments in Christmas variety and music show history:

Judy Garland versus the Velvet Fog - The Judy Garland Christmas Special (1963)

This whole special was super awkward and forced, from Garland and her kids doing dance routines in their fake living room to mother-daughter singing. Sometime after the ads for pills and Pall Mall cigarettes (really!), Garland invited "neighborhood caroler" Mel Torme over to the piano so they could sing a duet of Torme's classic "The Christmas Song." Garland bungled a line at one point, and a slightly perturbed Torme called her out on it in the middle of the song! Judy then exacted her revenge by intentionally switching the word "reindeer" to "rainbows" (a nod to her *Wizard of Oz* days). As she delivers the changed line, she stares at Torme like they're in a prison yard. It's very rare to see a duet where the two performers seemingly hate each other.

The Old Crooner and the White Duke - *Bing Crosby's Merry Olde Christmas* (1977)

In this special, Bing's long-lost relative invited the family to spend Christmas with him in England. So Bing packed up the family (they all were adults who seemed to live at home) and flew across the Atlantic. By this point the faded Bing Crosby was wearing a level of makeup you just don't see outside a coffin.

There was a knock at the door, and—WHAT ARE THE ODDS?!?—it's neighbor David Bowie! The White Duke seemed just as confused to be in this special as the world was to see him in it. At the time, Bowie was trying to normalize his image, so he played along. Kind of. He hated the song that he and Bing were originally supposed to sing ("The Little Drummer Boy"), so producers scrambled to come up with a solution. After about an hour, they emerged with "Peace on Earth," which would be sung in a medley with Crosby's "Drummer Boy." The end result was so bizarre, it was perfect.

The seventy-seven-year-old Crosby died six weeks after filming the duet.

The Divorcees with Captain Kangaroo - *The Sonny and Cher Christmas Special* (1976)

Sonny and Cher got divorced in the summer of 1975. A few days later, she married rock star Gregg Allman. Sonny and Cher's variety show was toast. But a year later, there was enough demand for a television reunion (and unfunny comedy sketches) that they revived the show. In the Christmas episode on December 5, 1976, the awkwardness of the divorced couple seemed to spill over in the Christmas medley at the end. Sonny and Cher's seven-year-old, Chastity, is forced to join in the singing. The family is joined by Bernadette Peters (the best part of this medley) and, inexplicably, children's host Captain Kangaroo (Bob Keeshan), who was wearing his famous red jacket with the big pockets. Just when it appears it can't get weirder, Cher brings out her infant son, Elijah Blue Allman (the child she conceived with Gregg Allman shortly after leaving Sonny), who promptly bursts into tears.

The Star Wars Holiday Special (1978)

From the moment it came out on May 25, 1977, the Star Wars franchise was a cultural phenomenon. Demand was off the charts. And so, as a way to keep the audience warm until its sequel (*Empire Strikes Back*) came out in 1980, George Lucas produced *The Star Wars Holiday Special*. It was an unmitigated disaster.

Despite bringing back the bulk of the *Star Wars* cast as well as Bea Arthur, Art Carney, Diahann Carroll, Jefferson Starship, and Harvey Korman, this was a failure on every level. The main premise was that Han Solo and Chewbacca were trying to get back to Chewy's home planet in time to celebrate Life Day, a fictional, Christmas-like holiday. Somehow, that's where the coherence of this special cuts off. Art Carney plays a human who is friends with the Chewbacca family. Harvey Korman bounces around in different roles that seem to be rejected bits from *The Carol Burnett Show*. Chewbacca's dad, at one point, seems to be trying to have an erotic experience with Diahann Carroll through his VR headset. She sings "I am your pleasure" while dancing around to psychedelic music and effects. Rock band Jefferson

Starship somehow find a career lowlight, even though they were involved with the Altamont Free Concert and "We Built this City." Bea Arthur brought her usual sass while playing the bartender at the famous cantina.

It was a career embarrassment for Lucas, who did his best to destroy every copy. His attempts failed, and the doomed holiday special lives on in infamy on the internet.

Thirsty Octogenarian - *The George Burns (Early) Early, Early Christmas Special* (1981)

The main premise of this Christmas special was that eighty-five-year-old George Burns had a cigar and a thirst for young women. Led on stage by a sleigh pulled by Playboy Playmates, Burns soon introduces a stripped-down Ann-Margret singing "Hold Me Squeeze Me" while dancing seductively with a crazed look in her eyes. Burns calls her "delicious," then goes on to a scene where he flirts with more Playmates.

Rankin/Bass

In the mid-'60s and early '70s, Rankin/Bass produced some of the best-loved Christmas specials ever to air on television. Although the company stopped producing specials more than a generation ago, it is nearly impossible to go a day in December without seeing the influence of their holiday "animagic." When given the script for the movie *Elf*, director Jon Favreau wanted to make a timeless Christmas classic. He later revealed that one of his first choices to establish tone was to make the North Pole look like the Christmas specials from his childhood—the ones with stop-motion animation. He was talking about Rankin/Bass specials.

In 1964, a fortuitous series of events led Arthur Rankin, Jr. and Jules Bass to Rudolph the Red-Nosed Reindeer. In the late '40s, a copywriter named Robert L. May wrote a book for the Montgomery Ward department store to give away free to children. It was a massive hit. May then convinced his composer brother-in-law, Johnny Marks, to write a song based on *Rudolph*. The song was a big hit for Gene Autry. A few years later, Marks' next-door neighbor in Greenwich Village was a filmmaker named Arthur Rankin. Rankin liked the underdog nature of the song, so he added some layers to the story, and pretty soon, he had the general framework for an animated special. Rankin/Bass then wanted to get the special aired on the GE Fantasy Hour. That's where May comes back into the picture. May's employer (Montgomery Ward) had a good relationship with General Electric's vice president of housewares, Willard Sahloff. Sahloff pulled some strings and, within a few years, Rankin/Bass had a deal. On December 6, 1964, the stop-motion animated special (using a special GE bulb for the main character's nose), *Rudolph the Red-Nosed Reindeer*, aired and was a massive success.

Rankin/Bass released another nineteen Christmas specials (fourteen of them stop-motion animation). While people have fond memories of some of the iconic Rankin/Bass specials (*Rudolph the Red-Nosed Reindeer, Frosty the Snowman, Santa Claus Is Comin' to Town*, and several others), there are many that range from depressing and dull to absolutely bonkers.

Rankin/Bass Christmas specials from 1964 to 2001:

Rudolph the Red-Nosed Reindeer (1964)

The most famous Christmas special in history does not paint Santa in a positive light. Just a couple minutes into it, Santa stops by the cave where his "Lead Reindeer" Donner and his wife are celebrating the birth of their calf, Rudolph. When Santa sees Rudolph's nose glow, he implies that if Rudolph is going to have any future on the sleigh team, he will need to stifle out any "nonconformity." So Donner covers up Rudolph's nose with mud. When Rudolph's shiny nose pokes through the mud, Santa tells Donner, "You should be ashamed of yourself." Whaaat?!? What kind of inimical game is Santa playing with these reindeer? He also treats the elves like garbage too.

Luckily, Rudolph befriends a sad elf named Hermey and a delightful weirdo prospector named Yukon Cornelius. The three go on an adventure where each prove their usefulness. While Rudolph gets hero treatment and a spot at the front of the reindeer team in the end, we still haven't heard an "I'm sorry" out of Santa.

Cricket on the Hearth (1967)

The year after the massive success of stop-motion *Rudolph*, Rankin/Bass followed it up with a 2D adaptation of a lesser-known Charles Dickens Christmas story. The animated special actually got a live introduction from Danny Thomas (don't worry, no coffee tables were used). It's a pretty grim tale of a guy being presumed dead, his fiancé going blind out of sadness, poverty, and a potentially unhappy wedding on the horizon. Roddy McDowall plays the cricket narrator.

The Little Drummer Boy (1968)

The first few years of Rankin/Bass were all over the map, tonally. Much like they did with *Rudolph*, the animation studio made another stop-motion story from a song. But, instead of a jolly ballad about a glowing reindeer, they chose the "Pa-rum-pum-pum-pum" song about a poor kid who drummed for baby Jesus. They fleshed out the character with a brutal backstory—he watched his parents get set on fire by bandits, so now he dabbles in nihilism. He does get to play that drum for the newborn, which must've thrilled new parents Mary and Joseph.

Frosty the Snowman (1969)

There isn't a ton of story to *Frosty the Snowman*. He comes to life, gets hot, and wants to move to the North Pole, where he will never melt. But the casting is fantastic. Jackie Vernon's gentle deadpan delivery gave off a sweetness that made you pull for the dimwitted snowman. Gravelly-voiced Jimmy Durante made everything the narrator said sound cool. And Billy de Wolfe, as the antagonistic Professor Hinkle, plays the perfect cartoon villain. "Think nasty, think nasty, think nasty!" But there is one glaring question that never gets answered at the end: How does Karen get down from her roof without breaking her neck? Santa gives her a lift home but just drops her off on a steep, snow-covered roof in the middle of the night. Considering she doesn't appear in any of *Frosty*'s sequels, you have to wonder if things took a much darker turn that Christmas Eve.

Santa Claus Is Comin' to Town (1970)

The most clever and interesting Rankin/Bass special stars Fred Astaire as a mailman who systematically answers every question about Santa (Why the red suit? Why the name Santa? Why does he bring toys to kids? Why go down chimneys? Why put toys in stockings? Why does he laugh like that? Why and how do his reindeer fly?). Unlike the L. Frank Baum Santa origin story, which spent a lot of time focusing on nymphs, dark creatures, and axes, *Santa Claus Is Comin' to Town* is just a fun look at the big man's backstory. And in the scenes where Santa has to go against the sadistic mayor of Sombertown (Burgermeister Meisterburger), Santa keeps finding new ways to dunk on him. Aside from that confusing scene where the future Mrs. Claus goes on an "Aquarius / Let the Sunshine In" psychedelic trip for no apparent reason, the special is a well-paced, enjoyable hour.

Festival of Family Classics: A Christmas Tree (1972)

For the 1972-1973 television season, Rankin/Bass produced a fairy tale and folklore cartoon that told a different story each week. About a week before Christmas in 1972, they animated Charles Dickens' tale, *A Christmas Tree*. Well, sort of. *A Christmas Tree* is mostly about Dickens staring at the ornaments on his tree and telling semi-autobiographical stories. This is more of an imagining of Charles Dickens huffing ether next to his decorated tree. The episode begins with Dickens telling a couple of kids about ornaments. Then the Peter Piper ornament comes to life and tells the kids that the essence of Christmas has been stolen by the giant at the top of Jack's beanstalk. Soon the kids are sassing Bigfoot, riding a magic carpet, and giving a dragon a hot foot.

'Twas the Night Before Christmas (1974)

This is another bad special for Santa. Inexplicably, he is ready to blow off an entire town because one of its residents doubted his existence. Still, *'Twas the Night Before Christmas* features the best song to appear in any Rankin/Bass special—"Even a Miracle Needs a Hand."

The Year Without a Santa Claus (1974)

Yet another special where Santa is kind of a bad guy. He's not feeling loved enough, so he just declares he's calling out sick. Mrs. Claus, however, has other plans, and soon she, Vixen the reindeer, and two elves named Jingle and Jangle are making clandestine trips to America to gauge interest in the holiday. But the perseverance of Mrs. C and the gang is all secondary to the real stars of this special: Snow Miser and Heat Miser. The egomaniacal, climate-controlling, dueling sons of Mother Nature steal the show. These guys aren't just gangsters. They are accompanied by theme songs whenever they burst on the scene. Mr. Ten-Below and Mr. Hundred-and-One are the best part of any Rankin/Bass special. In 2008, they got their own non-Rankin/Bass special that was just okay.

The First Christmas: The Story of the First Christmas Snow (1975)

Once again, the people at Rankin/Bass dipped into the temporary blindness well. This time, it's a shepherd boy who was struck by lightning. Some nuns take him in. His only wish is for Christmas snow (which, shockingly, cures his blindness). Angela Lansbury does a bang-up job singing "White Christmas" at the end. The biggest question remains—what's up with that title?

The Little Drummer Boy, Book II (1976)

In the year of America's Bicentennial, there was a fever and the only prescription was more Drummer Boy. Despite a tidy ending to the first one, the percussionist is back, and this time he's teaming up with one of the Three Kings to protect some silver bells. Roman soldiers with really gross arm hair are the bad guys this time. But, since the whole special is about silver bells, at least it will probably end with a nice rendition of that song. Right? Nope. It's "Do You Hear What I Hear?"

Frosty's Winter Wonderland (1976)

Jackie Vernon is back playing Frosty the Snowman. And he has emotional and physical needs. So the children are guilted into building him a wife.

Rudolph's Shiny New Year (1976)

This special is pure insanity. The story plays out like a screenplay was written with *Mad Libs*. Head-scratching appearances and locations present themselves in every scene. In a nutshell, Rudolph is told he needs to find Baby New Year before midnight on New Year's Eve or the world will be stuck on December 31 forever. Baby New Year (a.k.a. Happy) ran away because people made fun of his giant ears. So Rudolph, the poster child of bullied runaways, is uniquely qualified to track him down. With the help of a caveman, a medieval knight, Benjamin Franklin, and Goldilocks' three bears, Rudolph finds Happy, defeats a murderous vulture, and, in the process, saves all of humankind. Bonkers.

Nestor, the Long-Eared Christmas Donkey (1977)

This is *Rudolph the Red-Nosed Reindeer*, but just swap a reindeer for a donkey, a glowing nose for long ears, the abominable snowman for the Roman Empire, and Santa Claus for baby Jesus. They based this special off a song written by Gene Autry. But, unlike "Rudolph," which gave the "Singing Cowboy" his greatest hit, the song "Nestor, the Long-Eared Christmas Donkey" is a plodding song devoid of a hook. Also, Nestor's mom dies in a snowstorm while protecting her long-eared son. Then, after helping Mary get to the stable to deliver Jesus, Nestor goes back to celebrate… *with the farmer who forced his mother into the deadly snowstorm*! Whaaat?!?

The Stingiest Man in Town (1978)

Tom Bosley plays a narrator named the London Humbug in the Rankin/Bass adaptation of *A Christmas Carol*. It's actually pretty good. Walter Matthau does the Grumpy Old Man thing pretty well as Scrooge. There were a few too many songs, which compressed some of the story, but overall, it was a pretty solid special. Too bad it wasn't stop-motion.

Jack Frost (1979)

This special falls into the so-weird-it's-kind-of-good category. There's a whole side story where Jack Frost is battling an oppressive robot army for the fate of a town called January Junction, which doesn't make a ton of sense. And Buddy Hackett plays Punxatawny Phil, a groundhog, which also doesn't make a ton of sense for a Christmas special. But the main plot is a pretty intriguing love story that actually doesn't have a super happy ending. Jack Frost is ready to give it all up to marry a woman he adores. Father Winter gives him a chance to become human as long as she comes to love him back by spring. She falls for someone else, and Jack has the bittersweet ending of seeing her happy but knowing he won't ever get to be with her.

Rudolph and Frosty's Christmas in July (1979)

Like a gambler on a hot streak, the people at Rankin/Bass let a decade-plus of adulation for their iconic characters, Rudolph the Red-Nosed Reindeer and Frosty the Snowman, build up and then pushed all their chips to the center of the table. They made a full feature-length movie starring the pair. It was a disaster.

The basic premise is that some warlock named Winterbolt wakes up from a long coma caused by the Queen of the Northern Lights (not worth explaining) and gets jealous of Santa Claus. So, he uses his magic to try to ruin Christmas. Most of the story takes place at a circus during the summer. Some ice cream man takes a hot air balloon to the North Pole and asks Rudolph and Frosty if they can travel south with him to work at his girlfriend's circus. It's a complete mess. Frosty, his wife, and their two kids get amulets that prevent them from ever melting. Ethel Merman plays a singing circus owner. Rudolph gets tricked into committing a crime. Frosty and his whole family die. Jack Frost gets to town riding a whale. It's probably best Christmas isn't celebrated in July.

Pinocchio's Christmas (1980)

It's kind of like a sequel to *Pinocchio* but, unless you're really familiar with the details of the original story, you'd be kind of lost. Why is he still made of wood? Wasn't the whole point of the original story that he was turned into a boy at the end? Pinocchio and Geppetto do a *Gift of the Magi* thing in the beginning, which sets off a whole series of events that leads Pinocchio to prostitute himself at a carnival. Also, Geppetto has a horrendous toupee.

The Leprechaun's Christmas Gold (1981)

"What's a Christmas song that isn't going to cost us an arm and a leg for the rights?"

"How about 'Christmas in Killarney'?"

"Let's do it!"

This special is Christmas in name only. It feels like a St. Patrick's Day special starring Art Carney as the main leprechaun. It's kinda boring except for the antagonist, a shape-shifting banshee named Mag the

Hag. Mag is always one step ahead of everyone but, in lucky leprechaun fashion, they get bailed out by a rainbow.

The Life and Adventures of Santa Claus (1985)

The fundamental problem with this animated adaptation of L. Frank Baum's 1902 Santa origin story is it contrasts the 1970 Fred Astaire classic, *Santa Claus is Comin' to Town*. Plus, it's kind of creepy.

Santa, Baby! (2001)

The final Rankin/Bass special was kind of like watching Michael Jordan on the Wizards. They hit some of the same marks (Rankin/Bass in the credits, a special based off a famous song, a magical twist of fate at Christmas) but it just felt like it was missing something. Its biggest legacy will probably be that it was the first animated Christmas special starring a predominantly black cast since Fat Albert in the 1970s. *Santa, Baby!* starred Vanessa Williams, Gregory Hines, Patti LaBelle, and Eartha Kitt (who made the titular song famous nearly a half century earlier). Some little girl stumbles upon a magical partridge in a pear tree who can grant wishes. So she wishes for her songwriter dad to overcome writer's block and kick out a hit. The town then comes together to save an animal shelter and inspires her dad to write "The Heart and Soul of Christmas," which raises the question about whether that partridge was really all that magical. Oddly enough, one of the writers of this special gained fame a few years later by writing *The Hunger Games*.

ANIMATED SPECIALS

While Rankin/Bass gets most of the credit for their famous Christmas specials, their run of success only lasted about fifteen years (from the mid-1960s to the late 1970s). Aside from a few hits (*Mister Magoo*, *The Grinch*, *Charlie Brown*), other animation companies failed to keep up during that run. Bland animal tales like *The Night the Animals Talked* (1970), *Santa and the Three Bears* (1970), Hanna-Barbera's *A Christmas Story* (1972), *The Bear Who Slept Through Christmas* (1973), and *A Very Merry Cricket* (1973) all fell pretty flat.

Then, in the late 1970s, animators started realizing the power of taking established brands (Fat Albert, Yogi Bear, the Flintstones, Pink Panther, Raggedy Ann and Andy, Berenstain Bears, Bugs Bunny) and turning them into successful Christmas specials. Several comic strips made specials as well: *A Family Circus Christmas* (1979), *B.C.: A Special Christmas* (1981), *Ziggy's Gift* (1982), *A Wish for Wings That Work* (which was from the comic strip *Opus* in 1991).

By the 1990s, the backlog of all the old specials started to pile up. With a glut of cable channels and home videos, appetite for new Christmas specials waned. There still were a few unremarkable stand-alone specials (like *Up on the Housetop* in 1992, *A Wish That Changed Christmas* in 1992, and *Jingle Bell Rock* in 1995), but, for the most part, new Christmas specials are still a rarity today.

Here are the biggest animated specials in television history:

***Mister Magoo's Christmas Carol* (1962)** - The first made-for-television animated Christmas special might not be as popular as other '60s specials, like *Rudolph* and *Frosty*, but it might be the most important. In the early days of television, it wasn't clear what would capture the public's imagination. There were three networks and advertisers with a lot of clout. If the first animated Christmas special was a flop, it would be years before someone tried another. Anyway, in

1959, a man named Henry Saperstein bought the animation studio UPA. After releasing a disastrous movie called *1001 Arabian Nights,* UPA came pretty cheap. The one bright spot from that movie was a vision-challenged, clumsy millionaire named Mister Magoo. Saperstein wanted to showcase Magoo and thought plugging him into a proven Christmas story (*A Christmas Carol*) would be the best bet. He worked out a deal with the advertiser Timex and sold it to television to air a week before Christmas in 1962. Rather than change Magoo into a Victorian London character, they made him starring as Scrooge on Broadway. He tried to hire Broadway legend Richard Rogers but ended up getting composer Jule Styne and lyricist Bob Merill (who would make *Funny Girl* two years later). *Mister Magoo's Christmas Carol* was a huge hit. NBC aired it in prime time each December for five years before it went into syndication. Mister Magoo walked so Rudolph could run.

***A Charlie Brown Christmas* (1965)** - *Peanuts* comic strip creator Charles Schulz and his friend, producer Lee Mendelson, pitched animated shows about Charlie Brown to networks, but nobody seemed to care. Then, in the summer of 1965, Coca-Cola reached out to Schultz and Mendelson to see if they'd consider making an animated special that they could sponsor. Schultz agreed, with two conditions: First, all the voices had to be actual children; second, one minute of the special had to be dedicated to Linus reading the Nativity chapter from the Bible. And so, on December 9, 1965, *A Charlie Brown Christmas* aired. It has been on television ever since. In recent years, the special has aired with tacked-on Charlie Brown Christmas episodes (1992's *It's Christmastime Again, Charlie Brown,* 2002's *Charlie Brown's Christmas Tales,* and 2003's *I Want a Dog for Christmas, Charlie Brown*) but the original is really the only one anyone is looking for.

How the Grinch Stole Christmas **(1966)** - Theodor "Dr. Seuss" Geisel had been burned by Hollywood before, both financially and creatively. So it was unlikely that he was going to let anyone option his books again. Then along came animation legend Chuck Jones (of *Looney Tunes* fame). Jones and Geisel had worked together on US Army Air Force training and propaganda films during World War II. Geisel believed in Jones, so he let him give it a shot. Dr. Seuss wrote the lyrics for the theme song. Jones then got deep-voiced Thurl Ravenscroft (Tony the Tiger from Frosted Flakes commercials) to sing it and horror icon Boris Karloff to narrate and star. The whole book only took about twelve minutes to read, so Jones created a bunch of scenes with the Grinch's dog, Max, to fill it out. It was an instant classic. *How the Grinch Stole Christmas* has aired in prime time every December since and has inspired two movies that have grossed about $900 million combined.

The Fat Albert Christmas Special **(1977)** - Before the Civil Rights movement, the only black animated characters on TV were awful stereotypes. Then, in 1972, Bill Cosby produced a positive, lesson-based Saturday morning cartoon called *Fat Albert and the Cosby Kids* ("If you're not careful, you just might learn somethin'"). The entire cast featured black teenagers who resembled ones from Cosby's childhood growing up in North Philadelphia. In 1977, the show was given its own special. It's a pleasant tale that hits on a couple of standard Christmas tropes: Fat Albert and his friends generously help a poor couple find shelter in their clubhouse before the woman gives birth, and they also help an old rich miser find the Christmas spirit. Hey, hey, hey!

Bugs Bunny's Looney Christmas Tales **(1979)** - The greatest cartoon character of all time finally got his own dedicated Christmas special in

1979 that featured three eight-minute shorts: Bugs Bunny and Yosemite Sam's version of a *Christmas Carol*, Wile E. Coyote chasing Road Runner around in the snow, and Bugs Bunny stopping the Tasmanian Devil from destroying Christmas.

Yogi's First Christmas **(1980)** - Christmas revelry at Jellystone Park wakes Yogi Bear and Boo-Boo up from hibernation. Soon they join in the fun and help overcome a Scrooge-like Hermit and a rotten kid from destroying Christmas. A couple of years later, they slapped the whole crew together for the much, much worse *Yogi Bear's All-Star Comedy Christmas Caper*. Stay away from that one.

A Chipmunk Christmas **(1981)** - Armenian-American grape farmer Ross Bagdasarian moved his family to Hollywood so he could become a big star. The best he could come up with was a role as a piano player in Hitchcock's 1954 thriller *Rear Window*. As he approached fifty, he started experimenting more with his music. So he started messing around with a reel-to-reel tape recorder and found that if he recorded in half speed then played it back at regular speed, it would sound like a high-pitched insect or animal—a chipmunk, for example. In 1958, he released "The Chipmunk Song." It was an instant success, selling twenty-five million records and reaching number one on the Billboard Hot 100. He died in 1972, but the popularity of that song continued. Finally, in 1981, it was turned into an animated special. Despite it being pretty weird (doctors are ready to give up on a kid's life, but suddenly a harmonica gifted by a rodent makes him better), that special inspired multiple television shows and several movies.

The Smurfs' Christmas Special **(1982)** - In 1958, a Belgian comic artist named Pierre Culliford (pen name "Peyo") created little characters inspired by trolls of Nordic folklore and called them Les

Schtroumpfs. They became very popular in Belgium and had a few animated specials. They eventually spread into the Netherlands (where the name translated to "the Smurfs"). Then in 1976, an animated special called *The Smurfs and the Magic Flute* caught the eye of American producers. In 1981, Hanna-Barbera created an animated show called *The Smurfs*. It was an instant smash, and Smurf figurines became one of the hottest toys on the market. In 1982, NBC gave them a prime-time Christmas special.

The Snowman **(1982)** - This beloved British Christmas special is about a boy who builds a snowman that comes to life and takes him to see Santa. The dialogue-free special was based on a popular 1978 picture book by Raymond Briggs.

A Garfield Christmas **(1987)** - The world's most widely syndicated comic strip (it brings in about a billion dollars per year in merchandise) finally got its own Christmas special in 1987. Jon brings his cat, Garfield, and dog, Odie, to his mom's house so they can all spend Christmas with his weird family. Despite the fact that Garfield is miserable and ungrateful to everyone, this special actually has one of the nicer endings, as Garfield discovers long-lost letters that Jon's grandfather wrote to his grandmother. Plus, there's a peppy Lou Rawls song at the beginning.

Winnie the Pooh and Christmas Too **(1991)** - Disney finally got into the network television Christmas special game with its famous gluttonous bear, Winnie the Pooh. Pooh and his friends all write letters to Santa, then send them into the wind. When his letter blows south, Winnie goes on a quest to hand-deliver a new one to the North Pole. The most remarkable part of this special was that it was originally introduced on ABC by Walt Disney Company CEO Michael Eisner and some terrifying Pooh, Tigger, Rabbit, and Eeyore mascots.

***Olive, the Other Reindeer* (1999)** - In 1997, Vivian Walsh and J. Otto Seibold wrote a charming Christmas book called *Olive, the Other Reindeer*. When one of Santa's reindeer is injured, Santa says he needs "all of the other reindeer" if Christmas is going to continue. Olive hears this line incorrectly and thinks he's talking about her. One of the fans of the book was Simpsons creator Matt Groening, who read it to his children. As the creator of the most successful show in the history of the Fox network, Groening quickly had it turned into a Christmas special, starring Drew Barrymore.

***Shrek the Halls* (2007)** - DreamWorks kicked off a new genre of Christmas special in 2007 by taking the characters and voice actors from their successful movie franchise (this took place between *Shrek the Third* and *Shrek Forever After*) and giving them a separate show at the end of the year. Mike Myers, Eddie Murphy, Cameron Diaz, and Antonio Banderas all returned to their roles to make it an A-list special. In the years after *Shrek the Halls*, DreamWorks also produced *Merry Madagascar* in 2009 and *Kung Fu Panda Holiday* in 2010, while Pixar produced *Toy Story That Time Forgot* in 2014.

***Prep & Landing* (2009)** - Unlike just about every other Christmas special in history, Disney created the concept for this one from scratch. Prep and Landing weren't known characters from a movie, TV show, song, or book. They were just new characters for a CGI special about the elves that get everything ready for Santa when he arrives at a home. *Prep & Landing* has spawned two sequels (2010's *Operation: Secret Santa* and 2011's *Naughty vs. Nice*).

It's a SpongeBob Christmas! **(2012)** - After 174 episodes, SpongeBob Squarepants made a stop-motion Christmas special for network TV. The beautifully made special was a tip of the cap to Rankin/Bass Christmas specials (with specific nods to *Santa Claus Is Comin' to Town* and *Rudolph the Red-Nosed Reindeer*). Apparently, the inspiration for the special came from a song written by the voice of SpongeBob (Tom Kenny) and his writing partner: "Don't Be a Jerk (It's Christmas)." In short, Plankton (the bad guy) hands out jerktonium-laced fruitcake that turns all of the residents of Bikini Bottom into jerks… all except for SpongeBob, whose pure heart and optimism are unable to be changed. This is one of the best.

The Snowy Day **(2016)** - It would be tough to do a better job with making the illustrated pages of a book come to life than did the 2016 adaptation of Ezra Jack Keats' book, *The Snowy Day*. Much like Raymond Briggs' *The Snowman*, *The Snowy Day* was a popular book involving snow but not necessarily Christmassy. Their animated specials, on the other hand, expanded to talk about the holiday. Actually, *The Snowy Day* expands beyond just Christmas. While a great deal of attention of the 1962 book was about the protagonist being a black child (a rarity still but especially so in 1962), this special does a great job of including Hanukkah and the way different cultures celebrate Christmas. The story remains mostly the same as the book as it follows a boy exploring the limitless possibilities before him on a winter day (only now during the holiday season). The voice actor talent is impressive with Laurence Fishburne, Regina King, and Angela Bassett.

Some head-scratching specials:

Christmas Comes to Pac-Land **(1982)** - In the early '80s, there were a couple of things people were really into: arcade games and cocaine.

Pac-Man was king of the former and was given his own Saturday morning cartoon AND prime-time Christmas special. There's a good chance, cocaine factored into those decisions.

***Deck the Halls with Wacky Walls* (1983)** - There were a few months in 1983 where Wacky WallWalkers were the hottest toy. Think Slinky or fidget spinners. They were like sticky octopi that would be thrown against the wall and could slowly "walk" their way down (and, depending on the wall you were using, leave a stain that Mom wouldn't be too happy about). Anyway, during those few months, someone green-lit a Christmas special with animated Wacky WallWalkers, possibly in hopes to turn the phenomenon into the next Smurfs. It didn't.

***He-Man and She-Ra: A Christmas Special* (1985)** - He-Man and She-Ra are twin superheroes who had their own weird shows in the '80s. For one magical night in syndication, they shared top billing. In this insane holiday special, Orko (the floating comic relief of the show) accidentally transports two young children from Earth to an alternate universe. They are then captured by Skeletor (the show's villain). Over the span of about a half hour, little Miguel and Alisha teach the He-Man/She-Ra gang about Christmas. By the end, He-Man is dressed as Santa and lecturing about the true meaning of the holiday.

***A Claymation Christmas Celebration* (1987)** - In 1986, the California Raisin Advisory Board launched an ad campaign to promote dried grapes. The ad, featuring animated humanoid raisins singing Marvin Gaye's "I Heard It Through the Grapevine," was wildly popular. So much so that Gaye's 1967 song reached number eight on the 1986 contemporary charts. The animator for that commercial, Will Vinton Productions, landed a Christmas special deal from it. The result was a claymation nightmare featuring singing camels, animated bells, and, yes, the Motown-themed California Raisins.

Frosty Returns **(1992)** - After a couple of decades of buildup, people were ready for a *Frosty* sequel. The last anyone saw of him was when he got married in the 1976 sequel. Sixteen years later, he returned, except this wasn't a Rankin/Bass production and it appears that the animation budget was slashed significantly. Instead of a scarf, Frosty is wearing a bow tie, like some sort of Chippendales dancer. Not even the voices of John Goodman, Jonathan Winters, Brian Doyle-Murray, and a young Elisabeth Moss can rescue this monstrosity.

Grandma Got Run Over by a Reindeer **(2000)** - A special based off the worst Christmas song of all time should inspire sufficiently low expectations. Somehow, *Grandma Got Run Over by a Reindeer* falls below them. Jake Spankenheimer's grandmother runs a family store that somehow sells clocks, bread, and robots. On Christmas Eve, he looks out of the window and sees her getting trucked by Santa. She went missing for a year, returns, claims amnesia, and Santa is put on trial. F-minus. Would not recommend.

Cabbage Patch Kids: Vernon's Christmas **(2003)** - The Cabbage Patch Kids are putting on a Christmas play at school, and Vernon's younger cousins Amy and— Nope, I'm stopping right there. All you need to know is this stop-motion Cabbage Patch Kids video features pulsating dolls in a universe with no parents. The dolls make the animatronic Chuck E. Cheese band look lifelike. Never EVER try to find this unsettling nightmare fuel on YouTube. It will haunt you forever.

VeggieTales **"Merry Larry and the True Light of Christmas" (2013)** - VeggieTales looks like it was designed by a middle schooler in an

"Intro to Programming" course. Even if you can get past the awful animation, it's death by a thousand cuts. VeggieTales starts with a somewhat normal premise (if you can suspend disbelief enough to get past how the anthropomorphic vegetables kind of look like thumbs)—Bob the Tomato and Larry the Cucumber want to have a really cool Christmas display at the mall. Over time, they are guilted into tearing down all the decorations, as Jesus would have wanted. This special is about as subtle as a pipe bomb.

Saturday Morning and After-School Cartoons

Part of the reason there aren't as many new Christmas specials anymore is because of the rapid expansion of animated shows over the past few decades. Now just about every kids show has its own holiday episode in December. There were a few in the early years of television (*Popeye, Casper the Friendly Ghost, The Flintstones, Scooby-Doo*), but the real explosion of cartoons happened in the '80s and '90s. Seemingly every hit movie (*Ghostbusters, Back to the Future, Rambo, Ace Ventura, Men in Black*), comic book superhero (Batman, Superman, Justice League, X-Men, the Tick, Teenage Mutant Ninja Turtles), action star (Jackie Chan), and even stand-up comic (Louie Anderson, Howie Mandel) got their own show and Christmas episode. They all fell into one of three categories: dysfunctional family gatherings, turning a mean person (a Scrooge) nice for one night, or helping out troubled kids.

Here are the best:

The Flintstones **"Christmas Flintstone" (1964)** - Fred gets a job as a mall Santa to earn some extra cash. He does such a good job that, when the real Santa falls ill, Fred is tapped to deliver the presents.

Animaniacs "'Twas the Day Before Christmas / Jingle Boo / The Great Wakkorotti: The Holiday Concert / Toy Shop Terror / Yakko's Universe" (1993) - Much like the show itself, this episode of Christmas-themed vignettes is equal parts slapstick, absurdities, and clever references. The highlights are a riff on *'Twas the Night Before Christmas* and a concert performance of "Jingle Bells" done entirely by burping.

SpongeBob Squarepants "Christmas Who?" (2000) - In the second season of SpongeBob, Sandy the squirrel teaches SpongeBob about Christmas. Predictably, he's super amped about it and shares what he knows with everyone. After Santa fails to show up in Bikini Bottom on Christmas Eve, SpongeBob and his friends are crushed. His normally Scrooge-like neighbor, Squidward, takes a turn as Santa to lift everyone's spirits.

What's New, Scooby-Doo? "A Scooby-Doo! Christmas" (2002) - There have been many iterations of Scooby-Doo, and just about each one did a Christmas episode. Aside from the ones involving Scrappy-Doo, they've all been pretty good. In this one, the gang travels to a village that is being terrorized by a headless snowman and, therefore, don't really get into the holiday. Just like in every episode, Scooby and Shaggy are not brave, get hyper focused on eating, and then are used as bait. The snowman is one of the better villains in the show's history.

Here are some confusing ones:

Popeye the Sailor "Spinach Greetings" (1960) - In quite possibly the first Christmas cartoon episode, Popeye has to save Santa after the Sea Hag kidnaps him. He takes his spinach, gets all jacked up, and then murders a vulture and alligator on the way to saving Santa. The only problem is all the action is implied, not shown. Looks like the animators took a Christmas break early.

G.I. Joe: The Real American Hero **"Cobra Claws Are Coming to Town" (1985)** - The Cobras fool the Joes with the old Trojan horse trick. Apparently, they were not familiar with the *Iliad*. In the end, Shipwreck's pet parrot, Polly, grows to be, like, sixty feet tall and saves the day—and Christmas—while singing "Jingle Bells." Typical Christmas stuff.

Rambo **"When S.A.V.A.G.E. Stole Santa" (1986)** - The cartoon adaptation of a movie series about a guy who just wanted to be left alone shows Rambo desperate to be around people. In this episode, Rambo is tasked with saving an orphan and a nuclear weapons scientist-turned-toy maker, all while showing off his massive biceps. It ends with Rambo snowboarding shirtless on a hubcap. There's a good chance this show was written by a fifth-grade boy.

Arthur **"Arthur's Perfect Christmas" (2000)** - While it's encouraging that the PBS show targeted for four-to-eight-year-olds shows how not everyone celebrates Christmas the same way (and even shows a nice depiction of Hanukkah), it harps a bit too much on not having enough money at Christmas and doubting the existence of Santa. It's a bit heavy for preschoolers (and adults).

PRIME-TIME ANIMATION

The show that kick-started prime-time animation was a Christmas special. (Yes, *The Flintstones* was in prime time but is now considered a kids' cartoon.) For a few years, you'd see *The Simpsons* in short bumpers going into the commercial breaks during *The Tracey Ullman*

Show. But it wasn't until December 17, 1989 that the (now) longest running scripted program in the history of television got its own full-length show. "Simpsons Roasting on an Open Fire" was a much sweeter version of the show we all know today. Instead of a moronic clown, Homer was just a down-on-his-luck dad who would do anything for his family. The Christmas special had its humorous moments but was pretty tame compared to future episodes. Most importantly, the groundbreaking special introduced the world to Homer, Marge, Bart, Lisa, and Maggie and laid the foundation for a completely new genre of television.

Here are the best prime-time animated Christmas shows:

The Simpsons **"Marge Be Not Proud" (1995)** - At this point, the show can boast of dozens of excellent Christmas episodes. There are Homer-centric ones, like "'Tis the Fifteenth Season," in which a selfish Homer falls asleep to a version of *A Christmas Carol* and becomes disgustingly altruistic. There's typical Bart ones, like "Miracle on Evergreen Terrace," where he starts a fire and ruins Christmas. There are a couple of great school ones, like "Skinner's Sense of Snow" and "Grift of the Magi," where adult incompetence leads to disastrous results right around Christmas. There's a solid one called "She of Little Faith" where Lisa struggles with commercialization. But the strongest Christmas episode of all is one that focuses on the relationship between Marge and Bart. Bart really wants the hot new video game and gets caught stealing it right before Christmas. The rest of the episode is about Bart trying to keep his parents from finding out and dealing with the consequences when they do. This season seven offering is touching but still full of typical Simpsons hilarity (Krusty hosting a pathetic Christmas special, Milhouse getting obsessed with a ball and cup, and the line, "Christmas is a time when people of all religions come together to worship Jesus Christ").

Beavis and Butt-Head "Beavis and Butt-Head Do Christmas" **(1995)** - Two dimwitted teenaged heavy metal fans read some viewer letters and did two Christmas movie parodies. The first was "Huh-Huh-Humbug," a spoof of *A Christmas Carol*, as Beavis is visited by ghosts who interrupt him while he's watching an X-rated movie. In the second, "It's a Miserable Life," Butt-Head sees what life would be like if he was never born. Neither learns any lessons.

South Park "Mr. Hankey, the Christmas Poo" **(1997)** - While it certainly has some competition from "Woodland Critter Christmas," in which Stan accidentally assists in the birth of the antichrist, and "Merry Christmas, Charlie Manson!" in which the famous murderous cult leader teaches Stan about the importance of family, the best *South Park* Christmas show is this season one episode. The town is hell-bent on eliminating all offensive content at Christmastime. Meanwhile, Kyle is trying to convince everyone there is a sentient turd that comes each holiday season called Mr. Hankey, the Christmas Poo.

The PJs "How the Super Stole Christmas" **(2000)** - This claymation show about life in the projects opened its second season with Thurgood, the super, repossessing various things from his tenants' apartments so he can buy a good gift for his wife. The Grinch parallels are intentional, but let's just say the people in his building aren't quite as forgiving as the Whos down in Whoville.

Family Guy "A Very Special Family Guy Freakin' Christmas" **(2001)** - A series of mishaps mostly caused by her selfish and boorish husband have driven Lois Griffin over the edge at Christmas. Meanwhile, Peter is consumed with watching a Christmas special (that's really a spoof of all bad 1980s animated specials)—*KISS Saves Santa*.

Rick and Morty **"Anatomy Park" (2013)** - Rick shrinks Morty and injects him into a homeless man in a Santa outfit who is dying of tuberculosis. Meanwhile, Morty's grandparents have recently entered into a three-way relationship.

Other solid prime-time animation Christmas shows: *Space Ghost Coast to Coast* "A Space Ghost Christmas" in 1994, *King of the Hill* "Pretty Pretty Dresses" (1998), *Sealab 2021* "Feast of Alvis" (2002), *Moral Orel* "The Best Christmas Ever!" (2005), *The Boondocks* "A Huey Freeman Christmas" (2005), *Robot Chicken* "Misery, My Sweet Baboo (Linus & Sally Misery)" (2007), *BoJack Horseman* "Sabrina's Christmas Wish" (2014), *F is for Family* "O Holy Moly Night" (2015), *Mike Tyson Mysteries* "The Christmas Episode" (2019)

PUPPETS

Ever since *Sesame Street* premiered in 1969, Jim Henson's marionette-puppet hybrids—Muppets—have been in big demand for Christmas specials.

Here are some of the puppet standouts:

Emmet Otter's Jug-Band Christmas **(1977)** – Notwithstanding his own creations of Kermit, Ernie, Cookie Monster, Miss Piggy, and Big Bird, Jim Henson and his crew took on the challenge of adapting a beloved children's Christmas book to the Muppet universe. The sweet—and mildly depressing—story is, essentially, a twist on *The Gift of the Magi*. Emmet and his mom sell off important work tools so they can compete in the local talent show and, hopefully, win the grand prize.

***Christmas Eve on Sesame Street* (1978)** - There was no better thrill for a kid than seeing Oscar, Ernie, and Big Bird hit the ice at the start of Sesame Street's first (and best) Christmas special. The special gives all of the characters a platform to do what they do best (Ernie and Burt—being friends, Oscar—raining on parades, Cookie Monster—eating, and Big Bird—being earnest).

***John Denver and the Muppets: A Christmas Together* (1979)** - There was a stretch from the mid-'70s to the mid-'80s when it was impossible to avoid John Denver. The "Country Roads" singer somehow linked up with the Muppets on multiple occasions. The best one was his 1979 special where he played it completely straight and had a music/variety show (like Bing Crosby) except the singers were Muppets. "The Twelve Days of Christmas" opening is the highlight.

***A Muppet Family Christmas* (1987)** - Kermit and the gang go to Fozzie Bear's mom's house for Christmas and sing songs. The best of the bunch is a pretty great version of "Jingle Bell Rock."

***A Muppet Christmas: Letters to Santa* (2008)** - Another one of the better Muppet Christmas specials has the gang needing to hand-deliver a letter to the North Pole after the post office closes on them.

The puppet universe has had its share of clunkers as well. Here are the worst:

***The Spirit of Christmas* (1953)** - This marionette retelling of *'Twas the Night Before Christmas* has a haunting aura. All the characters' eyes and expressions replace Christmas spirit with agita.

D.C. Follies "Reagan Accidentally Gives Fred a Nuke for Christmas" **(1987)** - The political satire puppet-human show *D.C. Follies* made fun of the circus inside of the Beltway. With a bevy of dated references (Jim and Tammy Fay Bakker, cassette tapes), it would be tough for a show to hold up worse. Cher, Sylvester Stallone, and Dolly Parton puppets appear.

Mr. Willowby's Christmas Tree **(1995)** - This story about a tree at a rich guy's estate is just kind of sad. Robert Downey, Jr. and Leslie Nielsen collected a paycheck for the special. That's about it.

COPS, DETECTIVES, AND LAWYERS

There is no better bet for television executives than shows about law enforcement officers, private investigators, or lawyers. There's an endless supply of storylines and opportunities to make these types of protagonists look like heroes. Starting with sheriffs in old Westerns, these shows have put out many, many Christmas episodes. Some familiar tropes:

1. Pregnant women need help like the Virgin Mary on Christmas Eve.
2. Lots and lots of orphans need saving.
3. Children are constantly separated from their parents.
4. Santa Clauses tend to commit crimes. Law enforcement is always chasing criminals hiding behind white beards.
5. A member of the cast is having trouble getting into the holiday spirit.

Here are the standout Christmas episodes involving cops and lawyers:

Adam-12 "**Log 122: Christmas—The Yellow Dump Truck**" **(1968)** - It was a simpler time for cop shows. Two LAPD officers are tasked with delivering toys to underprivileged families. The episode involves a car thief, stolen toys, a DUI (for comic relief, which was a common thing on shows back then), a domestic disturbance, and a hardened cop's melted heart. It's about as un-gritty as a cop show will ever get but definitely has a healthy amount of Christmas spirit.

Kojak "**How Cruel the Frost, How Bright the Stars**" **(1975)** - The unintentional comedic brilliance of Telly Savalas is on full display with his portrayal of Theo Kojak, the rule-breaking, tough-talking NYC detective. While working his way through about three packs of smokes, Kojak spends Christmas Eve with his partner tracking down an at-large gunman and helping a young woman find her boyfriend. This is a great episode if you're feeling nostalgic about New York City in the 1970s or just want to watch Savalas get creepy with some mistletoe. He closes the episode by shouting, "LOVE THY NEIGHBOR, BABY!" into the night.

Starsky & Hutch "**Little Girl Lost**" **(1976)** - The father of a young girl (played by Kristy McNichol) has just been murdered and it's up to the undercover detective duo working the streets of the fictional Bay City (it's Los Angeles) to save her. At the same time, one-half of that duo (Hutch) isn't feeling the Christmas spirit. Combine those two elements, sprinkle in the help of informant and bartender-dressed-like-a-pimp Huggy Bear, and you've got yourself an excellent Christmas episode.

Police Woman "**Merry Christmas, Waldo**" **(1977)** - An old man dresses up like Santa Claus and robs banks. Undercover Sgt. "Pepper"

Anderson (Angie Dickinson) can't figure out why. This episode does a good job tackling loneliness and giving at Christmas, and showcases an old lady who eats cat food.

Moonlighting "'Twas the Episode Before Christmas" (1985) - Bruce Willis and Cybill Shepherd's private investigator dramedy actually had two strong Christmas episodes (the other being 1986's "It's a Wonderful Job" in which Maddie Hayes imagines life without her owning a detective agency). But this episode is one of the best in the entire series. The Blue Moon Detective Agency tries to find the mother of an abandoned baby (who was found by the receptionist). Meanwhile, mob henchmen who killed that baby's father are also looking for that mother and baby.

The Equalizer "Christmas Presence" (1987) - It's Christmas 1987, and goons are trying to drive a boy with AIDS and his grandmother from their New York City apartment. In steps the retired secret agent-turned-guardian angel and one of his partners. In real life, the Equalizer (Edward Woodward) was recovering from a massive heart attack, so his partner does most of the heavy-lifting in this episode. But it's still satisfying and delivers a nice family reunion.

Matlock "The Gift" (1987) - During a party filled with Santa Clauses, one of them murders a woman. Her ex-husband (played by a young Bryan Cranston) is arrested, and it's up to the folksy criminal defense lawyer Ben Matlock to defend him so he can spend Christmas with his daughter. It's tough not to love Andy Griffith and even tougher to dislike anything with Bryan Cranston in it. Family separation at Christmas is the big theme. One (hopefully) small issue—at the beginning of the episode, we learn that Cranston's character had no visitation rights whatsoever but don't know why. Are we sure Matlock should be trying so hard to reunite him with his daughter?

NYPD Blue **"From Hare to Eternity" (1993)** - The cantankerous Detective Sipowicz isn't too jazzed to be playing Santa Claus at the annual Christmas party at the station. But, before the party, he and his partner Kelly have to track down a kidnapped child. It's an episode that features a dead rabbit, some good Christmas spirit (partially undercut by Sipowicz's casual racism), and the quote, "I tell ya, whoever invented cellular phones should be hung by their nuts."

The Wire **"Final Grades" (2006)** - The best episode of the best season of the best dramatic series in television history takes place at Christmastime. While some holiday episodes are heartwarming stories of people changing for the better, Christmas in this episode only serves as a backdrop for the conclusion of season four, when many things take turns for the worse. Good intentions lead to terrible consequences. Good people are facing brutal conditions. Also unlike other cop shows' holiday episodes, this one wouldn't make a whole lot of sense out of context. But it takes place at Christmas and it's fantastic… just not in the usual way.

Monk **"Mr. Monk and the Secret Santa" (2005)** - Tony Shalhoub's show about a quirky private investigator who works with the police actually had four good Christmas episodes during its eight-season run. In 2006, Monk met his estranged dad. In 2007, he got accused of shooting a man in a Santa costume. In 2008, he helped three homeless men find out who killed their friend. Even in the series finale in 2009, there were flashbacks to Christmas. But the best of all is from season four, when someone sent a poisoned bottle of port to the captain (played by Ted Levine, a.k.a. Buffalo Bill from *The Silence of the Lambs*!). Part of the search for the guy trying to kill the captain was having the extreme germaphobe Monk having to play a mall Santa.

Other solid ones: *S.W.A.T.* "Silent Night Deadly Night" (1975), *Magnum, P.I.* "Thank Heaven for Little Girls (and Big Ones Too)" (1980), *Hill Street Blues* "Santaclaustrophobia" (1982), *T.J. Hooker* "Slay Ride" (1983), *Homicide: Life on the Street* "All Through the House" (1994), *Dexter* "Truth Be Told" (2006), *Psych* "Gus's Dad May Have Killed an Old Guy" (2007), *Sherlock* "A Scandal in Belgravia" (2012)

Here are some head-scratching Christmas episodes involving cops and lawyers:

Dragnet **"The Big .22 Rifle for Christmas" (1952)** - This early cop show took real LAPD cases and turned them into fictionalized ones for Detective Joe Friday to solve. For this Christmas episode, they picked the darkest story imaginable. Two boys open a Christmas present early. It doesn't go well. Joe Friday concludes the episode by saying, "You don't give a kid a gun for Christmas."

CHiPs **"Christmas Watch" (1979)** - A couple of thieves are bouncing around Los Angeles, stealing things left and right, including one family's car and all of their Christmas presents. But angry Ponch is most fixated on a stolen fifteenth-century bell. For some reason, it can't be Christmas without hearing that bell. Also, there's a drunk driving scene used as comic relief.

Hart to Hart **"A Christmas Hart" (1982)** - The show about middle-aged millionaires who love getting romantic and solving mysteries has the Harts trying to stop a "Jingle Gram" burglary ring. The couple's crummy detective work is evident throughout. Eventually, Mrs. H gets out of trouble by applying blunt force to the head of one of the bad guys. Any detective agency that relies on a chauffeur's ability to act is a lousy one.

Knight Rider **"Silent Knight" (1983)** - Michael and his talking car, K.I.T.T., accidentally hit a "gypsy" (the name they use many times during the episode) while he's trying to run away from bank robbers. Most of the episode is Hasselhoff and his perm trying to protect the teenager while listening to Fleetwood Mac's "Gypsy." Also, Michael teaches K.I.T.T. about Christmas, and the bank robbers are dressed like clowns.

MacGyver **"The Madonna" (1989)** – This season five Christmas episode of the show about a hyper-intelligent, military-trained government contractor who is short on cool solutions and long on shots of Richard Dean Anderson's mullet. In fact, the only creative thing MacGyver did in the entire episode was applying gauze to a homeless woman's hand. (In the episode, she's referred to as "bag lady" many times.) Most of "The Madonna" is about MacGyver struggling with the Christmas blues, a community center putting on a holiday show, and a missing Madonna statue (which was a clear reference to *Dragnet's* 1951 Christmas episode, "The Big Little Jesus").

Baywatch **"Silent Night, Baywatch Night" (1994)** - David Hasselhoff's 1990s crime-fighting-lifeguards show spreads its fifth-season Christmas over two (seemingly endless) episodes. The Hoff's Mitch Buchannon is looking out for a ten-year-old con artist whose mother is locked in jail. Meanwhile, lifeguard Matt is convinced that a group of little people are really Santa's elves. And C.J.'s (Pam Anderson) new friendship with a priest has him potentially willing to give up his vows to the Church. It ends with the little people throwing presents at a bad guy on an ATV, then kicking sand in his face.

Ally McBeal **"Silver Bells" (1997)** - This relationship-heavy legal dramedy tackles a polygamy case in this episode. Also, Ally's boss at the law firm (Peter MacNicol) is actively trying to date her. The episode feels like just an excuse for everyone to sing Christmas songs at the end—to varying degrees of success.

DOCTOR SHOWS

Medical dramas offer high tension, tugs at the heartstrings, and constant chances at winning the day. TV doctors might not always play by the rules but, dammit, they're gonna do what it takes to save their patients! And, at Christmastime, the hero factor ratchets up even more. Here are a few Christmas episode tropes from the doctor show world:

1. The most fertile month of the TV universe is obviously March, judging by the onslaught of Christmas deliveries.
2. Christmas is a time for miracles, and every television hospital has a kid in bad need of one.
3. Grouchy, Scrooge-like patients find the Christmas spirit during their hospital stay.
4. It's not just the patients. Some of our favorite TV doctors are in bad need of saving themselves from crippling drug and alcohol problems.

Here are a few standout medical Christmas episodes:

M*A*S*H **"Death Takes a Holiday" (1980)** - The Korean War medical dramedy (with an inexplicable laugh track) had a few solid Christmas episodes, but the best was in season nine. In one storyline, the staff is throwing a party for local orphans in the mess tent. Since the supply shipment is delayed, the staff has to donate stuff to give to the kids. While this is happening, Hawkeye, Hot Lips, and B.J. are frantically trying to keep a mortally wounded soldier alive past midnight so his death certificate won't read Christmas.

***Northern Exposure* "Seoul Mates" (1991)** - This fish-out-of-water show, about a New York doctor who is assigned to a quirky town in Alaska, celebrated Christmas in 1991 by having the Jewish Dr. Joel Fleischman buy his first Christmas tree (because he always admired them from afar). Also, Maurice, the wealthy retired Marine in town, gets visited by the son he didn't know he fathered during the Korean War.

***Chicago Hope* "Christmas Truce" (1995)** - A man is in critical condition after a fall while doing some home construction. Thanks to gang violence in the neighborhood, ambulances aren't going to come. The only way the man can be saved is if two of the show's doctors (Nyland and Hancock) brave the gunfire and treat him at the site. Also, a promising young high school pitcher has to have a tricky surgery that could derail his athletic career.

***ER* "I'll Be Home for Christmas" (2001)** - With the exception of the episode where Dr. Benton miraculously cured a man's blindness with his touch, ER had a number of powerful holiday episodes over its fifteen-season run, often involving a child emergency and some personal life heaviness for the staff. Probably the best of the bunch was this season eight episode, which was Eriq LaSalle's final appearance as a regular cast member. Facing the possibility of losing his son in a custody battle, Dr. Benton is forced to leave County and take a job with more reasonable hours for a single father. Also, Carter deals with the divorce of his parents, a mom accidentally shoots her son, and a woman in a coma is ready to give birth.

House **"Damned If You Do" (2004)** - The show about an irritable doctor who shows a Sherlock Holmes-like ability to diagnose the greatest of mystery illnesses on a weekly basis had its best Christmas episode in its first season. A nun enters the hospital with a weird skin condition on her hands. After a misdiagnosis leads to a horrible reaction, the hospital staff scrambles to save her life and find the real problem.

Huff **"Christmas Is Ruined" (2005)** - This short-lived Hank Azaria series about a psychiatrist and his family had a strong Christmas episode in its first season. Family is visiting for Christmas, and Huff's wife's mother announces she is stopping her chemo treatments. Also, Huff's buddy (played by Oliver Platt) brings a prostitute to Christmas dinner.

And here are a couple of head-scratching doctor shows:

Doogie Howser, M.D. **"Doogie the Red-Nosed Reindeer" (1989)** - Doogie, the child prodigy doctor, wants to get out of working the Christmas shift at the hospital so he can go to a party. So he pretends to be sick and is given the night off. The rest of this season one episode is Doogie feeling guilty about his selfish choice. Why would he make such an unprofessional and irresponsible decision? Because he is sixteen! That's what sixteen-year-olds do. And that's why you don't employ them as surgeons at high-profile hospitals! The episode finishes (like all the others) with Doogie typing some sanctimonious words into his computer diary as an electric keyboard plays.

Grey's Anatomy **"Adrift and at Peace" (2010)** - Every scene in this episode seems to feature either a good-looking doctor or nurse spouting righteous indignation or hooking up with a coworker. For the capper, a doctor proposes to a handsome patient who is without insurance so he doesn't have to die.

TEEN DRAMAS AND NIGHTTIME SOAPS

By nature, teen dramas and soap operas are over-the-top all year long. Characters get together, break up, get back together, get caught in love triangles, have dysfunctional families, have substance issues, have a baby, have custody disputes, and sometimes murder each other. At Christmastime, they keep doing that stuff, but there's often a tree and holiday music in the background. Also, gift giving has been known to create headaches.

Here are few standout teen dramas and nighttime soap episodes:

The Wonder Years "Christmas" (1988) - The main premise of this dramedy is a boy's struggle through adolescence, from pursuing the affections of his childhood crush (Winnie Cooper) to processing the horrors of the Vietnam War while he deals with middle school. This Christmas episode perfectly captures it all, as Kevin frets about getting Winnie the perfect gift. Meanwhile, the Cooper family are trying to make it through their first Christmas since Winnie's older brother was killed in Vietnam. Also, Kevin and his brother, Wayne, lobby their simmering-with-rage dad for a color TV.

Beverly Hills, 90210 "A Walsh Family Christmas" (1991) - No teen drama could match *BH90210*'s run of nine crazy Christmas episodes. Each December, Dylan, Brandon, Kelly, Steve, Andrea, Donna, David, and company tackled whatever nonsense was thrown at them (cocaine, abstinence, Secret Santa drama, a potential plane crash, infidelity, the Brian Setzer Orchestra, love triangles, a parrot that keeps saying "damn bird," a meddlesome mother paying off boyfriends, unknown siblings, emergency dental surgery, midnight mass drama, a dance marathon, an incarcerated parent, third-degree burns, sexual harassment in the workplace, Hilary Swank, parental divorce, racism, heroin runs to Mexico, and much more). The best of the bunch was probably in season two, when Brenda brought a homeless man dressed as Santa to Casa Walsh. Meanwhile, Steve went on a quest to find his biological mother and Brandon paid a visit to his ex-girlfriend Emily in a mental hospital.

Melrose Place "Oy! to the World" (1995) - The *BH90210* spin-off's season four Christmas episode had a little bit of everything: The FBI questions Amanda, Jo decides not to force Jane out at Hart Mancini Designs, Brooke fakes a pregnancy, Alison recovers from addiction by curling up on the couch and watching *It's a Wonderful Life*, and Sydney slips a tranquilizer into Jane's drink (to stop her from hooking up with Michael). Plus, it includes the line, "First you seduce my father, then you kill him. Two weeks later, you're after my husband?!?"

The O.C. "The Best Chrismukkah Ever" (2003) - Yet another *Beverly Hills, 90210* emulator had a strong first season of teen drama fun before having to crank up the nonsense to unwatchable levels. Essentially, it's about a rich family in Orange County, California who takes in a kid from the wrong side of the tracks. In this episode, the Cohens' son, Seth, excitedly explains to their new housemate, Ryan, their family tradition of combining Hanukkah and Christmas (since the dad is Jewish and the mom is Christian) into one holiday—Chrismukkah. There's some family drama, the bad girl next door has a drinking problem, and Seth ends up in a nerd fever dream (having to choose between two girls who are way out of his league).

Orange Is the New Black "Can't Fix Crazy" (2013) - The Christmas episode of this women-in-prison show has the inmates putting on a Christmas talent show. Meanwhile, the main character (Chapman) is dealing with a woman trying to kill her. A well-timed Secret Santa gift proves to be a big boost.

Cobra Kai "Feel the Night/December 19" (2020) - The final episodes of the third season of the *Karate Kid* spin-off series take place at Christmastime. An old flame of Johnny's is back in town for the holiday. Also, the nerd karate crew's Christmas party is crashed by the villainous karate crew, leading to an epic, fun showdown (which should have led to many, many arrests).

And here are a couple of head-scratching episodes:

Beverly Hills, 90210 "It's a Totally Happening Life" (1992) - The writers gave the teen drama the *It's a Wonderful Life* treatment in this season three Christmas offering. Angels discuss a group of teens who are in trouble (their school bus is about to get T-boned by a garbage truck). The episode then shows the gang's terrible behavior over the previous week. Unlike George Bailey, the entire West Beverly High gang is thoroughly unlikable this episode. Plus, the extras riding the bus along with the protagonists are a glee club that won't stop singing. None of these high school kids seem worthy of saving... except for maybe Steve Sanders (played by twenty-eight-year-old Ian Ziering).

Dawson's Creek "Merry Mayhem" (2002) - *Dawson's Creek* was a show that followed the lives of a group of high school friends in a fictional Massachusetts town. The problem was, by year six, they were adults. Their cute twenty-five-cent words and soliloquies weren't so cute anymore. This final season episode has all the main characters returning to Capeside for Christmas. Joey brings home a loser boyfriend. Pacey is inexplicably a high-powered, full-of-himself businessman, and Dawson is a production assistant who is dating a movie star. And *Dawson* is the one not satisfied with his relationship. How did this movie star fall for a guy with the sensibilities of someone's great-grandmother? This group is a collective bummer. One of their drunk friends drives a car into the house during dinner.

Desperate Housewives "**Boom Crunch**" **(2009)** - The show that started as "these four typical housewives aren't quite as perfect and happy as they seem" quickly devolved into a *Mad Libs*-on-PCP abomination. In what seems like a parody of a soap opera, one of the housewives is suing another. Someone's son has amnesia. A neighbor stabs herself and blames it on someone else's husband. One woman from the neighborhood is blackmailing another. And a man played by Dan Castellaneta (the voice of Homer Simpson) has a heart attack while flying a small plane. Now it's about to crash into a Christmas party with all the housewives on Wisteria Lane.

SCI-FI, FANTASY, AND HORROR

Some television shows offer true escape from reality by taking place in alternate universes. That doesn't prevent those shows from incorporating Christmas into their December storylines. Superheroes, vampires, aliens, angels, ghosts, anti-Santa demons, and even characters stuck in other dimensions celebrate the holiday. How does Will in *Stranger Things* communicate with his mom from the Upside Down? Through Christmas lights.

Here are the standout sci-fi, fantasy, and horror Christmas episodes:

Alfred Hitchcock Presents **"Together" (1958)** - The "Master of Suspense" had three great Christmas episodes in the 1950s. One involved a paroled convict struggling to stay on the straight and narrow while working as a department store Santa ("Santa Claus and the Tenth Avenue Kid" in 1955). Another featured a husband bumping off his wife ("Back for Christmas" in 1956). But the best was this one about a guy who gets stuck in a locked office with the mistress he just murdered.

The Twilight Zone **"The Night of the Meek" (1960)** - Art Carney plays Henry Corwin, a down-and-out Santa who just lost his job. As he's being escorted out of the department store, Corwin wonders aloud why a regular person can't be Santa. "On one Christmas, I'd like to see the meek inherit the earth. And that's why I drink… and that's why I weep." Corwin's journey over the rest of the powerful episode has touches of *A Christmas Carol*, *Miracle on 34th Street*, and *It's a Wonderful Life*.

Amazing Stories **"Santa '85" (1985)** - Santa Claus trips a burglar alarm while delivering presents in this Christmas episode of Steven Spielberg's fantasy anthology series. When he gets tossed in the slammer with a bunch of fake Santas, it looks like Christmas is ruined. Luckily, an eight-year-old boy is determined to save him.

Tales from the Crypt **"And All Through the House" (1989)** - A woman kills her husband for the insurance money. At the same time, an escaped convict wearing a Santa suit is roaming her neighborhood. Bloody hijinks ensue.

Black Mirror **"White Christmas" (2014)** - The Christmas episode of this dystopian sci-fi anthology series opens with two guys (Jon Hamm and Rafe Spall) sharing a meal on Christmas at a remote snowy outpost. The two share stories about what led them to this grim location. Hamm used to help men pick up women. Spall had a relationship go south.

Some other solid episodes: *Voyagers!* "Merry Christmas, Bogg" in 1982, *Tales from the Darkside* "Seasons of Belief" (1986), *The X-Files* "How the Ghosts Stole Christmas" (1998), *Smallville* "Gemini" (2007), *Pushing Daisies* "Corpsicle" (2007), *Lost* "The Constant" (2008), *American Horror Story: Asylum* "Unholy Night" (2012)

And here are a few head-scratching episodes:

***Wonder Woman* "The Deadly Toys" (1977)** - On a weekly basis in the late '70s, Wonder Woman was "fighting for your rights… in her satin tights." But, at Christmastime in season two, Diana Prince found herself in a battle with her clone. An evil toy maker and an evil general were trying to start a clone army at Christmas. Not even two Wonder Women could save television at Christmas that year.

***Beauty and the Beast* "God Bless the Child" (1988)** - A few years before Disney turned it into a wildly popular animated musical, CBS turned the eighteenth-century fairy tale into a TV show set in the tunnels under New York City. In this episode, Linda Hamilton's Catherine ("Beauty") helps a pregnant hooker escape so she can give birth at Christmastime. While under the city, the prostitute falls in love with Ron Perlman's Vincent ("Beast"). The real thing is somehow even weirder than this description.

***Lois & Clark: The New Adventures of Superman* "Seasons Greedings" (1994)** - Superman himself, Dean Cain, wrote this episode. Viewers quickly learn that the Man of Steel is not a man of letters. Evil toy makers (played by George and Weezy Jefferson,

Sherman Hemsley, and Isabel Sanford) create a toy that causes all the people of Metropolis to act like spoiled, petulant children. In reality, it created some of the worst overacting in television history.

Hercules: The Legendary Journeys "A Star to Guide Them" (1996) - The late-'90s-syndicated show's not-so-subtle attempt at a Nativity-themed episode has Hercules' friend, Iolaus, following a mysterious star up north. There, he and Hercules find a King Herod-type who is killing newborns. One of those newborns is giving off a Jesus vibe. This episode answers the age-old question—what would happen if sixth graders wrote a play starring adult-film-caliber actors?

OTHER DRAMA

Most shows fit into neat categories. Police shows beget more police shows. Same is the case for hospital or law office shows. Through most of television history, that's the way it was. There were the occasional departures (*Little House on the Prairie, The Waltons, B.J. and the Bear, Our House, Thirtysomething*), but, for the most part, they were uneventful shows. Most of their Christmas episodes reflected that.

Then, in the late '90s, cable television networks really started investing in original programming. As a result, the new millennium has experienced a new Golden Age of Television. Suddenly, there were tons of great shows that didn't feature cops, lawyers, or doctors.

Here are the standout Christmas episodes from those shows:

The Sopranos "To Save Us All from Satan's Power" (2001) - The week before the greatest *Sopranos* episode ("Pine Barrens") was a pretty good offering in season three. It's the first Christmas since Tony murdered his old friend-turned-FBI informant, Big Pussy. Tony is struggling with flashbacks and deciding who should take his place as Santa at the holiday party. The mob boss is also not too pleased about his daughter's boyfriend.

Six Feet Under "It's the Most Wonderful Time of the Year" (2002) - The show about a family who runs a funeral home had a strong Christmas episode in its second season. It begins with a Santa on a motorcycle getting hit by a bus in front of children and somehow gets darker from there. Christmas marks the one-year anniversary of patriarch Nathaniel Fisher's death. Each child remembers their last time seeing him. Also, Nate is forced to have a Christmas dinner with his girlfriend's dysfunctional family.

Mad Men "Christmas Comes But Once a Year" (2010) - *Mad Men* had a few good Christmas episodes. The best of them was in season four, when the cash-strapped ad agency is forced to throw a massive, budget-shattering Christmas party to keep an important client happy. Also, Don struggles with the loneliness of the holidays after getting divorced.

Friday Night Lights "Always" (2011) - The final episode of the Texas high school football show takes place at Christmastime. The former quarterback is back in town and wants to marry the coach's daughter. Coach Taylor is weighing options for his future. And the team is preparing for the state final. The episode puts a perfect bow on the five-season drama.

The Crown "War" (2020) - Christmas is the backdrop as two prominent figures in British life, Margaret Thatcher and Princess Diana, are headed for significant life changes. Thatcher is on the verge of being pushed out of office by her own party after serving as prime minister for eleven and a half years. Meanwhile, Diana's loveless nine-year marriage is nearing its end.

Some other solid episodes: *Little House on the Prairie* "Christmas at Plum Creek" (1974), *B.J. and the Bear* "Silent Night, Unholy Night" *look out for a young Ted Danson appearance* (1979), *The West Wing* "In Excelsis Deo" (1999), *Parenthood* "What to My Wondering Eyes" (2012)

Here are a couple of head-scratchers:

Window on Main Street **"Christmas Memory" (1961)** - Hot off the heels of the beloved sitcom *Father Knows Best*, Robert Young starred in a bizarre show where a guy returns to his hometown and writes about his neighbors. In this episode, Young's character gets invited to a Christmas party with relative strangers and he bums everyone out by talking about the butter churner that his late wife once gave him.

Downton Abbey **"Christmas at Downton Abbey" (2011)** - The stakes could not be lower as lots of rich people in tuxedos and gowns stick their noses into each other's business and have a very stiff Christmas party. Cousins Matthew and Mary hook up but then get engaged, so it's not a scandal.

SITCOMS

The absolute kings of the Christmas episode genre are sitcoms. From the early days of *Father Knows Best* and *I Love Lucy*, sitcoms have embraced December episodes about the holiday. Today, it's pretty much expected from every situation comedy. Because of that, you start to notice a lot of similarities.

Even though the famous song begs for it, it really almost never is a "white Christmas" in most of America. There has been snow on Christmas only three times in New York City in the past half century. Los Angeles has had zero during that span. Even Chicago gets a white Christmas less than half the time. For sitcom Christmases, though, it's practically a mandate. Some show it falling or dusting the ground just to set the tone. Others use snowstorms to cause travel delays or cancellations. The list of Christmas-themed sitcom episodes that don't feature snow is shorter than the list of ones that do.

Snow isn't the only Christmas sitcom trope. Here are a few others:

1. Family gatherings are an excuse for sitcoms to share old clips or flashbacks.
2. Characters are asked to perform in a big Christmas show.
3. Sometimes, the actors themselves just want to show off their singing bona fides, so they break into song at the end of the Christmas episode.
4. There has to be a character dressed as Santa Claus. Whether it's working as a department store Santa for an episode, being festive for a party, donning the suit to convince a kid the big man has arrived, or wearing it for a local production, one of the main characters will be in a red suit.

Here are the standout sitcom Christmas episodes:

The Andy Griffith Show **"A Christmas Story" (1960)** - One of the best Christmas episodes in sitcom history was written by a guy using a fake name. Frank Tarloff had been blacklisted in 1953 by the House Un-American Activities Committee (McCarthyism). So "David Adler" wrote this sweet story about Mayberry's town Scrooge and his relentless push to punish a man caught making moonshine on

Christmas Eve. Since the man had a family, Sheriff Andy has to come up with a clever way for everyone to still have a merry Christmas.

The Mary Tyler Moore Show **"Christmas and the Hard-Luck Kid II" (1970)** - This groundbreaking show about an independent woman dealt with one of the challenges of having a career during the holidays. For the first Christmas at her new job, Mary Richards is forced to cancel all her festive plans and work at the television station on both Christmas Eve and Christmas Day. (The "II" in the title is a reference to the "Christmas and the Hard-Luck Kid" episode of *That Girl*, also written by Jim Brooks four years earlier.)

Bewitched **"Sisters at Heart" (1970)** - While there were funnier Christmas episodes of *Bewitched* (like "A Vision of Sugar Plums" in 1964), "Sisters at Heart" is the most important holiday offering. The show was on the fade by 1970 (they had dumped the original Darren Stephens the year before). In an unusual twist, writers worked with a group of inner-city Los Angeles high school sophomores ("Story by: 5th Period English – Room 309 Thomas Jefferson High School") for this season seven Christmas episode. Elizabeth Montgomery opens the show by introducing it to the audience and explaining the episode was "conceived in the image of innocence and filled with truth." Samantha's daughter, Tabitha, has a close friend whom she refers to as her sister. That the girl happens to be black causes problems with one of her dad's racist clients. There's a goofy situation where Tabitha's novice witchcraft turns the two girls into polka-dotted sisters (and a super uncomfortable blackface scene which attempts to prove racism), but the groundbreaking episode was an earnest shot at righting some wrongs at Christmastime.

The Bob Newhart Show **"His Busiest Season" (1972)** - *The Bob Newhart Show* was a rarity, in that it was about an adult married couple who didn't have kids and weren't really interested in talking about them. In this season one episode, the Chicago psychologist is dealing with a group session awash with sad holiday memories, so he invites them all to his home for Christmas Eve.

Happy Days **"Guess Who's Coming to Christmas" (1974)** - In the second season of this '50s-era sitcom, Fonzie hadn't yet taken over the show and was still a bit of a dangerous mystery. Richie realizes that Fonzie will be all alone on Christmas Eve, so he and Mr. C come up with a way to get him to their house (while preserving the Fonz's pride). When Fonzie realizes what has happened, he finally warms up to Richie and thanks him "for having all your freckles in the right place."

Good Times **"Penny's Christmas" (1977)** - A major story arc on season five of *Good Times* was the arrival of Penny (played by a young Janet Jackson), a girl who had been abused by her biological mother but was about to be adopted by the loving Willona. As a way to show appreciation and love for her soon-to-be adoptive mother, Penny tries to buy a gift for Willona. Before she can pay for it, a pickpocket steals her money. When Penny tries to shoplift the gift instead, she gets caught and throws into question her chance at adoption.

Taxi **"A Full House for Christmas" (1978)** - Christmas episodes give shows a chance to redeem their least deserving. In season one, *Taxi* writers opted for the cheapskate boss, Louie de Palma (Danny DeVito). Louie's even less likable professional gambler brother is in town from Vegas, and Louie wants him to visit their mother. The only way the brother will do that is if he loses at poker. It's a fun showdown and features the legendary DeVito at his peak.

Married... with Children **"You Better Watch Out" (1987)** - There were a few strong *Married... with Children* Christmas episodes (Al working as a mall Santa, Al getting the *It's a Wonderful Life* treatment) but the best is from season two, when a publicity stunt mishap involving a parachuting Kris Kringle leads to the Bundys having a dead body in their backyard.

Cheers **"Christmas Cheers" (1987)** - Several funny storylines intersect in this season six Christmas episode. Rebecca is forcing everyone to work Christmas Eve, leading to sour moods. While running out to get Rebecca a last-minute gift, Sam—literally—runs into a beautiful flight attendant. Norm is working a side job as a mall Santa. And Cliff is on a quest to win a canned food drive which will net him a free trip to Disney.

Wings **"A Terminal Christmas" (1990)** - This season two episode touches on a very un-sitcommy subject—loneliness. Thanks to cancelled plans across the board, the gang drops in on Fay's Christmas party, only to find her sitting alone. It's the first Christmas she has had without her late husband, and the airline's receptionist is unable to move forward. There still is a funny twist involving a Dustbuster, but this is one of the more poignant Christmas sitcom episodes.

Frasier **"Miracle on Third or Fourth Street" (1993)** – In almost every season, the *Cheers* spin-off had a strong holiday episode. The best was its first, when a depressed Frasier clashes with his father and is separated from his son. Frasier opts to work the Christmas Day shift, which proves to be an even bigger downer. On his way home, the disheveled radio shrink gets mistaken for a homeless man at a diner, which leads him to finding his holiday spirit.

Seinfeld "**The Strike**" **(1997)** - While the nearly perfect sitcom had several great Christmas episodes ("The Red Dot" in season three, "The Pick" in season four, and others), season nine boasts the most iconic. In this episode, we learn that George's father invented an alternative holiday to Christmas that revolved around airing out grievances—Festivus. Other intertwining storylines involve Jerry dating a woman whose appearance drastically changes in different lighting, George making up a fake charity, Elaine giving out a fake phone number to creepy guys, and Kramer picketing a bagel shop where he used to work.

Spin City "**Miracle Near 34th Street**" **(1997)** - This season two Christmas episode of the New York City Hall comedy has Michael J. Fox's character scrambling to undo the damage of a mayor's blunder in front of a child. Meanwhile, negotiations with City Hall Santa Clauses turn violent, which creates even more damage. This prompts the staff to go to great lengths to restore the boy's faith in Christmas.

Curb Your Enthusiasm "**Mary, Joseph and Larry**" **(2002)** - Christmas proves to be a chaotic time for the Jewish Larry David as his wife's Christian family overruns his house by putting up a tree and singing carols loudly. Larry finds himself in deep trouble when he accidentally eats a baby Jesus cookie that was meant for Christmas. Other storylines include Larry covering for his philandering friend, Jeff, and Larry accidentally double-tipping a worker at his country club.

The Office (BBC) "**Christmas Special**" **(2003)** - The original *Office* was a cultural phenomenon. Unfortunately, Stephen Merchant and Ricky Gervais only made twelve episodes, leaving many open questions about the beloved characters (David Brent, Dawn, Tim, and company). A year later, the show returned for a two-part Christmas special, answering those questions. The mockumentary still featured plenty of hilarious awkwardness but delivered one of the most satisfying conclusions to a show in television history, all at the Wernham Hogg Christmas party.

Arrested Development "**Afternoon Delight**" **(2004)** - This dysfunctional family comedy moved at such a rapid pace and with such long-running jokes that just watching this season two episode on its own would probably be a bit confusing. But the basic premise is the Bluth Company is hosting its annual Christmas party while everyone is in chaos. The incompetent Gob is running the company into the ground, Michael is worried that he's drifting apart from his son, Buster is trying to get out of military service, Lindsay is trying to cheat on her husband, and Lucille needs to unwind. It culminates with an unfortunate uncle-niece karaoke duet and an accident at the Banana Stand.

The Office (US) "**Christmas Party**" **(2005)** - The American workplace mockumentary had a great season two Christmas episode. Boss Michael Scott wants to impress everyone at the twenty-dollar-limit Secret Santa game by contributing a $400 iPod. When he receives a disappointing gift in return, he changes the rules and turns it into a Yankee Swap. This creates chaos, as everyone wants the iPod, and Jim's heartfelt gift for Pam gets lost in the shuffle.

30 Rock "**Ludachristmas**" **(2007)** - Liz Lemon's loving parents are in town for Christmas, and they show themselves to be the complete opposite of her boss Jack Donaghy's miserable mother. Liz's brother Mitch (Andy Richter) is also visiting. He had a head injury in high school and still believes he is seventeen years old. Meanwhile, Kenneth thinks the rest of the office doesn't understand the true meaning of Christmas, so he cancels their annual night of revelry ("Ludachristmas").

Modern Family "Undeck the Halls" (2009) - This family sitcom shines a light on an underrated parenting tradition—using the threat of cancelling Christmas as a cudgel on misbehaving kids.

It's Always Sunny in Philadelphia "A Very Sunny Christmas" (2009) - This degenerates-running-a-bar sitcom had a fantastic Christmas special in which Dennis and Dee try to shame their father for being a bad dad at Christmas by giving him the Ebenezer Scrooge treatment. Meanwhile, Charlie and Mac learn some uncomfortable truths about their childhood Christmases.

Community "Abed's Uncontrollable Christmas" (2010) - Abed wakes up in a Rankin/Bass-style stop-motion universe and is determined to find the true meaning of Christmas. The rest of the gang at Greendale Community College are concerned he is having a psychotic break. The unique sitcom journey teaches maybe the most important holiday lesson of all—that Christmas means something different to everyone, and that's okay.

Brooklyn Nine-Nine "Yippie Kayak" (2015) - The Andy Samberg / Andre Braugher NYPD comedy had several fun Christmas episodes. The best was this season three installment. While trying to shop for a last-minute Christmas present, Jake Peralta and the gang get trapped in a *Die Hard* hostage situation. The John McLain-idolizing detective is now tasked with saving the day while living out his fantasy.

Veep "Camp David" (2016) - The blistering, satirical show about the ugly world of politics had a hilarious Christmas episode in season five.

President Selena Meyer and her family head to Camp David for a Christmas getaway. Her real goal at the retreat is to secretly negotiate with the Chinese government. Christmas presents from her family get regifted as diplomatic offerings to foreign leaders, and brutal insults are frequently leveled at all of her staff.

Ted Lasso "Carol of the Bells" (2021) - This feel-good comedy had a great season two Christmas episode, which showed how Christmas can be celebrated in a multitude of ways. Ted and his boss deliver toys to the less fortunate, members of his soccer team gather with friends and family, and team captain Roy Kent goes on a Christmas scramble to help his niece suffering from halitosis. This episode boasts the best Christmas playlist of any television episode in history, a stop motion animation sequence, and a handful of classic Christmas movie references.

Some other solid Christmas sitcom episodes: *The Honeymooners* "'Twas the Night Before Christmas" (1955), *I Love Lucy* "The I Love Lucy Christmas Special" (1956), *Mr. Ed* "Ed's Christmas Story" (1963), *The Addams Family* "Christmas with the Addams Family" (1965), *Welcome Back, Kotter* "Hark, the Sweat Kings" (1976), *All in the Family* "The Draft Dodger" (1976), *What's Happening!!* "A Christmas Story" (1976), *The Jeffersons* "984 W. 124th St., Apt 5C" (1977), *Three's Company* "Three's Christmas" (1977), *WKRP in Cincinnati* "Jennifer's Home for Christmas" (1979), *Newhart* "No Room at the Inn" (1982), *Benson* "Mary and Her Lambs" (1982), *Night Court* "Santa Goes Downtown" (1984), *The Golden Girls* "'Twas the Nightmare Before Christmas" (1986), *It's Garry Shandling's Show* "It's Garry Shandling's Christmas Show" (1988), *Friends* "The One with Phoebe's Dad" (1995), *NewsRadio* "Xmas Story" (1996), *Just Shoot Me!* "Jesus, It's

Christmas" (1997), *The Jamie Foxx Show* "Christmas Day-Ja Vu" (1998), *Everybody Loves Raymond* "The Toaster" (1998), *Scrubs* "My Own Personal Jesus" (2001), *Extras* "The Extra Special Series Finale" (2007), *The Inbetweeners* "Xmas Party" (2008), *Parks and Recreation* "Christmas Scandal" (2009), *Broad City* "Under the Mistletoe" (2010), *Workaholics* "The Strike" (2011), *Louie* "New Year's Eve" (2012), *How I Met Your Mother* "The Final Page" (2012), *The Mindy Project* "Josh and Mindy's Christmas Party" (2012), *Schitt's Creek* "Merry Christmas, Johnny Rose" (2018), *Dave* "Bar Mitzvah" (2021)

Here are some head-scratching Christmas sitcom episodes:

Dennis the Menace **"The Christmas Story" (1959)** - Mr. Mitchell is afraid Dennis will find the wrapped presents, so he stores them at neighbor Mr. Wilson's house. Then the show tries to paint Wilson as the villain for getting cranky when Dennis torments him in search of those presents. Shame on the Mitchells for raising an awful boy. He's not some little scamp in overalls. Dennis Mitchell is a sociopath.

Laverne & Shirley **"Oh Hear the Angels' Voices" (1976)** - The Schotz Brewery odd couple and their friends are tasked with performing a Christmas show at a hospital. When they arrive, they find out it's a mental hospital, Shirley freaks out, and the audience laughs. The gang makes a handful of lame mental illness jokes (clearly the writers had just seen *Cuckoo's Nest*) and television viewers are treated to some bad singing and comedy, capped off by Big Ragu doing an unintentionally haunting song-and-dance routine to "Jingle Bell Rock."

Silver Spoons **"The Best Christmas Ever" (1982)** - The show about a boy who moves in with the filthy-rich father he never knew had a Christmas episode in its first season. Ricky discovers a homeless family lives in a cave on their property. He and his dad decide to help. They bring a few gifts to the cave, Edward Stratton hooks up the homeless dad up with a job at his factory, and they all sing "Silent Night." No invitation to join the Strattons indoors was ever on the table.

ALF **"ALF's Special Christmas" (1987)** - There will never be a worse moment in television history than "ALF's Special Christmas." The Borscht-belt-joke-spewing alien from the planet Melmac joins the Tanner family on a Christmas trip to a cabin in the woods. ALF angers everyone by opening everyone's presents and ruining the surprise. Then he sneaks into a guy's truck to open more presents (which were about to be delivered to sick kids at a hospital). Next, ALF poses as an ugly stuffed animal, makes his way inside the hospital, and befriends a dying eight-year-old girl named Tiffany. There are a handful of bad jokes accompanied by a laugh track. After overhearing a doctor say this will be Tiffany's last Christmas, ALF helps deliver a baby, then tells the mom to name her "Tiffany" (presumably, to replace the Tiffany on her way out). There's a subplot about the guy delivering toys being unable to go on without his wife (who died earlier in the month), but ALF stops him from committing suicide. When the credits roll, we learn there really was a girl named Tiffany who died. It's profoundly sad, and the funny parts aren't remotely funny.

COMEDY SHOWS

In the first few decades of television, the only Christmas comedy offerings were on sitcoms or late-night talk shows. Right before Christmas each December on *The Tonight Show*, Johnny Carson would do a Christmas sketch after his monologue and maybe read a few charming letters to Santa. But it really wasn't until *Saturday Night*

Live in 1975 that television offered truly funny Christmas-related comedy.

Here are the strongest offerings from comedy programs at Christmas:

Saturday Night Live **(1975-present)** - It would be impossible to pick a single episode or sketch to encapsulate SNL's contributions to Christmas comedy. Each December, over a dozen Christmas-related sketches are spread out over a few episodes.

Sketches include recurring characters, like Dan Aykroyd's dangerous toy manufacturer Irwin Mainway in 1976, Eddie Murphy's Mister Rogers-parody Mister Robinson, Jon Lovitz's egomaniacal Shakespearian actor Master Thespian in 1987, Chris Farley's motivational speaker Matt Foley playing Santa in 1993, and Rachel Dratch's Debbie Downer in 2005.

Other classic Christmas sketches include famous movie parodies, like when Dana Carvey recreated an even more satisfying ending to *It's a Wonderful Life* in 1986 or when Alec Baldwin put a *Glengarry Glen Ross* spin on Santa's workshop in 2005 ("Always Be Cobbling!").

SNL is constantly making song parodies. Christmas is no exception. In 1990, the cast promoted a fake Christmas album called Dysfunctional Family Christmas, with such hits like "Someday I'll Get Christmas Right," "I've Got My Drinking Under Control for the Holidays," and "Fruitcake and Shame." In 2014, the women of the cast talked about hooking up while home at their parents' during the Christmas break with "(Do It on My) Twin Bed." In 2020, Kristen Wiig sang the ballad of the forgotten moms on Christmas with "Christmas Morning" (a.k.a. "I Got a Robe").

Robert Smigel's "TV Funhouse" animated segments have made many contributions to the SNL Christmas canon. In "The Harlem Globetrotters' First Christmas," the famous basketball team plays the Three Kings to see who gets to sleep at an inn instead of in a manger. Also, Smigel did a *Charlie Brown Christmas* parody in which Linus' blanket doesn't just transform Charlie Brown's tree into something great—it also turns a broken-down vehicle into a fancy sports car and a down-and-out junkie into a younger, more attractive prostitute.

Sometimes, SNL just gets weird and funny. In 1986, Steve Martin warmly shared his "Christmas Wish" but kept adding increasingly selfish requests to it. In 1999, Will Ferrell played a guy named Mark Jensen who was trying to sing Christmas songs on a rotating stage only to be overcome with motion sickness.

The SNL Christmas episodes even had some terrific non-Gentile sketches, like when Jon Lovitz's "Hanukkah Harry" filled in for Santa in 1989 ("On Moishe, on Herschel, on Schlomo"), Adam Sandler sang his "Chanukah Song" in 1994, and Robert Smigel's "Christmas Time for the Jews" was performed by Darlene Love in 2005.

Late Night with David Letterman **"Christmas with the Lettermans" (1984)** - Before the annual Christmas visits by Darlene Love and Jay Thomas, Dave did a parody of every cheesy Christmas special, complete with a fake family, fake snow, and fake emotions. During "Christmas with the Lettermans," his staged family clearly didn't care for each other and Dave exhibited some questionable parenting. Pat Boone appeared as a guest to promote, in earnest, his cheesy upcoming Christmas special. Things got awkward.

In Living Color "Homey Claus" (1990) - Damon Wayans' surly ex-convict character, Homey D. Clown, gets a job as a mall Santa for his mandated community service.

Late Night with Conan O'Brien "Christmas Caroling" (2004) - The best of Conan's Christmas bits over the years have come when the ginger late-night host goes out into the field, whether that's checking out Christmas decorations on people's lawns or going around the office looking for gift ideas for his Secret Santa recipient. But the funniest sketch of all is when Conan joins a Victorian-era-costumed caroling group in New Jersey.

Nathan For You "Santa" (2013) - Nathan Fielder is a business advisor who advises clients of bizarre strategies to grow their businesses. In this episode, he tries to assist a mall Santa with a criminal record in getting Christmas work in the summer.

Drunk History "Drunk History Christmas Special" (2017) - The show, in which people act out the words of drunk people, focuses on three Christmas moments in history: Washington crossing the Delaware River, Charles Dickens writing *A Christmas Carol*, and Teddy Roosevelt being convinced to have a tree in the White House.

Other solid comedy Christmas episodes: *Mystery Science Theater 3000* "Santa Claus Conquers the Martians" (1991), *Chappelle's Show* "Nat King Cole Christmas" (2003), *MadTV* "Santa Gets Caught" (2008), *Tim and Eric Awesome Show, Great Job!* "Chrimbus Special" (2010), *Key & Peele* "Baby It's Cold Outside" (2012), *I Think You Should Leave* "Scrooge Encounters a Cyborg from Christmas in 3050" (2019) and "Detective Crashmore" (2021)

YULE LOG

All that Christmas programming… and yet some prefer to watch a good ol' Yule log burning on their television sets. The tradition started in 1966, when New York's WPIX (Channel 11) manager Fred Thrower wanted the station to do "something a little different and special" for Christmas. On Christmas Eve, he had his station air three hours of the view of the fireplace in the mayor's mansion on a continuous seventeen-second film loop. The log was accompanied by classic music by artists like Nat King Cole. It was a ratings hit. New York City residents didn't have fireplaces. This was the next best thing.

The log burned every Christmas Eve for the next twenty-three years. Network executives pulled the plug in 1990, saying the three hours of commercial-free programming was a bad business move. People were livid. "Bring Back the Log" petitions circulated and soon, the log was back… for four hours! By 2003, the log was broadcast nationwide. The idea has since been copycatted by giants like Netflix and YouTube, but the original idea is still going strong on Channel 11.

DICKENS

There have been many prolific authors over the years who have had their writing adapted to film and television—Stephen King, Jules Verne, Ian Fleming, and Robert Louis Stevenson, to name a few. Some have had the same story adapted multiple times (William Shakespeare's *Romeo and Juliet*, Jane Austen's *Emma*). And then there's Charles Dickens' *A Christmas Carol*. Seemingly every year there's at least a few new adaptations of the story about a nasty miser who gets visited by three ghosts on Christmas Eve. And the reason why the 1843 novella still resonates today is because it's nearly perfect.

Charles Dickens' story of redemption may be timeless, but it was very much influenced by Victorian London in "the Hungry '40s." In the spring of 1843, the famous author attended a fundraising dinner with a bunch of rich guys. Despite the fact that they were at a charity function, Dickens found the men distastefully self-indulgent. In a letter to a friend, he called them "sleek, slobbering, bow-paunched, overfed, apoplectic, snorting cattle."

Around the same time, one of Dickens' friends had just written a pretty comprehensive government report on child labor. The results were grim. Kids were working at factories up to sixteen hours a day, six days a week. At night, they were sleeping above the factory floors. Victorian London had seen an explosion in population and manufacturing, and the divide between rich and poor grew. There were no labor laws to speak of, so the bottom rung of society (poor kids) were treated the worst.

It was easier for the "haves" to believe that their own successes were completely earned and that "have-nots" were unscrupulous or lazy and needed to be taught proper work ethic in workhouses.

Well, Charles Dickens knew that the whole system was both rigged and immoral. When Charles was twelve, his father John Dickens fell on hard times and was sent to Marshalsea debtors' prison. Charles was forced to work at Warren's Blacking, a boot polish factory. When John was eventually released from the prison, he pulled Charles from the factory and sent him back to school. But those traumatic few months stayed with Charles Dickens the rest of his life. So, when he read that government report on children working in factories, the now-famous author set out to write a pamphlet for the privileged to read. He planned to call it "An Appeal to the People of England on behalf of the Poor Man's Child."

He realized that to make a bigger impact, he needed to use his talents to make his point in a more clever way. For his protagonist, Ebenezer Scrooge, he created a hard-working, miserly rich man whose selfishness and disdain for others has placed him at a crossroads. While legend has it that the name itself was inspired by a tombstone epitaph he saw in Edinburgh a couple of years earlier ("Ebenezer Lennox Scroogie — MEAN MAN (1792-1836)"), the most likely inspiration for the character was former member of Parliament John Elwes. Born John Meggot in 1714, he changed his name at an early age to match his uncle's, so he could inherit his fortune. Elwes' stinginess was so legendary (restricted use of light in his home to save money on candles, barely ate to save money on food, resisted paying for doctor's services when he was injured, took the long way on trips to avoid turnpike tolls, and so on), a famous book was written about him by Edward Topham after his death in 1789. When he died, his estate was worth £500,000 (about $80 million today).

As a contrast to Scrooge, Dickens wrote a hard-working poor person who has no chance at upward mobility (Bob Cratchit). He based Tiny Tim on his crippled nephew Harry Burnett, who died from tuberculosis at age nine. He sprinkled in ghosts, which were common in Christmas tales at the time. On December 2, just six weeks after starting, *A Christmas Carol* was completed. (Side note: In 2017, a fun movie starring Dan Stevens and Christopher Plummer detailed those frantic six weeks—*The Man Who Invented Christmas*.)

Dickens' publishers were not impressed and therefore weren't interested in committing to a big rollout. The author ended up covering most of the costs and barely broke even during the first printing. Luckily, demand for *A Christmas Carol* was immediate. *A Christmas Carol* was published on December 19, 1843 and all six thousand copies were sold by Christmas Eve. Two subsequent printings sold out by New Year's Eve.

The novella's cultural impact was also quite swift. In a review for *Fraser's Magazine*, novelist William Thackeray said, "It seems to me a national benefit, and to every man or woman who reads it a personal kindness." Charitable giving around the holidays spiked and has done so ever since.

A Christmas Carol represents what is truly great about Christmas: kindness, generosity, and an appreciation for life. Ever since the winter solstice celebrations of thousands of years ago, humans have been using this time to take a step back from their day-to-day activities, gather with loved ones, and celebrate what truly matters—each other. Ebenezer Scrooge represents the people who have lost their way, those who have overlooked the importance of the Golden Rule, and gives them a chance at redemption. It's never too late to change and become our best selves.

Thanks to its timeless themes, rarely a year has gone by without some sort of movie or television adaptation. Not all of them are perfect (although most are decent), but they will keep re-making *A Christmas Carol* until the end of time. Here are, arguably, the top hundred so far:

1. *Scrooge* **(1951)** - Alastair Sim's portrayal of Scrooge is widely considered the best, and for good reason. Scrooge is miserable, we all know that part, but this film captures the truly terrible moments that shaped his life (the death of his sister, his awful behavior upon Marley's death). His giddiness in the final act is the payoff we want to see.

2. *Scrooged* (1988) - Although derided for being "mean" and "uneven" by critics, this is easily the best alternative version of *A Christmas Carol* (and possibly the best of all). America in the 1980s was plagued by lots of the same issues as Victorian England. The divide between rich and poor was growing. Consumerism had engulfed society. A win-at-all-costs mentality began to prevail at the corporate level. Michael Douglas had just won an Oscar for his realistic portrayal of a vicious corporate executive ("Greed is good"). Bill Murray's Frank Cross was the perfect '80s Scrooge. And he was hilarious in the process.

3. *The Muppet Christmas Carol* (1992) - Michael Caine does a great Scrooge (by playing it perfectly straight as if he's acting with other humans), and the Muppets are perfectly cast in the right spots.

4. *Disney's A Christmas Carol* (2009) - Robert Zemeckis' CGI retelling of the story feels like he sampled the best versions over the years and put them all into this visually stunning version. Jim Carrey does a great Scrooge (kind of an Alastair Sim impression) as well as the ghosts. Since it was all CGI, Zemeckis had the freedom to recreate Victorian London and take creative chances that would be impossible with a regular production (Fezziwig's Party, Ghost of Christmas Future).

5. *BBC/FX's A Christmas Carol* (2019) - By far the darkest portrayal of all of the versions, Guy Pearce takes Scrooge's awful behavior to a new level in this mini-series. Given more time to tell the story, creator Steven Knight is able to flesh out the novella and go in directions that would have gotten Charles Dickens banned in the nineteenth century. This version will haunt you (and make you question how much

redemption a guy deserves) but also makes you care for the people around Scrooge significantly more.

6. *It's Always Sunny in Philadelphia* "A Very Sunny Christmas" (2010) - Frank Reynolds (Danny DeVito) is a terrible father, so his children try to show him the error of his ways by dressing up his old business partner as a ghost, sewing him into the couch so he can overhear the present, and then taking him to a graveyard.

7. *A Christmas Carol* (1999) - Patrick Stewart and Richard Grant excel in this traditional portrayal.

8. *The Simpsons* "'Tis the Fifteenth Season" (2003) - Homer acts super selfishly and then falls asleep while watching *Mr. McGrew's Christmas Carol* (parody of Mister Magoo). He wakes up the least selfish man in Springfield, which annoys his do-gooder neighbor Ned Flanders. Homer then has an epiphany about Christmas without consumerism, turns into the Grinch, and steals everyone's gifts.

9. *Scrooge* (1935) - Seymour Hicks plays an excellent Ebenezer. A weird "God Save the Queen" part in the middle is a little unsettling.

10. *Bugs Bunny's Christmas Carol* (1979) - In seven minutes, a ghost Bugs Bunny tortures Yosemite Sam as Scrooge enough that he gives away all his money.

11. *A Christmas Carol* (1984) – This one would be higher on the list if not for George C. Scott's pretty gross phlegmy smoker's cough and the jarring appearance of the Ghost of Christmas Past (who looks like she just pulled an all-nighter at Studio 54).

12. *Beavis and Butt-Head* "Huh-Huh-Humbug" (1995) - Beavis falls asleep while cooking a rat on the grill at Burger World and dreams he is the boss. Ghosts interrupt him from watching a Scrooge-themed adult film, but he learns no lessons.

13. *Saturday Night Live* **"Bankrupt Scrooge" (1988)** - Danny DeVito plays Scrooge a year after his fateful night. He's now broke from being so generous. "I've really taken it in the pants, financially."

14. *A Christmas Carol* **(1938)** - Reginald Owen's Scrooge is crusty… and possibly an extreme hoarder. Lots of newspapers are stacked up.

15. *Family Ties* **"A Keaton Christmas Carol" (1983)** - Michael J. Fox's Alex gets visited by the Ghosts of Past and Future (played by his sisters on the show).

16. *I Think You Should Leave* **"Scrooge Encounters A Cyborg From Christmas In 3050" (2019)** - After encountering all three ghosts, Ebenezer Scrooge is visited by the "Ghost of Christmas Way Future" and is forced to fight off attacking skeletons with his cane.

17. *Quantum Leap* **"A Little Miracle" (1990)** - Sam leaps into a Scrooge-like industrialist who is trying to shut down a Salvation Army. Sam then plays the role of the ghosts to guilt him.

18. *Sanford and Son* **"Ebenezer" (1975)** - Redd Foxx's Sanford gets visited by ghosts, then delivers a pretty cool, bluesy "Christmas Song."

19. *The Stingiest Man in Town* **(1978)** - Rankin/Bass does a solid animated version starring Walter Matthau and Tom Bosley.

20. *Mickey's Christmas Carol* **(1983)** - This version gave birth to the greatest Disney animated character of all—Scrooge McDuck.

21. *Bewitched* **"Humbug Not Spoken Here" (1967)** - Samantha uses her powers to be the "Spirit of Christmas" for her husband's Scrooge-like client (played by Charles Lane, the gold standard of cranky sitcom foils in the 1960s).

22. *Saturday Night Live* **"Scrudge" (2017)** - Old Scrooge lives in present day with a roommate and treats everyone like garbage.

23. *Scrooge* **(1970)** - Albert Finney plays a great Ebenezer in a musical with a hit-or-miss soundtrack. Only issue is he could've used some acting help with playing drunk. One sip and he acted like Mel Gibson at Moonshadows.

24. *The Real Ghostbusters* **"X-Mas Marks the Spot" (1986)** - The Ghostbusters enter a portal that takes them to Victorian England. They bust the ghosts that were meant to scare Scrooge into kindness and, in the process, destroy future Christmases. So they pose as ghosts and haunt Ebenezer on their own.

25. *WKRP in Cincinnati* **"Bah Humbug" (1980)** - Mr. Carlson eats one of Johnny Fever's special brownies, then dreams of three ghosts who convince him to be more generous with the staff.

26. *Be Cool, Scooby-Doo!* **"Scroogey Doo" (2017)** - The gang travels back to 1843 London and runs into a scared Scrooge who has encountered a ghost. Meanwhile, Velma realizes that the ghosts are meant for her as she questions her association with Mystery, Inc.

27. *Family Guy* **"Don't Be a Dickens at Christmas" (2017)** - The Ghost of Patrick Swayze takes Peter on a journey around Quahog and shows him the Christmas spirit.

28. *Back to the Future: The Animated Series* **"A Dickens of a Christmas" (1991)** - A pickpocket steals the keys to the DeLorean in nineteenth-century London. Meanwhile, Marty McFly pretends to be the Ghost of Christmas to scare Ebiffnezer Tannen from foreclosing on a toy store.

29. *A Christmas Carol: A Thomas Edison Production* **(1910)** - This silent film amazingly covered it all (Scrooge's boarding school, Fezziwig, redemption) in just ten minutes.

30. *Ebbie* **(1995)** - Soap Opera legend Susan Lucci does an impressive job as a ruthless businesswoman visited by ghosts.

31. *A Flintstone Christmas Carol* **(1994)** - Fred gets the lead in a community theater production of *A Christmas Carol*, while also being a selfish jerk in real life. He gets let off the hook pretty easy.

32. *Aqua Teen Hunger Force* **"Cybernetic Ghost of Christmas Past from the Future" (2002)** - This bizarre Adult Swim version features Christmas ghosts showing forced carpet-eating, robots, and a swimming pool full of blood.

33. *The Six Million Dollar Man* **"A Bionic Christmas" (1976)** - Lee Majors' Steve Austin uses his powers to scare a Scrooge-ish industrialist played by Ray Walston.

34. *A Christmas Carol: The Musical* **(2004)** - Kelsey Grammer, Jesse Martin, and Jason Alexander do a pretty solid job in this well-produced TV movie musical.

35. *Blackadder* **"Blackadder's Christmas Carol" (1988)** - Rowan Atkinson's revisionist history British sitcom uses the ghosts to teach the main character being nice is a bad thing and Tiny Tim is super annoying.

36. *A Carol for Another Christmas* **(1964)** - This TV movie written by Rod Serling uses the Dickens framework to speak out about war.

Written right as the Cold War and Vietnam were ramping up, Sterling Hayden (Captain McCluskey in *The Godfather)* leads an impressive cast (Peter Sellers, Robert Shaw, Eva Marie Saint, Ben Gazzara) in a heavy-handed yet thought-provoking version.

37. *A Sesame Street Carol* **(2006)** - Obviously, Oscar is the natural fit for Scrooge and this special uses some *Sesame Street* greatest Christmas hits, but… to paraphrase the words of Dave Chappelle, HE LIVES IN A TRASH CAN! Of course he's grouchy!

38. *Saturday Night Live* **"Christmas Past" (2013)** - The Ghost of Christmas Past takes Scrooge back to Fezziwig's party and he realizes his love life didn't work out because he is actually gay.

39. *Animaniacs* **"A Christmas Plotz" (1993)** - The Warners haunt the CEO as three ghosts for firing a security guard on Christmas Eve.

40. *Ms. Scrooge* **(1997)** - A quality rendition that brings race and gender into the story is somewhat undercut by Cicely Tyson's confusing decision to do the role in an Edward G. Robinson voice.

41. *Peter Pan and the Pirates* **"Hook's Christmas" (1991)** - Unlike the normal Captain Hook, this version looks like a jacked Johann Sebastian Bach. Ghosts convince Hook to believe in celebrating Christmas… and to be an even nastier villain in the future.

42. *The Odd Couple* **"Scrooge Gets an Oscar" (1970)** - Oscar's poker buddies haunt him after he refuses to play Scrooge in a local play and kicks Felix out of the apartment.

43. *The Looney Tunes Show* **"A Christmas Carol" (2012)** - It's 104 degrees outside and Bugs isn't feeling Christmas. So Lola Bunny puts on *A Christmas Carol* production to get the town into the spirit.

44. *Northern Exposure* **"Shofar So Good" (1994)** - A clever take on *A Christmas Carol* has a visiting rabbi showing Joel Yom Kippur past, present, and future.

45. *Robot Chicken* **"Scrooge's Lesson" (2013)** - Scrooge bursts out of his home on Christmas morning screaming about how ghosts are real.

46. *General Hospital* **"General Hospital's Christmas Carol" (2019)** - In a surprising stand-alone episode, Finn learns about the spirit of Christmas in a solid, straightforward telling of the story.

47. *Melrose Place* **"Holiday on Ice" (1994)** - Amanda (Heather Locklear) has nightmares about the awful way she has treated people in the past and how it affects her future.

48. *The Venture Bros.* **"A Very Venture Christmas" (2004)** - This Adult Swim cartoon pokes fun at all of the Christmas special tropes, including *A Christmas Carol's* gravestone scene and giddy Christmas morning, a heart growing two sizes too big like the Grinch, a glowing nose like Rudolph, and a crazed run through town yelling "Merry Christmas" like George Bailey.

49. *Martin* **"Scrooge" (1996)** - Martin buys himself Jordans and everyone else nonsense, then is visited by three ghosts and, randomly, Jackie Chan.

50. *Ebenezer* **(1998)** - Jack Palance plays a crusty Old West version of Scrooge. His teeth whitening took a bit of realism out of the setting.

51. *Camp Candy* **"Christmas in July" (1990)** - In the late '80s, everyone loved John Candy and wanted him in more projects. This manifested into a Saturday morning cartoon where Candy plays the leader of a summer camp. His meanest camper rejects his "Christmas in July" idea, eats bad chocolate, and then gets visited by spirits.

52. *DuckTales* **"Last Christmas" (2018)** - This is kind of a follow-up to *Mickey's Christmas Carol,* in that Scrooge McDuck is now friends with the ghosts. Also, his nephew Dewey is hanging out with the younger version of his deceased mother.

53. *An American Christmas Carol* **(1979)** - Henry Winkler ("the Fonz") stars as a Scrooge-like Benedict Spade (cool name!) in an adaptation set in Depression-era New Hampshire. He does a solid job, but the old man makeup is one of the worst in history (worse than *J. Edgar*).

54. *Mister Magoo's Christmas Carol* **(1962)** - This is the first-ever animated Christmas special. The near-sighted titular character stars in *A Christmas Carol* production on Broadway.

55. *Dr. Quinn, Medicine Woman* **"Mike's Dream: A Christmas Tale" (1993)** - Jane Seymour's character struggles with being a doctor during a stressful Christmas (which involves a baby being born in a manger). Her ghosts set her straight.

56. *The Smurfs: A Christmas Carol* **(2011)** - Grouchy Smurf gets what's coming to him.

57. *Christmas Carol: The Movie* **(2001)** - A pretty impressive cast (Simon Callow, Kate Winslet, and Nicholas Cage) leads a relatively straightforward telling of Dickens' tale. The animation is a bit drab (like *Watership Down*).

58. *A Christmas Carol* **(1971)** - This hand-drawn animated rendition features the great Alastair Sim reprising his role.

59. *It's Christmas, Carol!* (2012) - Carrie Fisher plays Eve, the boss of a heartless executive who has lost her way. A few *Star Wars* references are made throughout the movie.

60. *Mr. Belvedere* "A Happy Guy's Christmas" (1989) - Mr. Belvedere, the snobby, persnickety live-in butler for a middle-class Pittsburgh family, gets the ghost treatment. The backdrop is a community theater production where the Owens family gets all the parts.

61. *A Different World* "For Whom the Bell Tolls" (1989) – After Whitley is mean, she is shown her actions. Then, at a festive party, revelers sing about M.C. Hammer.

62. *The Dukes of Hazzard* "The Great Santa Claus Chase" (1980) - Boss Hogg steals a Christmas tree shipment, and later the Dukes pretend to be spirits feeding him messages over the CB while he sleeps. Boss reads Dickens, then joins them at a party.

63. *The Chipmunks* "Merry Christmas, Mr. Carroll" (1989) - Alvin is a selfish paperboy.

64. *Las Vegas* "A Cannon Carol" (2007) - The nerdy casino concierge is a bit Scrooge-ish, then gets knocked out. Ghosts remind him he's boring.

65. *American Dad* "The Best Story Never Told" (2006) - The main character of this Seth McFarland cartoon uses the Ghost of Christmas Past to go back to 1970 to try to kill anti-war protester Jane Fonda. It ruins America.

66. *Jake and the Neverland Pirates* "Captain Scrooge" (2015) - Pirate Captain Hook gets the little kids' *Christmas Carol* treatment.

67. *The Adventures of Ozzie and Harriet* "The Busy Christmas" **(1956)** - Ozzie, the dad, is so consumed with his starring role in the local theater production of *A Christmas Carol* that he ignores Christmas at his house.

68. *The Dukes* "A Dickens of a Christmas" **(1983)** - People couldn't get enough of the CBS action-comedy show that it was turned into a Saturday morning cartoon. Boss Hogg is Scrooge and the General Lee (the protagonist's Confederate Flag-topped car!) was turned into a garbage truck.

69. *Highway to Heaven* "Another Christmas" **(1984)** - Michael Landon haunts a used car dealer, seemingly, as both the Ghost of Exposition and the Ghost of Guilt-Trip Present.

70. *Sabrina: The Animated Series* "A Witchmas Carol" **(1998)** - Sabrina's rival, Gem, is mean, so she and her friends pretend to be ghosts. Gem is still mean afterward.

71. *The Spooktacular Adventures of Casper* "A Christmas Peril" **(1990)** - Dickens' story told from the ghosts' perspective.

72. *A Dennis the Menace Christmas* **(2007)** - Mr. Wilson gets visited by ghosts so he can feel bad about being mean to Dennis, but the real villains are Dennis the Menace's parents. Why won't they hold him accountable for being a monster?

73. *Doctor Who* "A Christmas Carol" **(2010)** - A time-traveling alien is visited by holograms… and a sky full of fish.

74. *Xena: Warrior Princess* "A Solstice Carol" **(1996)** - Xena (kind of a dollar-store Wonder Woman) uses her powers to pretend to be ghosts that haunt a king with a terrible orphan policy.

75. *Dolly Parton's Christmas on the Square* **(2020)** - Dolly Parton plays a cheery ghost who keeps popping up around town and haunts the town villain. Christine Baranski's acting and Dolly's singing rescue a pretty corny version.

76. *Star Trek: The Next Generation* **"Devil's Due" (1991)** - Data, an AI character, shows his learning of human customs by performing a Scrooge monologue scene for Captain Picard.

77. *A Jetson Christmas Carol* **(1985)** - George's boss, Mr. Spacely, gets visited by some lazy ghosts after being so stingy. Aside from Jane, this show is pretty light on likable characters.

78. *A Christmas Carol* **(1982)** - This animated Australian version makes the ghost of Jacob Marley look like a member of the band KISS.

79. *Christmas Cupid* **(2010)** - The USA Network took a shot at a Hallmark-type version of *A Christmas Carol*. It's essentially beautiful people interacting without adding a ton to the story.

80. *Fame* **"Ebenezer Morloch" (1985)** - The show about a fine arts high school focuses this episode on Vice Principal Morloch. The ghosts might redeem him for one episode. The highlight of the episode was Debbie Allen doing a beautiful rendition of "Have Yourself a Merry Little Christmas."

81. *The Alcoa Hour* **"The Stingiest Man in Town" (1956)** - Famous Sherlock Holmes actor Basil Rathbone stars in this shaky musical version. Rathbone is decent. The musical part isn't.

82. *Shower of Stars* **"A Christmas Carol" (1954)** - Yet another live-action musical from the early days of television. Scenes are interrupted for six- and seven-minute-long vibrato-laden songs which don't move the story forward. Even Tiny Tim, who is dying of tuberculosis, has the energy to belt out opera-styled singing while putting the star on the Cratchit tree.

83. *Rich Little's Christmas Carol* **(1979)** - Rich Little was a talented impersonator. Unfortunately, there is a short shelf life for most impressions. Therefore, this traditional telling of the story just seems tedious. W.C. Fields, Richard Nixon, Edith Bunker, John Wayne, Walter Matthau, Paul Lynde, Johnny Carson, Stan Laurel, Oliver Hardy, Columbo, and George Burns were all parodied.

84. *Alice* **"Mel's Christmas Carol" (1981)** - Mel, the soul-crushing owner of the diner where Alice works, is so stingy that everyone quits. Sadly, Flo already departed the show a year earlier. "This episode can kiss my grits!"

85. *101 Dalmatians: The Series* **"Christmas Cruella" (1997)** - The Ghost of Christmas Past reminds Cruella de Vil that she is a psychopath because she had absentee parents.

86. Smallville "Lexmas" (2005) - The show about the origin story of Superman focuses mostly on his nemesis, Lex Luthor. Lex gets shot, then is visited by the ghost of his mother. The only super thing Clark Kent does is run fast for two seconds.

87. *Barbie in A Christmas Carol* **(2008)** - A mean Barbie doll named Eden Starling gets haunted by ghosts.

88. *Dora the Explorer* **"Dora's Christmas Carol Adventure" (2009)** - Dora helps the show's resident kleptomaniac, Swiper, visit the past and future to get back on Santa's good side.

89. *The New Scooby-Doo Mysteries* "The Nutcracker Scoob" (1984) - The Ghost of Christmas Never haunted a Christmas pageant. Way too much Scrappy-Doo in this episode.

90. *DIC's A Christmas Carol* (1997) - Tim Curry, Whoopi Goldberg, Michael York, and Ed Asner star in this uninspiring version.

91. *Thomas and Friends* "Diesel's Ghostly Christmas Tale" (2015) - This is one of the more cruel versions. Everyone gives Diesel the train a hard time for being outdated, and yet *he's* the bad guy who has to redeem himself?

92. *One Life to Live* "Asa's Christmas Carol" (1989) - The industrialist patriarch of the Buchanan family does a lot of yelling when forced to confront his past, present, and future.

93. *The Young and the Restless* "Victor's Christmas Carol" (2015) - Victor and his mustache are forced to confront some of his dead ex-wives.

94. *The Suite Life on Deck* "A London Carol" (2010) - This broad Nickelodeon comedy forces a girl named London to look in a mirror and face her past, present, and future. Also, one of the main characters creates an elaborate robot to fill in for him at the juice bar.

95. *The Christmas Carol* (1949) - This version narrated by Vincent Price feels like a bad sixth-grade production.

96. *A Carol Christmas* (2008) - Tori Spelling plays a mean talk show host who gets visited by ghosts played by William Shatner and Gary Coleman. No.

97. *Gumby* "Scrooge Loose" (1957) - Scrooge steps out of Dickens' book, says "humbug" about 3,500 times, and then steals a bag of

Santa's toys. Gumby, wearing a Sherlock Holmes hat for no apparent reason, lassos him.

98. *EastEnders* "A Christmas Carol" (2011) - Scrooge and housekeeper are seemingly woken by the Ghost of Bad Acting Christmas Past.

99. *Annoying Orange* "Orange Carol" (2012) - The sole purpose of this children's show is to be annoying. Mission accomplished.

100. *An American Carol* (2008) - *Airplane!* writer David Zucker made a *Christmas Carol*-style, pro-Iraq War movie where ghosts visit a Michael Moore parody (played by Chris Farley's brother), showing him that opposing war is un-American and evil. *An American Carol* starred Kelsey Grammer, Jon Voight, Kevin Sorbo, James Woods, and Bill O'Reilly. While the overly dramatic Moore isn't impervious to parody, defending the Iraq War was probably not the best hill to die on.

OTHER STUFF THAT HAPPENED ON CHRISTMAS

With Christmas hogging all of the December 25 attention, it would be remiss not to acknowledge these major events and milestones on this day.

DECEMBER 25 BIRTHS

Here are some influential humans not named Jesus who had a Christmas birthday:

- Isaac Newton (1642) - Astronomer and mathematician. (They used the Julian calendar back then. Today, his birthday would be January 4.)
- Clara Barton (1821) - Nurse and founder of the American Red Cross.
- Helena Rubenstein (1870) - Cosmetics mogul and philanthropist.
- Muhammad Ali Jinnah (1876) - Founder of Pakistan.
- Humphrey Bogart (1899) - Actor from *Casablanca* and *The Maltese Falcon*.
- Cab Calloway (1907) - Singer and bandleader. Called the Cotton Club home during the Harlem Renaissance.
- Anwar Sadat (1918) - Egyptian president and 1978 Nobel Peace Prize winner.
- Rod Serling (1924) - Television pioneer and creator of *The Twilight Zone*.
- Nellie Fox (1927) - Hall of Fame Chicago White Sox second baseman. Fifteen-time all-star.
- Kenny "the Snake" Stabler (1945) - Hall of Fame Oakland Raiders quarterback.
- Larry Csonka (1946) - Hall of Fame Miami Dolphin running back. Was a star on the NFL's only undefeated team in history.
- Jimmy Buffett (1946) - Musician and philanthropist. Famous for the song "Margaritaville."
- Barbara Mandrell (1948) - Country music star and variety show host.
- Sissy Spacek (1949) - Academy Award-winning actress (*Coal Miner's Daughter*).

- Annie Lennox (1954) - Singer-songwriter ("Sweet Dreams (Are Made of This)") and philanthropist.
- Joaquin "El Chapo" Guzman (1954) - Influential in a bad way. One of the most violent drug traffickers in history.
- Ricky Henderson (1958) - Greatest leadoff hitter in Major League Baseball history and the stolen base king.
- Shane MacGowan (1957) - Lead singer of Celtic punk band the Pogues. Sings a great Christmas song, "Fairytale of New York."
- Florian O'Malley Armstrong, a.k.a. Dido (1971) - English singer-songwriter ("Thank You").

DECEMBER 25 DEATHS

Some major figures passed away on Christmas, including:

- W.C. Fields (1946) - Comedic actor. Hated working with kids and dogs.
- Charlie Chaplin (1977) - Comedic actor. Created United Artists and is considered one of the major figures in motion picture history.
- Billy Martin (1989) - New York Yankee second baseman and manager.
- Dean Martin, a.k.a. "The King of Cool" (1995) - Singer, actor, comedian, and "Rat Pack" member.
- James Brown, a.k.a. "The Godfather of Soul" (2006) - Singer, songwriter, dancer, and activist.
- Eartha Kitt (2008) - Singer, dancer, and activist.
- George Michael (2016) - English singer-songwriter.
- K.C. Jones (2020) - Boston Celtic guard and head coach.

DECEMBER 25 WORLD LEADERS

Christmas has been used as a day to crown leaders:

— Charles the Great, a.k.a. Charlemagne (AD 800) - Founder of the Holy Roman Empire and killer of pretty much anyone who wasn't Christian.
— Henry III (1046) - Very strict Roman emperor. Sometimes called "the Black" or "the Pious."
— William the Conqueror (1066) - Norman king of England who was known for, believe it or not, conquering. Violently put down uprisings by the English to kick out their French overlord.
— Hirohito (1926) - Japanese emperor. Oversaw a brutal invasion of China and the attack on Pearl Harbor.

A couple of world leaders saw their exit on Christmas Day:

— Romanian dictator Nicolae Ceausescu's thirty-four year reign of terror came to an end by way of firing squad. (1989)
— Mikhail Gorbachev stepped down as leader of the Soviet Union. (1991)

DECEMBER 25 IN AMERICAN HISTORY

— General George Washington used the holiday as the perfect time to attack fourteen hundred unsuspecting troops in Trenton, New Jersey. Washington crossing the Delaware River is one of the most famous paintings in American history. (1776)
— America and Britain ended the War of 1812 at the Treaty of Ghent. (1814) *Christmas Eve

DECEMBER 25 FIRSTS

— Jupiter Hammon became the first black published artist in American history with her poem "An Evening Thought." (1760)
— Kentucky doctor Ephraim McDowell performed the first-ever ovarian tumor surgery. His forty-five-year-old patient lived another thirty-three years. (1809)
— Seventeen-year-old Richard Starkey got his first drum set. Five years later, Ringo Starr was playing drums for the Beatles. (1957)

DECEMBER 25 UNFORTUNATE ANNIVERSARIES

Christmas Day has sadly sometimes been a day of loss.

Natural disasters have caused catastrophe on Christmas:

— Flooding hit the coastlines of the Netherlands, Germany, and Scandinavia, killing fourteen thousand people. (1717)
— A cyclone hit the town of Darwin, Australia, killing seventy-one, destroying 80 percent of the homes, and leaving forty-one thousand people homeless. (1917)
— A flash flood washed away a bridge minutes before a train rolled through in New Zealand. The train plunged into the Whangaehu River and 151 people died. (1951)
— An earthquake hit Bam, Iran, killing over twenty-six thousand and leaving more than one hundred thousand homeless. (2003)

— A tsunami with the power of twenty-three thousand atomic bombs crushed Indonesian and Thai cities, leaving 230,000 dead or missing. (2004)

Christmas tragedy isn't just about Mother Nature. Humans have caused plenty of Yuletide misery:

— A group of dejected racist Confederate veterans didn't like how the South was forced to incorporate Northern policies, so they formed a secret club of losers called the Ku Klux Klan. (1865)
— A race war erupted in Mayfield, Kentucky after a black man was lynched. (1898)
— Hundreds of striking mine workers were celebrating a Christmas Eve dinner with their families at Italian Hall in Calumet, Michigan when someone yelled, "FIRE!" A stampede for the exits left seventy-three dead. Fifty-nine of them were children. (1913)

DECEMBER 25 SPORTS

Christmas (and Boxing Day in the UK) is big for sports. The NBA (basketball), NFL (football), NHL (hockey), and the English Premier League (soccer) have all had standout moments:

— The California Golden Seals defeated the Los Angeles Kings 3–1 in the final NHL game on Christmas. (1971)
— The Miami Dolphins defeated the Kansas City Chiefs in double overtime 27–24 in the longest game in NFL history. (1971)
— New York Knicks Hall of Famer Bernard King scored sixty points against the New Jersey Nets. (1984)

— Arsenal legend Thierry Henry scored a hat trick and had two assists as Arsenal defeated Leicester City 6–1. (2000)
— Title-winning Los Angeles Laker teammates Shaquille O'Neal and Kobe Bryant faced each other for the first time. Shaq's Miami Heat defeated the Lakers despite Kobe's forty-two points. (2004)

DECEMBER 25 MOVIES

Many major films have premiered on Christmas Day. Here are a few of the best:

— *To Kill a Mockingbird* (1962) - Gregory Peck won an Oscar for his performance as Atticus Finch and Horton Foote won one as well for his screenplay adaptation of Harper Lee's story.
— *The Sting* (1971) - Director George Roy Hill reunited with actors Paul Newman and Robert Redford in this movie about lovable conmen. The film won seven Academy Awards, including Best Picture and Best Director.
— *Catch Me If You Can* (2002) - Steven Spielberg directed Leonardo DiCaprio as a charming con artist and Tom Hanks as the determined FBI agent who is chasing him.
— *Django Unchained* (2012) - The most successful of Quentin Tarantino's Christmas Day releases was this revisionist Western starring Jamie Foxx. Tarantino won the Academy Award for Best Screenplay and Christoph Waltz won for Best Supporting Actor.

FINAL THOUGHTS

Mark Twain once wrote, "Explaining humor is a lot like dissecting a frog. You learn a lot in the process, but in the end you kill it." As I found myself writing about the 1987 *ALF* Christmas special in the middle of April, I feared I may be doing the same to Christmas. But, upon further reflection, I realized that the unfunny Reagan-era sitcom is a perfect reason why this holiday is great. Christmas has evolved from very specific celebrations to a cultural phenomenon that permeates an entire season each year around the globe.

Thanks to its myriad of roots, rarely does Christmas mean the same thing to two people. Much like the United States itself, American Christmases tend to be a hodgepodge of traditions from different cultures: Christmas tree from Germany, mistletoe from Norse folklore, Santa Claus from the Dutch (but also from Turkey), modern Christmas music from a Jewish immigrant (Irving Berlin), and so on. Naturally, no two families have the exact same traditions. Christmas is special to so many Americans—just in a variety of ways.

Christmas, at its core, is about love. It's about taking stock in who or what you love. It's about showing appreciation for the people you love. It's about giving and generosity of spirit. It's about loving yourself and being the best person you hope to be. Or it's about stepping back from your ordinary schedule and doing something that you love, whether it's hugging your grandma or watching six straight hours of pro basketball.

The goal of this book was to give some explanation about why we celebrate the way we do, tap into the nostalgia that this season so heavily relies upon, and point out a few new great things that might enhance future Yuletide celebrations. New songs, movies, and traditions will emerge, old customs will evolve, but the message of this book will remain the same—embrace it all!

Merry Christmas!

ACKNOWLEDGEMENTS

Thanks to my Jewish wife, who encouraged me to write this book.

Thanks to my boys, who have given me the opportunity to relive the joy of childhood Christmas. Also, sorry for letting you watch *Die Hard* at way too young of an age.

Thanks to my sisters, with whom I have had many, many great Christmas memories (except for suffering through Mannheim Steamroller).

Thanks to my childhood, college, and adult friends. Many of my fondest Christmas memories have involved friends (comparing gifts on the phone every Christmas morning with my friend Charles, going to the movies after family stuff with my friend Jake, my buddy Dan playing "Blue Christmas" on repeat until my weirdo freshman year roommate left, annual Christmas drinks at Rolf's, Old Town, and Pete's Tavern with Saro and Jill, and so many more terrific memories with great friends). As corny as it seems, Clarence was right when he wrote in George Bailey's book, "Remember no man is a failure who has friends."

Thanks to my friend, Sally, who made me promise I would publicly thank her for answering a few questions about British Christmas.

Thanks to Santana Moss, whose three touchdowns on Christmas Eve in 2005 against the Giants were a delightful early gift. Santana Claus delivered.

Thanks to the great Juan Dixon.

RANDOM TV NOTES

As discussed earlier, television shows tend to cling to a few familiar tropes at Christmastime. Here are the specific episodes in which they appear:

Cop shows where pregnant women need to be helped like the Virgin Mary on Christmas Eve:
Daniel Boone "A Christmas Story" in 1965, *Spencer for Hire* "The Hopes and Fears" in 1986, *Jake and the Fat Man* "What Child Is This?" in 1989, *JAG* "All Ye Faithful" in 2002, *NCIS* "Newborn King" in 2011

Cops shows where orphans are saved:
The Untouchables "The Night They Shot Santa Claus" in 1962, *Branded* "A Proud Town" in 1965, *Gunsmoke* "P.S. Murray Christmas" in 1971, *Starsky & Hutch* "Little Girl Lost" in 1976, *The Fall Guy* "Escape Claus" in 1985, *21 Jump Street* "Christmas in Saigon" in 1987, *Matlock* "The Scrooge" in 1989, *The Wire* "Final Grades" in 2006

Cop shows reuniting children with their parents:
Highway Patrol "Christmas Story" in 1956, *Have Gun - Will Travel* "The Hanging Cross" in 1957, *The Mod Squad* "Kristie" in 1972, *Vega$* "Christmas Story" in 1980, *Knight Rider* "Silent Knight" in 1983, *L.A. Law* "The Nut Before Christmas" in 1991, *Matlock* "The Gift" in 1987, *NYPD Blue* "From Hare to Eternity" in 1993, *Baywatch* "Silent Night, Baywatch Night" in 1994, *Homicide: Life on the Street* "All Through

the House" in 1994, Walker, Texas Ranger "A Ranger Christmas" in 1996, *JAG* "Jaggie Bells" in 1998

Cop shows with Santa Clauses committing crimes:
Rawhide "Twenty-Five Santa Clauses" in 1961, *McCloud* "'Twas the Fight Before Christmas" in 1976, *Police Woman* "Merry Christmas, Waldo" in 1977, *Cagney & Lacey* "I'll Be Home for Christmas" in 1982, *Remington Steele* "Dancer, Prancer, Donner and Steele" in 1985, *Jake and the Fatman* "Have Yourself a Merry Little Christmas" in 1987, *Kung Fu: The Legend Continues* "A Shaolin Christmas" in 1996, *Walker, Texas Ranger* "A Matter of Faith" in 1999, *Chuck* "Chuck Versus Santa Claus" in 2008, *Hawaii Five-0* "Oni Kalalea Ke Ku a Ka La'au Loa" in 2017

Cop shows with cast members struggling to get into the holiday spirit:
Have Gun - Will Travel "The Hanging Cross" in 1957, *The Man from U.N.C.L.E.* "The Jingle Bells Affair" in 1966, *Adam-12* "Log 122: Christmas — The Yellow Dump Truck" in 1968, *CHiPs* "Christmas Watch" in 1979, *Starsky and Hutch* "Little Girl Lost" in 1976, *T.J. Hooker* "Slay Ride" in 1983, *L.A. Law* "Sydney, the Dead-Nosed Reindeer" in 1986, *MacGuyver* "The Madonna" in 1989, *Murder, She Wrote* "A Christmas Secret" in 1992, *NYPD Blue* "From Hare to Eternity" in 1993, *Homicide: Life on the Street* "All Through the House" in 1994, *Walker, Texas Ranger* "A Ranger Christmas" in 1996), *NCIS: Los Angeles* "Cancel Christmas" in 2014

Medical show delivering babies at Christmas:
Dr. Quinn, Medicine Women "Mike's Dream: A Christmas Tale" in 1993, *ER* "The Greatest of Gifts" in 2000, "I'll Be Home For Christmas"

in 2001, and "The High Holiday" in 2008, *House* "Joy to the World" in 2008, *Private Practice* "Georgia on my Mind" in 2012

Medical shows with grouchy, Scrooge-like patients:
Dr. Kildare "Season to be Jolly" in 1961 and "An Exchange of the Gifts" in 1964, *St. Elsewhere* "Santa Claus is Dead" in 1985). And, *sometimes*, it's the patients that help the doctor find that spirit (like *ER* "A Miracle Happens Here" in 1995, "Do You See What I See?" in 1997, "How the Finch Stole Christmas" in 1999, and "City of Mercy" in 2006, *Diagnosis Murder* "Santa Claude" in 1999

Medical show Christmas miracles:
Trapper John, M.D. "'Tis the Season" in 1981, *Doogie Howser, M.D.* "Doogie the Red-Nosed Reindeer" in 1988, *ER* "The Gift" in 1994, "The Miracle Worker" in 1998, "A Miracle Happens Here" in 1999, "I'll Be Home For Christmas" in 2001, "Hindsight" in 2002, and "All About Christmas Eve" in 2005, *Chicago Hope* "Christmas Truce" in 1995, *Providence* "The Eleventh Hour" in 2002, *Grey's Anatomy* "Grandma Got Run Over by a Reindeer" in 2005

Medical shows with doctors suffering from crippling drug and alcohol problems:
ER "The Miracle Worker" in 1998 and "The Greatest of Gifts" in 2000, *Chicago Hope* "Christmas Truce" in 1995 and "On Golden Pons" in 1997, *Nip/Tuck* "Reefer" in 2006, *House* "Merry Little Christmas" in 2006, *Grey's Anatomy* "Holidaze" in 2009

Gift-giving conundrums on Teen Dramas and Nighttime Soaps:
Dynasty "That Holiday Spirit" in 1984, *The Wonder Years* "Christmas" in 1988, *Beverly Hills, 90210* "A Walsh Family Christmas" in 1991,

"Gift Wrapped" in 1996, and "Santa Knows" in 1997, *Melrose Place* "A Tree Talks in Melrose" in 1997, *The O.C.* "The Best Chrismukkah Ever" in 2003, *Gossip Girl* "Roman Holiday" in 2009, and *Orange is the New Black* "Can't Fix Crazy" in 2013

Superheroes celebrating Christmas:
The Six Million Dollar Man in 1976, *Wonder Woman* in 1977 and 1978, *Lois and Clark: The New Adventures of Superman* from 1994 to 1996, *Xena: Warrior Princess* in 1996, *Hercules: The Legendary Journeys* in 1996, *Smallville* in 2005 and 2007, *The Flash* from 2014 to 2017, *Supergirl* in 2017, and *The Legends of Tomorrow* in 2017

Vampires celebrating Christmas:
Buffy the Vampire Slayer in 1998, *The Vampire Diaries* from 2012 to 2016, and *NOS4A2* in 2020

Aliens celebrating Christmas:
V: The Series in 1984 and *Roswell* in 2000 and 2001

Angels celebrating Christmas:
Highway to Heaven from 1986 to 1989

Ghosts celebrating Christmas:
X-Files in 1997 and 1998

"Anti-Santa" demons celebrating Christmas:
Supernatural in 2007

Witches celebrating Christmas:
Charmed in 2018

Sitcoms family gatherings flashback episodes at Christmas:

The Adventures of Ozzie and Harriet "The Miracle" in 1953, *I Love Lucy* "The I Love Lucy Christmas Show" in 1956, *Gilligan's Island* "Birds Gotta Fly, Fish Gotta Talk" in 1964, *Welcome Back, Kotter* "A Sweathog Christmas" in 1977, *Diff'rent Strokes* "Retrospective" in 1978, *Family Ties* "A Christmas Story" in 1982, *The Jeffersons* "Father Christmas" in 1983, *Gimme a Break!* "Snippets" in 1985, *We Got It Made* "Upstairs, Downstairs (aka Christmas Clip Show) in 1987, *The Big Bang Theory* "The Santa Simulation" in 2012

Sitcom characters performing in big Christmas shows:

Car 54, Where Are You? "Christmas at the 53rd" in 1961, *The Dick Van Dyke Show* "The Alan Brady Show Presents" in 1963, *The Adventures of Ozzie and Harriet* "Busy Christmas" in 1965, *The Brady Bunch* "The Voice of Christmas" in 1969, *The Odd Couple* "Scrooge Gets an Oscar" in 1970, *Laverne & Shirley* "Oh Hear the Angels' Voices" in 1976, *Good Times* "The Traveling Christmas" in 1978, *Saved by the Bell* "A Home For Christmas" (1991), *The Facts of Life* "Christmas in the Big House" in 1984, *Home Improvement* "'Twas the Blight Before Christmas" in 1993, *NewsRadio* "Stupid Holiday Charity Talent Show" in 1997, *8 Simple Rules* "All I Want for Christmas" in 2002, *The Middle* "Christmas Help" in 2012, *The Goldbergs* "Han Ukkah Solo" in 2016, *Brooklyn Nine-Nine* "Captain Latvia" in 2016

Sitcom actors showing off their singing bonafides:

The Andy Griffith Show "A Christmas Story" in 1960, *The Addams Family* "Christmas with the Addams Family" in 1965, *Benson* "Mary and Her Lambs" in 1982, *Silver Spoons* "The Best Christmas Ever" 1982, *Gimme a Break!* "Christmas in New York" in 1986, *My Two Dads*

"'Tis the Season" in 1987, *Charles in Charge* "Yule Laff" in 1987, *A Different World* "I'm Dreaming of a Wayne Christmas" in 1990, *30 Rock* "Christmas Special" in 2008, *Brooklyn Nine-Nine* "Captain Latvia" in 2016

Sitcom characters dressing as Santa Claus:
The Amos and Andy Show "The Christmas Story" in 1952, *I Love Lucy* "The I Love Lucy Christmas Show" in 1956, *The Adventures of Ozzie and Harriet* "Busy Christmas" in 1956, *The Andy Griffith Show* "A Christmas Story" in 1960, *Bewitched* "A Vision of Sugar Plums" in 1965, *The Addams Family* "Christmas with the Addams Family" in 1965, *All in the Family* "Christmas Day at the Bunkers" in 1971, *Happy Days* "All I Want for Christmas" in 1982, *Silver Spoons* "The Best Christmas Ever" in 1982, *Square Pegs* "A Child's Christmas in Weemawee" in 1982, *Gimme a Break!* "A Kanisky Christmas" in 1983, *Alice* "Tis the Season to be Jealous" in 1983, *Punky Brewster* "Yes, Punky, There is a Santa Claus" in 1984, *Mama's Family* "Santa Mama" in 1986, *Webster* "The Man in the Red Flannel Suit" in 1986, *Cheers* "Christmas Cheers" in 1987, *Married…with Children* "You Better Watch Out" in 1987 and "Christmas" in 1992, *Family Ties* "Miracle in Columbus" in 1987, *ALF* "ALF's Special Christmas" in 1987, *Full House* "Our Very First Christmas Show" in 1988 and "Arrest Ye Merry Gentlemen" in 1994, *Head of the Class* "Viki's Torn Genes" in 1990, *Roseanne* "Santa Claus" in 1991, *Saved by the Bell* "Home for Christmas" in 1991, *Baby Talk* "Away in a Manger" in 1991, *Home Improvement* "Yule Better Watch Out" in 1991 and "'Twas the Blight Before Christmas" in 1993, *The Hogan Family* "Ho Ho Hogans" in 1991, *Drexell's Class* "Silent Night, Holy Smokes" in 1991, *Martin* "I Saw Gina Kissing Santa Claus" in 1992, *Hangin' with Mr. Cooper*

"Miracle in Oaktown" in 1992 and "Christmas Show" in 1994, *Hearts Afire* "Blue Christmas" in 1993, *Boy Meets World* "Santa's Little Helper" in 1993, *Wings* "Happy Holidays" in 1993, *Seinfeld* "The Race" in 1994, *The Fresh Prince of Bel-Air* "Twas The Night Before Christening" in 1994, *Family Matters* "Fa La La La Laagghh!" in 1995, *Kenan & Kel* "Merry Christmas, Kenan" in 1996, *Frasier* "Perspectives on Christmas" in 1997, *Spin City* "MIracle Near 34th Street" in 1997 and "Toy Story" in 2000, *Sabrina the Teenage Witch* "Sabrina Claus" in 1997, *Boy Meets World* "Santa's Little Helpers" in 1998, *The Hughleys* "Miracle on 135th and Avalon" in 1999, *Friends* "The One with the Holiday Armadillo" in 2000, *Just Shoot Me!* "Christmas? Christmas!" in 2001, *Grounded for Life* "I Saw Daddy Hitting Santa Claus" in 2001, *According to Jim* "An According to Jiminy Christmas" in 2001, *That '70s Show* "Christmas" in 2003, *Hope & Faith* "Aru-Bah Humbug" in 2004, *30 Rock* "Ludachristmas" in 2007, *Parks and Recreation* "Christmas Scandal" in 2009, *The Office* "Christmas Party" in 2005, "Secret Santa" in 2009, and "Classy Christmas" in 2010, *New Girl* "The 23rd" in 2011, *Community* "Regional Holiday Music" in 2011, *Mike & Molly* "Christmas Break" in 2011, *Raising Hope* "The Chance Who Stole Christmas" in 2013, *Black-ish* "Black Santa/White Christmas" in 2014, *Brooklyn Nine-Nine* "The Pontiac Bandit Returns" in 2014, *Fresh Off the Boat* "The Real Santa" in 2015, *Superstore* "Christmas Eve" in 2017

BIBLIOGRAPHY

GENERAL HISTORY

Godlewski, N. (2018, December 25). *Where does Christmas get its name?* Newsweek. https://www.newsweek.com/christmas-word-name-where-1259923.

Hillerbrand, Hans J. "Christmas | Origin, Definition, Traditions, History, & Facts." *Encyclopedia Britannica*, https://www.britannica.com/topic/Christmas. Accessed 16 July 2021.

History.com Editors. History of Christmas. *History.com*, A&E Television Networks, 27 Oct. 2009, www.history.com/topics/christmas/history-of-christmas.

YULE

Gooden, Tai. "The Curious Past and Lasting Importance of Yule - Nerdist." *Nerdist*, 21 Dec. 2020, https://nerdist.com/article/yule-curious-past-and-present-day-importance/.

"The Origin of Yule & When Exactly to Celebrate Yule!" *Jolablot*, 13 Aug. 2019, https://jolablot.com/origin-of-yule/.

"YULE - Day of Winter Solstice." *National Day Calendar*, 16 July 2021, https://nationaldaycalendar.com/yule-day-of-winter-solstice/.

NORSE LIVING CONDITIONS

Hurstwic: Farms and Villages in the Viking Age. http://www.hurstwic.org/history/articles/daily_living/text/Villages.htm. Accessed 16 July 2021.

"Viking Homes." *National Museum of Denmark*, https://en.natmus.dk/historical-knowledge/denmark/prehistoric-period-until-1050-ad/the-viking-age/the-people/viking-homes/. Accessed 16 July 2021.

SATURNALIA

Encyclopaedia Britannica. "Saturnalia | Celebration, Sacrifice, & Influence on Christmas." *Encyclopedia Britannica*, https://www.britannica.com/topic/Saturnalia-Roman-festival. Accessed 16 July 2021.

Wigington, Patti. "Celebrating the Roman God Saturn at Saturnalia." *Learn Religions*, 25 June 2019, https://www.learnreligions.com/about-celebrating-saturnalia-2562994.

"WORKPLACE: The Wild History of Holiday Office Parties." *New Castle News*, 30 Nov. 2006, https://www.ncnewsonline.com/archives/workplace-the-wild-history-of-holiday-office-parties/article_4895ce64-538c-59ce-810f-1f37fa71b816.html.

JUVENALIA

Cranach. "Christmas Was NOT Based on the Roman Juvenalia." *Cranach*, 24 Dec. 2012, https://www.patheos.com/blogs/geneveith/2012/12/christmas-was-not-based-on-the-roman-juvenalia/.

SECULAR PERCENTAGE

Hrynowski, Zach. "More Americans Celebrating a Secular Christmas." *Gallup*, 20 Dec. 2019, https://news.gallup.com/poll/272378/americans-celebrating-secular-christmas.aspx.

DUTCH INFLUENCE

Boys, Bowery. "How Dutch New Amsterdam Helped Create the American Christmas Tradition - The Bowery Boys: New York City History." *The Bowery Boys: New York City History*, 8 Dec. 2020, https://www.boweryboyshistory.com/2020/12/very-special-new-amsterdam-christmas_17.html.

TREES

Inman, Michael. "O Tannenbaum: Or, a Brief History of the Christmas Tree." https://www.nypl.org/blog/2016/12/12/christmas-trees-arrival. Accessed 16 July 2021.

Waxman, Olivia. "How Christmas Trees Became a Holiday Tradition." *Time*, 21 Dec. 2020, https://time.com/5736523/history-of-christmas-trees/.

"What Happened to the Captured Hessians? | Washington Crossing Historic Park." *Washington Crossing Historic Park |*, 29 Jan. 2020, https://www.washingtoncrossingpark.org/captured-hessians/.

"Who Invented Electric Christmas Lights?" *The Library of Congress*, https://www.loc.gov/item/who-invented-electric-christmas-lights/. Accessed 16 July 2021.

"Why Do We Have Christmas Trees? The Surprising History behind This Holiday Tradition." *National Geographic*, 18 Dec. 2020, https://www.nationalgeographic.com/travel/article/christmas-tree-customs.

WREATHS

Moon, Kat. "Christmas Wreaths Are a Classic Holiday Decoration With a Surprisingly Deep History." *Time*, 21 Dec. 2018, https://time.com/5482144/christmas-wreath-origins/

Slater, Jack. "Why do we hang Christmas wreaths as decorations and where do they come from?" *Metro UK*, 8 Dec. 2019, https://metro.co.uk/2019/12/08/why-do-we-hang-christmas-wreaths-as-decorations-where-do-they-come-from-11410094/

MISTLETOE

"8 Mistletoe Facts That Are So Weird, They Might Make You Rethink This Holiday Tradition." *Bustle*, 2 Dec. 2015, https://www.bustle.com/articles/126992-8-mistletoe-facts-that-are-so-weird-they-might-make-you-rethink-this-holiday-tradition.

Andrews, Evan. "Why Do We Kiss Under the Mistletoe?" *HISTORY*, 22 Dec. 2020, https://www.history.com/news/why-do-we-kiss-under-the-mistletoe.

"The Death of Baldur - Norse Mythology for Smart People." *Norse Mythology for Smart People*, 16 July 2021, https://norse-mythology.org/tales/the-death-of-baldur/.

Norton, Lily. "Pucker Up! Why Do People Kiss Under the Mistletoe?" *Live Science*, 21 Dec. 2010, https://www.livescience.com/32901-why-we-kiss-under-mistletoe.html.

Passey, Brian. "What's the Deal with Mistletoe?" *The Spectrum*, https://www.thespectrum.com/story/life/2015/12/20/whats-deal-mistletoe/77522130/. Accessed 16 July 2021.

PAGAN ROOTS

"The Pagan Roots of Christmas." *Sky HISTORY TV Channel*, 16 July 2021, https://www.history.co.uk/article/the-pagan-roots-of-christmas.

Pappas, Stephanie. "Pagan Roots? 5 Surprising Facts About Christmas." *Live Science*, 23 Dec. 2012, https://www.livescience.com/25779-christmas-traditions-history-paganism.html.

JESUS' BIRTH

The Birth of Jesus. https://www.christianbiblereference.org/story_BirthOfJesus.htm. Accessed 16 July 2021.

Cooper, James. *The Christmas Story - An Angel Visits Mary*. https://www.whychristmas.com/story/angel_mary.shtml. Accessed 16 July 2021.

Graves, Dan. "The First Recorded Celebration of Christmas." *Salem Web Network*, 25 Dec. 336AD, https://www.christianity.com/church/church-history/timeline/301-600/the-1st-recorded-celebration-of-christmas-11629658.html.

Pruitt, Sarah. "Who Wrote the Bible?" *HISTORY*, 23 Mar. 2021, https://www.history.com/news/who-wrote-the-bible.

THREE KINGS

Cheng, Scarlet. "THE LEGEND OF THE THREE KINGS." *The Washington Post*, 10 Dec. 1989, https://www.washingtonpost.com/archive/lifestyle/style/1989/12/10/the-legend-of-the-three-kings/c58d1b2c-4615-47a9-be76-7ca057b7ed37/.

Hampshire, Robert. "What Is the Significance of the Three Wise Men and Their Gifts?" *Salem Web Network*, https://www.christianity.com/wiki/holidays/significance-of-the-three-wise-men-and-their-gifts.html. Accessed 16 July 2021.

OLIVER CROMWELL

Burton-Hill, Clemency. *When Christmas Carols Were Banned*. https://www.bbc.com/culture/article/20141219-when-christmas-carols-were-banned. Accessed 16 July 2021.

AMERICA BANS CHRISTMAS

Lange, Jeva. "When Americans Banned Christmas." *The Week*, 8 Jan. 2022, https://theweek.com/articles/479313/when-americans-banned-christmas.

CHRISTMAS CARDS

"Facts and Stats 2019." *Greeting Card Association,* https://www.greetingcard.org/wp-content/uploads/2019/09/Greeting-Card-Facts-09.25.19.pdf

Hanc, John. "The History of the Christmas Card." *Smithsonian Magazine*, 9 Aug. 2015, https://www.smithsonianmag.com/history/history-christmas-card-180957487/.

Ponti, Crystal. "Some of the Earliest Christmas Cards Were Morbid and Creepy." *HISTORY*, 17 Dec. 2020, https://www.history.com/news/victorian-christmas-cards.

"Rowland Hill's Postal Reforms | The Postal Museum." *The Postal Museum*, 15 July 2021, https://www.postalmuseum.org/discover/collections/rowland-hill-postal-reforms/.

ADVENT

Allen, Scott. "A Brief History of Advent Calendars." *Mental Floss*, 1 Dec. 2010, https://www.mentalfloss.com/article/26522/brief-history-advent-calendars.

Fairchild, Mary. "What Do the 3 Main Advent Candle Colors Mean?" *Learn Religions*, 7 Sept. 2020, https://www.learnreligions.com/symbolic-colors-of-advent-700445.

"History of Richard Sellmer Verlag." *Sellmer Adventskalender*, https://sellmer-adventskalender.com/en/pages/company-history. Accessed 16 July 2021.

Holcomb, Justin. "What Is Advent?" *Salem Web Network*, https://www.christianity.com/christian-life/christmas/what-is-advent.html. Accessed 16 July 2021.

Kosloski, Philip. "How to Fast during Advent." *Aleteia — Catholic Spirituality, Lifestyle, World News, and Culture*, 29 Nov. 2018, https://aleteia.org/2018/11/29/how-to-fast-during-advent/.

SANTA

Altman. Tory." How Santa Brought Coca-Cola in from the Cold." *National Museum of American History*, 17 Dec. 2014, https://americanhistory.si.edu/blog/santa-coca-cola.

Curtis, Polly. "Researchers Find the Real Face of Father Christmas." *The Guardian*, 13 Dec. 2004, http://www.theguardian.com/education/2004/dec/13/highereducation.uk.

Daley, Beth. "From St Nicholas to Santa Claus." *Home Collections Stories Log in / Join Home Collections Stories Teachers About Us Help Log in / Join*, 6 Dec. 2013, https://www.europeana.eu/en/blog/from-st-nicholas-to-santa-claus.

Editors, Biography. co. "Saint Nicholas." *Biography*, 12 Dec. 2019, https://www.biography.com/religious-figure/saint-nicholas.

"The History of How St. Nicholas Became Santa Claus." *National Geographic*, 25 Dec. 2018, https://www.nationalgeographic.com/history/article/131219-santa-claus-origin-history-christmas-facts-st-nicholas.

"How St. Nick Became Santa Claus and Moved to the North Pole." *Oceanwide Expeditions*, 25 Oct. 2021, https://oceanwide-expeditions.com/blog/st-nick-and-the-arctic-the-north-pole-christmas-connection.

Moy, Jeffrey V. *From Turkish Saint to Santa Claus: Thomas Nast and the Changing Face of St. Nick.* 24 Dec. 2018, https://morristowngreen.com/2018/12/24/from-turkish-saint-to-santa-claus-thomas-nast-and-the-changing-face-of-st-nick/.

Strauss, Valerie. "Why Is Christmas on Dec. 25? A Brief History Lesson That May Surprise You." *The Washington Post*, 25 Dec. 2015, https://www.washingtonpost.com/news/answer-sheet/wp/2015/12/25/why-is-christmas-on-dec-25-a-brief-history-lesson-that-may-surprise-you/.

SANTA'S ELVES

Pappas, Stephanie. "Elf on a Shelf: The Strange History of Santa's Little Helpers." *Live Science*, 18 Dec. 2013, https://www.livescience.com/42051-history-of-elves.html.

Westover, Jeff. "History of the Tradition of Elves | My Merry Christmas." *My Merry Christmas*, 21 Nov. 2016, https://mymerrychristmas.com/history-of-the-tradition-of-elves/.

Pruitt, Sarah. "What We Know About Vikings and Slaves." *HISTORY*, 27 June 2019, https://www.history.com/news/viking-slavery-raids-evidence.

AROUND WORLD

Alleyne, Caleigh. "20 Christmas Traditions Around the World That May Surprise You." *Country Living*, 17 Sept. 2020, https://www.countryliving.com/entertaining/g4933/christmas-traditions-around-the-world/.

Cooper, James. *Christmas Traditions, Christmas History, Christmas Around the World, The Christmas Story and Christmas Fun and Games! - Whychristmas?Com.* https://www.whychristmas.com. Accessed 17 July 2021.

Hillerbrand, Hans J. "Christmas | Origin, Definition, Traditions, History, & Facts." *Encyclopedia Britannica*, https://www.britannica.com/topic/Christmas. Accessed 16 July 2021.

EUROPE

"Christmas Celebrations around Europe." *ENIL – European Network on Independent Living*, 13 Dec. 2010, https://enil.eu/news/christmas-celebrations-around-europe/.

Galka, Max." The Strange and Sometimes Terrifying Santa Clauses of Europe - Metrocosm." *Metrocosm*, 22 Dec. 2015, http://metrocosm.com/santa-clauses-of-europe/.

Lanin, Colleen. "12 Christmas Traditions in Europe That Will Delight and Scare You." *TravelMamas.Com*, 22 Dec. 2020, https://travelmamas.com/christmas-traditions-in-europe/.

Steves, Rick. "Favorite Traditions of a European Christmas." *The Seattle Times*, 15 Dec. 2009, https://www.seattletimes.com/life/travel/favorite-traditions-of-a-european-christmas/.

BULGARIA

VisitMyBulgaria. "Celebrate Christmas in Bulgaria: What You Need to Know." *Travel Guide of Bulgaria*, 17 Dec. 2017, https://visitmybulgaria.com/celebrate-christmas-bulgaria/.

CZECH REPUBLIC

Czech Christmas. http://www.myczechrepublic.com/czech_culture/czech_holidays/christmas.html. Accessed 16 July 2021.

DENMARK

"7 Delightful Things to Know about Christmas in Denmark | VisitDenmark." *VisitDenmark*, https://www.visitdenmark.com/denmark/things-do/denmark-christmas-delights. Accessed 16 July 2021.

FINLAND

Wood, Jessica. "How Rovaniemi Became The Official Town Of Santa Claus." *Culture Trip*, https://theculturetrip.com/europe/finland/articles/how-rovaniemi-became-the-official-town-of-santa-claus/. Accessed 16 July 2021.

GERMANY

Kathy Lauer-Williams, Of The Morning. "The History of Belsnickel: Santa's Cranky Cousin." *Mcall.Com*, 29 Nov. 2013, https://www.mcall.com/entertainment/mc-xpm-2013-11-29-mc-belsnickel-christmas-pennsylvania-dutch-20131129-story.html.

GREAT BRITAIN

Christina. "Traditional British Christmas Pudding." *Christina's Cucina*, 3 Dec. 2016, https://www.christinascucina.com/traditional-british-christmas-pudding-make-ahead-fruit-brandy-filled-steamed-dessert/.

McDowell, Erin. "15 Quirky British Christmas Traditions Americans May Have Never Heard Of." *Insider*, 25 Dec. 2020, https://www.insider.com/quirky-british-christmas-traditions-americans-might-have-never-heard-of.

ICELAND

"Celebrating Christmas with 13 Trolls." *Iceland.Is Logo*, https://www.iceland.is/the-big-picture/news/celebrating-christmas-with-13-trolls/7916/. Accessed 16 July 2021.

ITALY

"The Legend of La Befana." *Rent Your Vacation Villa in Italy with Us!*, https://www.summerinitaly.com/traveltips/the-legend-of-la-befana. Accessed 16 July 2021.

Reilly, Lucas. "7 Facts About the Feast of the Seven Fishes." *Mental Floss*, 19 Dec. 2018, https://www.mentalfloss.com/article/567912/the-feast-of-the-seven-fishes-facts.

NETHERLANDS

McBain, Sophie. "Blacking up for Christmas in the Netherlands." *New Statesman*, 28 Nov. 2013, https://www.newstatesman.com/2013/11/blacking-christmas.

Swaab, Micah. "Black Pete: Is Time up for the Netherlands 'Blackface Tradition?" *Al Jazeera*, 2 Dec. 204AD, https://www.aljazeera.com/features/2020/12/4/the-netherlands-black-pete.

BIBLIOGRAPHY

NORWAY

Tours, Fjord. "The Traditions of Norwegian Christmas." *Fjord Tours*, 17 Dec. 2019, https://www.fjordtours.com/inspiration/articles/norwegian-christmas-traditions/.

SPAIN

"A Man With as Many Noses as There Are Days Left In the Year | Barcelona Lowdown." *Barcelona Lowdown*, 31 Dec. 2019, https://barcelonalowdown.com/man-of-many-noses/.

SWEDEN

Eveleth, Rose. "Every Year, a Swedish Town Builds a Giant Straw Goat, And People Just Can't Help Burning It Down." *Smithsonian Magazine*, 16 Aug. 2013, https://www.smithsonianmag.com/smart-news/every-year-a-swedish-town-builds-a-giant-straw-goat-and-people-just-cant-help-burning-it-down-180948158/.

SOUTH AMERICA

"7 Things That Make Christmas in South America Unique." *Matador Network*, 3 May 2021, http://matadornetwork.com/life/7-things-that-make-christmas-in-south-america-unique/.

"Latin America Christmas Traditions | VIP Journeys." *VIP Journeys*, 29 Nov. 2018, https://vipjourneys.com/latin-america-christmas-traditions/.

ARGENTINA

"Cultural Tidbit: Argentine Christmas Traditions." *Ecela Spanish*, 16 July 2021, https://ecelaspanish.com/cultural-tidbit-argentine-christmas-traditions/.

BRAZIL

Diakite, Parker. "Here's How Christmas Is Celebrated In Brazil - Travel Noire." *Travel Noire*, 21 Dec. 2018, https://travelnoire.com/heres-how-christmas-is-celebrated-in-brazil.

Farah, Ana. "13th Salary in Brazil." *The Brazil Business*, 14 Dec. 2012, https://thebrazilbusiness.com/article/13th-salary-in-brazil.

COLOMBIA

"Christmas in Colombia Is Unique | Colombia Country Brand." *Colombia Country Brand*, 22 Dec. 2018, https://www.colombia.co/en/colombia-country/9-reasons-that-make-christmas-in-colombia-unique/.

PERU

Herrera, Urpi. " The Chocolatada: A Peruvian Christmas Tradition That Gives Back." *Luxury Travel to Peru, Galapagos & Bolivia*, 4 Dec. 2018, https://www.kuodatravel.com/the-chocolatada-a-peruvian-christmas-tradition-that-gives-back/.

Infoamazingperu.com. "Christmas Traditions in Peru." *Amazing Peru Logo*, https://www.amazingperu.com/blog/christmas-traditions-in-peru.asp. Accessed 16 July 2021.

AUSTRALIA

Do, Suri. "How Do People in Australia Celebrate Summer Christmas?" *Medium*, 30 Nov. 2017, https://medium.com/@do_suri/how-do-people-in-australia-celebrate-summer-christmas-6ab9eec5eef3.

NEW ZEALAND

Naden, Liam. "How the Christmas Season Is Celebrated in New Zealand." *TripSavvy*, 22 Jan. 2019, https://www.tripsavvy.com/christmas-in-new-zealand-1606375.

ANTARCTICA

Miknaitis, Kathryn. "Like No Other: The South Pole Christmas Tree | Ice Stories: Dispatches From Polar Scientists." *Ice Stories: Dispatches From Polar Scientists*, 25 Dec. 2007, http://icestories.exploratorium.edu/dispatches/like-no-other-the-south-pole-christmas-tree/index.html.

ASIA

"How Do Different Asian Countries Celebrate Christmas?" *SBS PopAsia*, 16 July 2021, https://www.sbs.com.au/popasia/blog/2014/12/16/how-do-different-asian-countries-celebrate-christmas.

Nguyen, Kimberly. "How These 6 Asian Countries Celebrate Christmas." *NextShark*, 22 Dec. 2018, https://nextshark.com/christmas-holiday-celebration-asia/.

Rodgers, Greg. "There Are Plenty of Places to Celebrate Christmas in Asia." *TripSavvy*, 11 July 2019, https://www.tripsavvy.com/christmas-in-asia-1458350.

ARMENIA

Potter, Betty. "It's Still Christmas in Armenia." *Smithsonian Magazine*, 3 Aug. 2018, https://www.smithsonianmag.com/travel/its-still-christmas-armenia-180967689/.

JAPAN (KFC)

Barton, Eric. "Why Japan Celebrates Christmas with KFC." *Japan 2020*, https://www.bbc.com/worklife/article/20161216-why-japan-celebrates-christmas-with-kfc. Accessed 16 July 2021.

Fater, Luke. "How a White Lie Gave Japan KFC for Christmas." *Atlas Obscura*, 13 Dec. 2019, http://www.atlasobscura.com/articles/what-is-japanese-christmas.

Springer, Kate. "How KFC Became a Christmas Tradition in Japan." *CNN*, https://www.cnn.com/travel/article/kfc-christmas-tradition-japan/index.html. Accessed 16 July 2021.

PHILIPPINES

Tagalog Lang. "Filipino Christmas Eve: Noche Buena: Holiday Traditions." *TAGALOG LANG*, 25 Dec. 2020, https://www.tagaloglang.com/noche-buena-filipino-christmas-eve/.

AFRICA

"6 Christmas Traditions You'll Only Find in Africa." *Real Word*, 2 Dec. 2020, https://www.trafalgar.com/real-word/african-christmas-traditions/.

"Christmas Traditions Around the World - Lattitude Global Volunteering." *Lattitude Global Volunteering*, 14 Dec. 2017, https://lattitude.org/christmas-traditions-around-world/.

Wanderlust, Africa. "African Christmas Traditions: How People Celebrate Christmas in Africa?" *Africa Wanderlust*, 1 Nov. 2019, https://africawanderlust.com/destinations/african-christmas/.

ZAMBIA

Kubuka. "Christmas Kenya vs. Zambia - KUBUKA." *KUBUKA*, 17 Jan. 2018, https://kubuka.org/christmas-kenya-vs-zambia/.

NORTH AMERICA

CANADA

"Canadian Christmas Traditions You May Not Know." *Live & Learn: A Project of English Online Inc.*, 10 Dec. 2018, https://livelearn.ca/article/about-canada/canadian-christmas-traditions-you-may-not-know/.

"Christmas… by the numbers." Statistics Canada. https://www.statcan.gc.ca/eng/dai/smr08/2018/smr08_228_2018

CUBA

Gomez, Alan. "Christmas in Cuba." *USA TODAY*, https://www.usatoday.com/story/news/world/2014/12/25/cuba-havana-christmas/20897667/. Accessed 17 July 2021.

DOMINICAN REPUBLIC

"Feliz Navidad! 8 Dominican Christmas Traditions | Casa de Campo Living." *Casa de Campo Living*, 24 Dec. 2011, https://casadecampoliving.com/feliz-navidad-8-dominican-christmas-traditions-by-paola-marte/.

HAITI

St. Paulin, Ricot. "Christmas in Haiti." *Compassion International Blog*, 28 Dec. 2009, https://blog.compassion.com/christmas-in-haiti/.

HONDURAS

News. "Prepare for Christmas Like A Honduran - Olancho Aid Foundation." *Olancho Aid Foundation*, 14 Dec. 2017, https://olanchoaid.org/prepare-christmas-like-honduran/.

"Honduras Christmas Traditions at Our Little Roses | Our Little Roses." *Our Little Roses*, 21 Dec. 2020, https://www.ourlittleroses.org/blog/honduras-christmas-traditions-at-our-little-roses/.

MEXICO

Nowak, Claire. "This Is Why Poinsettias Are the Official Christmas Flower." *Reader's Digest*, 4 Dec. 2019, https://www.rd.com/article/poinsettias-official-christmas-flower/.

USA

Shaw, Gabbi. "5 of the Most Unusual Christmas Traditions in the US." *Insider*, 21 Dec. 2019, https://www.insider.com/unusual-us-christmas-traditions-2018-12.

FOOD

Keeler, Janet K. "The Origins of 10 Christmas Culinary Traditions." *Tampa Bay Times*, 17 Dec. 2013, https://www.tampabay.com/things-to-do/food/cooking/the-origins-of-10-christmas-culinary-traditions/2157403/.

Olver, Lynne. *The Timeline--Christmas Food History*. https://www.foodtimeline.org/christmasfood.html. Accessed 17 July 2021.

Rotkovitz, Miri. "Learn About the History Behind Christmas Food Traditions." *The Spruce Eats*, 28 Aug. 2020, https://www.thespruceeats.com/traditional-christmas-specialty-foods-1665645.

GOOSE

Sterling, Justine. "The Story Behind the Christmas Goose." *Delish*, 21 Dec. 2010, https://www.delish.com/food/recalls-reviews/history-of-the-christmas-goose.

TURKEY

Davison, Benjamin. "Perspective | The Hidden History of Christmas Dinner." *The Washington Post*, 22 Dec. 2017, https://www.washingtonpost.com/news/made-by-history/wp/2017/12/22/the-hidden-history-of-christmas-dinner/.

HAM

Clough, Jason. "The History of the Christmas Ham." *WFLA*, 17 Dec. 2016, https://www.wfla.com/news/the-history-of-the-christmas-ham/.

GINGERBREAD

Avey, Tori. "History of Gingerbread | The History Kitchen | PBS Food." *PBS Food*, 20 Dec. 2013, https://www.pbs.org/food/the-history-kitchen/history-gingerbread/.

Wilson, Antonia. "A Brief History of the Gingerbread House." *The Guardian*, 22 Dec. 2018, http://www.theguardian.com/travel/2018/dec/22/a-brief-history-of-the-gingerbread-house.

FRUITCAKE

Nachlas, Courtney. "Why We Eat Fruitcake on Christmas." *The Daily Meal*, 8 Dec. 2015, https://www.thedailymeal.com/holidays/why-we-eat-fruitcake-christmas.

"The Secret History of Fruitcake | CBC Kids." *CBC Kids*, https://www.cbc.ca/kidscbc2/the-feed/the-secret-history-of-fruitcake/. Accessed 17 July 2021.

"Ultimate Guide to Fruitcake." *HowStuffWorks*, 29 Nov. 2007, https://recipes.howstuffworks.com/menus/fruitcake.htm.

EGGNOG

Dias, Elizabeth. "A Brief History of Eggnog." *Time*, 21 Dec. 2011, https://time.com/3957265/history-of-eggnog/.

Miller, Ryan. "Eggnog Once Sparked a Military Riot: Here's the Story and 3 Other Facts about the Holiday Drink." *USA TODAY*, https://www.usatoday.com/story/news/nation/2019/12/04/eggnog-why-called-eggnog-started-riot-west-point/4297711002/. Accessed 17 July 2021.

Williams, Geoff. "A Brief History Of Eggnog: Its Past, Including The Infamous Eggnog Riot, Is Stranger Than You Think." *Forbes*, 29 Nov. 2016, https://www.forbes.com/sites/geoffwilliams/2016/11/29/a-brief-history-of-eggnog-its-past-is-stranger-than-you-think/.

CHESTNUTS

Castelow, Ellen. "Martinmas." *Historic UK*, https://www.historic-uk.com/CultureUK/Martinmas/. Accessed 17 July 2021.

Kruijs, Julie. "Roasted Chestnuts Lisbon, November 11 St. Martin's Day Traditions & Liqueur Jeropiga." *The Lisbon Connection A Lisbon Guide from the inside The Lisbon Connection A Lisbon Guide from the Inside*, 11 Nov. 2018, https://www.thelisbonconnection.com/roasted-chestnuts-lisbon-november-11-st-martins-day-traditions-liqueur-jeropiga/.

Morgan, Kate. "Why Don't We Roast Chestnuts for the Holidays Anymore?" *USA TODAY 10Best*, 16 Dec. 2020, https://www.10best.com/interests/food-culture/how-roasted-chestnuts-became-extinct-christmas-tradition/.

SUGARPLUMS

Rude, Emelyn. "The History That Explains Those 'Visions of Sugarplums.'" *Time*, 21 Dec. 2016, https://time.com/4606739/history-sugarplums/.

CANDY CANES

Eveleth, Rose. "We Don't Know the Origins of the Candy Cane, But They Almost Certainly Were Not Christian." *Smithsonian Magazine*, 11 Aug. 2012, https://www.smithsonianmag.com/smart-news/we-dont-know-the-origins-of-the-candy-cane-but-they-almost-certainly-were-not-christian-157380385/.

Kennedy, Lesley. "The Twisted History of Candy Canes." *HISTORY*, 7 Dec. 2018, https://www.history.com/news/candy-canes-invented-germany.

Rousseau, Dérick. "The History of Candy Canes and Why They Taste so Cool." *The Conversation*, 22 Dec. 2019, http://theconversation.com/the-history-of-candy-canes-and-why-they-taste-so-cool-128036.

CHRISTMAS COOKIES

Butler, Stephanie. "The Medieval History of the Christmas Cookie." *HISTORY*, 1 Sept. 2018, https://www.history.com/news/the-medieval-history-of-the-christmas-cookie.

Booth, Jessica. "The Fascinating History Behind Your Favorite Holiday Cookies." *Redbook*, 11 Dec. 2018, https://www.redbookmag.com/food-recipes/g25167408/christmas-cookies-history/.

Lee Ball, Aimee. "How Cookies Came to Be the Ultimate Christmas Treat." *Martha Stewart*, 15 Nov. 2017, https://www.marthastewart.com/1522801/christmas-cookies-sweet-history.

FIGGY PUDDING

Barksdale, Nate. "The History of Christmas Pudding." *HISTORY*, 1 Sept. 2018, https://www.history.com/news/the-holiday-history-of-christmas-pudding.

Blakemore, Erin. "A Brief History of Figgy Pudding." *Smithsonian Magazine*, 21 Aug. 2015, https://www.smithsonianmag.com/smart-news/brief-history-figgy-pudding-180957600/.

FEAST OF THE SEVEN FISHES

Adimando, Stacy. "An Eye-Opening Look at the Feast of the Seven Fishes." *Saveur*, 13 Dec. 2018, https://www.saveur.com/new-look-at-seven-fishes/.

Reilly, Lucas. "7 Facts About the Feast of the Seven Fishes." *Mental Floss*, 19 Dec. 2018, https://www.mentalfloss.com/article/567912/the-feast-of-the-seven-fishes-facts.

Trembath, Brian K. "What's the Meaning of The Feast of Seven Fishes?" *Denver Public Library History*, 15 Dec. 2015, https://history.denverlibrary.org/news/whats-meaning-feast-seven-fishes.

FASHION

Fashion History at Christmas. http://www.thepostmagazine.co.uk/brightonhistory/fashion-history-christmas. Accessed 17 July 2021.

UGLY SWEATERS

Cerini, Marianna. "A Cozy History of the Ugly Christmas Sweater." *CNN*, 21 Dec. 2020, https://www.cnn.com/style/article/ugly-christmas-jumpers/index.html.

"The History of Christmas Sweaters | Lands 'End | Lands 'End." *Lands 'End | Lands 'End*, https://www.landsend.com/article/the-history-of-christmas-sweaters/. Accessed 17 July 2021.

PAJAMAS

Fequiere, Roxanne. "The History of Matching Holiday Pajamas | Grok Nation." *Grok Nation*, 24 Dec. 2018, https://groknation.com/style/the-history-of-matching-holiday-pajamas/.

Spyker, Marisa. "How Matching Family Pajamas Became a Viral Holiday Tradition." *Southern Living*, 4 Dec. 2019, https://www.southernliving.com/christmas/family-tradition-christmas-pjs.

BOOKS

DICKENS

Eschner, Kat. "Why Charles Dickens Wrote 'A Christmas Carol.'" *Smithsonian Magazine*, 19 Aug. 2016, https://www.smithsonianmag.com/smart-news/why-charles-dickens-wrote-christmas-carol-180961507/.

IRVING

Heitman, Danny. "How Washington Irving Shaped Christmas in America." *The National Endowment for the Humanities*, https://www.neh.gov/humanities/2016/fall/feature/how-washington-irving-shaped-christmas-in-america. Accessed 17 July 2021.

SHEPHERD

Staff, Wide. "There's a Sequel to 'A Boy Named Sue 'From the Father's Perspective." *Wide Open Country*, 21 Jan. 2019, https://www.wideopencountry.com/father-of-a-boy-named-sue-shel-silverstein/.

Vlastelica, Ryan. "A Christmas Story Stayed on the Kid Side of a Coming-of-Age Book." *The A.V. Club*, 9 Dec. 2015, https://www.avclub.com/a-christmas-story-stayed-on-the-kid-side-of-a-coming-of-1798287241.

CAPOTE

Mathias, Cerith. "Remembering it the Way it Should Have Been: A Child's Christmas in Monroeville." *Deep South Magazine*. 23 Dec. 2020, https://deepsouthmag.com/2020/12/23/remembering-it-the-way-it-should-have-been-a-childs-christmas-in-monroeville/

'TWAS THE NIGHT BEFORE CHRISTMAS

Conradt, Stacy. "The Mystery Behind the World's Most Famous Christmas Poem." *Mental Floss*, 8 Dec. 2016, https://www.mentalfloss.com/article/26719/mystery-behind-worlds-most-famous-christmas-poem.

Foster, Don. "Who Was That Poet, Anyway?" *The Washington Post*, 24 Dec. 2000, https://www.washingtonpost.com/archive/opinions/2000/12/24/who-was-that-poet-anyway/9fa4e99f-476d-467d-b586-1538f3f9ac50/.

O. HENRY

Kornbluth, Jesse. "O. Henry Wrote His Christmas Classic, 'The Gift Of The Magi,' In 1905. In 'The Gift Of Gifts, 'I Update It." HuffPost. 23 Dec. 2015, https://www.huffpost.com/entry/ohenry-wrote-his-christma_b_8865788

RUDOLPH

Pupovac, Jessica. "Writing 'Rudolph': The Original Red-Nosed Manuscript." *NPR*, 25 Dec. 2013, https://www.npr.org/2013/12/25/256579598/writing-rudolph-the-original-red-nosed-manuscript.

YES, VIRGINIA

Tannenhauser, Carol. *Extra, Extra!Recent CommentsExplore Your Favorite Subject*. 24 Dec. 2019, https://www.westsiderag.com/2019/12/24/famous-virginia-who-questioned-the-existence-of-santa-claus-was-an-upper-west-girl.

Bever, Lindsey. "'Is There a Santa Claus?': How a Child's Letter Inspired the Classic 'Yes, Virginia ' Response." *The Washington Post*, 22 Dec. 2018, https://www.washingtonpost.com/history/2018/12/22/is-there-santa-claus-how-childs-letter-inspired-classic-yes-virginia-response/.

333

TOYS

"140 Most Popular Christmas Toys since 1900." *Visual.Ly*, https://visual.ly/community/Infographics/lifestyle/140-most-popular-christmas-toys-1900. Accessed 17 July 2021.

"The Most Popular Christmas Toy from the Year You Were Born." *Livingly*, https://www.livingly.com/The+Most+Popular+Christmas+Toy+from+the+Year+You+Were+Born. Accessed 17 July 2021.

Pocket-lint. "The Most Popular Christmas Toys and Tech from the Last Few Decades." *Pocket-Lint*, 15 Dec. 2020, https://www.pocket-lint.com/parenting/news/142866-most-popular-christmas-toys-and-tech.

Price, Lydia. "10 Toys That Have Caused Holiday Mayhem Through the Years." *PEOPLE.Com*, 19 Dec. 2019, https://people.com/parents/christmas-toy-crazes-through-the-years/.

Pruitt, Sarah. "10 Christmas Toys Through the Decades." *HISTORY*, 23 Aug. 2018, https://www.history.com/news/10-christmas-toys-through-the-decades.

TEDDY BEAR

The Story of the Teddy Bear - Theodore Roosevelt Birthplace National Historic Site (U.S. National Park Service). https://www.nps.gov/thrb/learn/historyculture/storyofteddybear.htm. Accessed 17 July 2021.

YO-YO

Baybrook, Jennifer. "A Rich History of a Simple Toy Called the Yo-Yo." *Yo-Yo*, https://www.yo-yo.com/blog/A-Rich-History-of-a-Simple-Toy-Called-the-Yo-Yo. Accessed 17 July 2021.

SLINKY

Sharp, Richard. *The Somewhat Shocking Story of the Slinky*. 15 Sept. 2015, https://www.linkedin.com/pulse/somewhat-shocking-story-slinky-richard-sharp.

FISHER-PRICE

Helmore, Edward. "Ninety and Still into Toys: How Fisher-Price Pulled a Town out of Depression." *The Guardian*, 13 June 2020, http://www.theguardian.com/lifeandstyle/2020/jun/13/ninety-and-still-into-toys-how-fisher-price-pulled-a-town-out-of-depression-and-may-do-so-again.

BARBIE

Holland, Brynn. "Barbie Through the Ages." *HISTORY*, 8 Mar. 2019, https://www.history.com/news/barbie-through-the-ages.

MessyNessy. "Meet Lilli, the High-End German Call Girl Who Became America's Iconic Barbie Doll." *Messy Nessy Chic*, 29 Jan. 2016, https://www.messynessychic.com/2016/01/29/meet-lilli-the-high-end-german-call-girl-who-became-americas-iconic-barbie-doll/.

LEGO

Blakemore, Erin. "The Disastrous Backstory Behind the Invention of LEGO Bricks." *HISTORY*, 29 Aug. 2018, https://www.history.com/news/the-disastrous-backstory-behind-the-invention-of-lego-bricks.

NERF

Duffley, John. "NERF Football Inventor Fred Cox, Ex-NFL Kicker, Dies at 80." *FanBuzz - Sports News - NFL | NCAA | NBA | WWE*, 21 Nov. 2019, https://fanbuzz.com/nfl/fred-cox-nerf-football/.

UNO

"Uno." *The Strong Logo*, https://www.toyhalloffame.org/toys/uno. Accessed 17 July 2021.

RUBIKS

"Rubik's Cube." *The Strong Logo*, https://www.toyhalloffame.org/toys/rubiks-cube. Accessed 17 July 2021.

CABBAGE PATCH KIDS

Friedrich, Otto. "The Strange Cabbage Patch Craze." *TIME.Com*, 12 Dec. 1983, http://content.time.com/time/magazine/article/0,9171,921419,00.html.

BEANIE BABIES

Ladybug. "Behind the Beanie Babies: The Secret Life of Ty Warner." *Chicago Magazine*, 22 Mar. 2021, https://www.chicagomag.com/Chicago-Magazine/May-2014/Ty-Warner/.

TICKLE ME ELMO

Hlavaty, Craig. "Remember the 'Tickle Me Elmo' Craze?" *Houston Chronicle*, 6 Dec. 2016, https://www.timesunion.com/life/article/Remember-the-Tickle-Me-Elmo-craze-Hot-10781630.php.

MUSIC

Berkowitz, Bonnie. "All We Want for Christmas Is ... These Songs. Here's Why." *The Washington Post*, 21 Dec. 2019, https://www.washingtonpost.com/graphics/2019/entertainment/holiday-music-popularity/.

"What Don't You Know About Holiday Music?" *Nielsen*, 7 Nov. 2017, https://www.nielsen.com/us/en/insights/article/2017/what-dont-you-know-about-holiday-music.

NUTCRACKER

Burton-Hill, Clemency. "How Tchaikovsky's Nutcracker became a Christmas classic." *BBC*, 22 Dec. 2015, https://www.bbc.com/culture/article/20151218-how-tchaikovskys-nutcracker-became-a-christmas-classic.

NPR. "How Tchaikovsky's Nutcracker Became a Holiday Tradition." *NPR Morning Edition*, 18 Dec. 2014, https://www.npr.org/2014/12/18/371597799/how-tchaikovskys-nutcracker-became-a-holiday-tradition.

NPR. "No Sugar Plums Here: The Dark, Romantic Roots Of 'The Nutcracker'." *NPR*, 25 Dec. 2012, https://www.npr.org/2012/12/25/167732828/no-sugar-plums-here-the-dark-romantic-roots-of-the-nutcracker.

Sandla, Robert. "How George Balanchine's THE NUTCRACKER Premiered at City Center." *New York City Center*, 16 Dec. 2016,https://www.nycitycenter.org/About/Blog/2016/how-george-balanchines-the-nutcracker-premiered-at-city-center/.

GOD REST YE MERRY GENTLEMEN

Christiansen, Connie. "God Rest Ye Merry Gentlemen, the Song and the Story." *Copyright © Sharefaith Inc. All Rights Reserved. 860 O hare Parkway Suite #200, Medford, OR, 97504, U.S.*, https://www.sharefaith.com. Accessed 17 July 2021.

WE WISH YOU A MERRY CHRISTMAS

Combest, Torie. "The History of We Wish You a Merry Christmas | Synonym." *Synonym*, https://classroom.synonym.com/the-history-of-we-wish-you-a-merry-christmas-12238050.html. Accessed 17 July 2021.

Webster, Audrey. "The Little-Known History of the Caroling Tradition." *Arcadia Publishing* https://www.arcadiapublishing.com/Navigation/Community/Arcadia-and-THP-Blog/November-2018/The-Little-Known-History-of-the-Caroling-Tradition

O TANNENBAUM

Flippo, Hyde. "Do You Know the Meaning of the German Carol 'O Tannenbaum.'" *ThoughtCo*, 4 Nov. 2019, https://www.thoughtco.com/german-versions-of-o-tannenbaum-4066932.

I SAW THREE SHIPS

Olsen, Ted. "Top Eight Historically Incorrect Christmas Songs." *Christian History*, 1 July 2021, https://www.christianitytoday.com/history/2008/december/top-eight-historically-incorrect-christmas-songs.html.

JOY TO THE WORLD

Moore, Sian. "The Lyrics and Composer of Christmas Carol 'Joy to the World.'" *Classic FM*, 2 Dec. 2020, https://www.classicfm.com/discover-music/occasions/christmas/joy-to-the-world-hymn-carol-lyrics-composer/.

Olsen, Ted. "Top Eight Historically Incorrect Christmas Songs." *Christian History*, 1 July 2021, https://www.christianitytoday.com/history/2008/december/top-eight-historically-incorrect-christmas-songs.html.

O COME ALL YE FAITHFUL

Adeste Fideles - Notes On The Carol. https://www.hymnsandcarolsofchristmas.com/Hymns_and_Carols/Notes_On_Carols/adeste_fideles.htm. Accessed 17 July 2021.

BIBLIOGRAPHY

Bell, Carolyn. "O 'Come All Ye Faithful: The Story Behind The Famous Christmas Carol." *MyNativity.Com*, 6 Apr. 2018, https://mynativity.com/blog/o-come-all-ye-faithful-the-story-behind-the-famous-christmas-carol/.

HARK! THE HERALD ANGELS SING

"Hark! The Herald Angels Sing." *Christmas with the Tabernacle Choir*, https://www.pbs.org/wgbh/christmas-tabernacle-choir/concert-2019/hark-the-herald-angels-sing/. Accessed 17 July 2021.

AULD LANG SYNE

Lewis, Robert. "Auld Lang Syne | History & Lyrics." *Encyclopedia Britannica*, https://www.britannica.com/topic/Auld-Lang-Syne. Accessed 17 July 2021.

"The History and Words of Auld Lang Syne | Scotland.Org." *Scotland*, https://www.scotland.org/features/the-history-and-words-of-auld-lang-syne. Accessed 17 July 2021.

SILENT NIGHT

Lewis, Susan. "The Story Behind The Beloved Christmas Carol 'Silent Night.'" *WRTI*, 19 Dec. 2020, https://www.wrti.org/post/story-behind-beloved-christmas-carol-silent-night.

ANGELS WE HAVE HEARD ON HIGH

"Angels We Have Heard on High." *Hymnary.Org*, https://hymnary.org/text/angels_we_have_heard_on_high. Accessed 17 July 2021.

Grimes, Taylor. "Angels We Have Heard On High — A Very Sufjan Christmas." *A Very Sufjan Christmas*, 24 Dec. 2019, https://www.sufjanchristmas.com/blog/2019/12/24/angels-we-have-heard-on-high.

THE FIRST NOEL

Acreman, Thomas. "The First Noël - A Christmas Revival." *Classic History*, 6 Dec. 2017, http://www.classichistory.net/archives/first-noel-carol.

"What Is the History of 'The First Noel 'in French?" *ThoughtCo*, 11 Feb. 2019, https://www.thoughtco.com/aujourdhui-leroi-des-cieux-french-christmas-1368139.

AVE MARIA

"What Are the Lyrics to 'Ave Maria', and Who Wrote It?" *Classic FM*, 27 Oct. 2020, https://www.classicfm.com/composers/schubert/ave-maria-schubert-lyrics/.

O HOLY NIGHT

"The Amazing Story of 'O Holy Night.'" *Beliefnet*, https://www.beliefnet.com/entertainment/movies/the-nativity-story/the-amazing-story-of-o-holy-night.aspx. Accessed 17 July 2021.

Ivry, Benjamin. "A Brief History of 'O Holy Night,' the Rousing Christmas Hymn That Garnered Mixed Reviews." *America Magazine*, 19 Nov. 2020, https://www.americamagazine.org/arts-culture/2020/11/19/brief-history-o-holy-night-christmas-hymn-review.

IT CAME UPON A MIDNIGHT CLEAR

"History of Hymns: 'It Came Upon a Midnight Clear.'" *Discipleship Ministries*, 18 July 2021, https://www.umcdiscipleship.org/resources/history-of-hymns-it-came-upon-a-midnight-clear.

"The Story Behind." *PraiseCharts*, 18 Dec. 2001, https://www.praisecharts.com/blog/the-story-behind-it-came-upon-a-midnight-clear/.

GOOD KING WENCESLAS

Davis, Elizabeth. "The Real Story behind the Carol Good King Wenceslas." *Classic FM*, 4 Dec. 2018, https://www.classicfm.com/discover-music/real-story-good-king-wenceslas-carol/.

JINGLE BELLS

Klein, Christopher. "8 Things You May Not Know About 'Jingle Bells.'" *HISTORY*, 1 Sept. 2018, https://www.history.com/news/8-things-you-may-not-know-about-jingle-bells.

WE THREE KINGS

Christiansen, Connie. "We Three Kings of Orient Are, the Song and the Story." *Sharefaith Inc.*, https://www.sharefaith.com. Accessed 17 July 2021.

DECK THE HALLS

O'Donnell, Dan. "The Forgotten History of 'Deck the Halls '| News/Talk 1130 WISN | Dan O'Donnell." *Dan O'Donnell*, 4 Dec. 2018, https://newstalk1130.iheart.com/featured/common-sense-central/content/2018-12-04-the-forgotten-history-of-deck-the-halls/.

Ruehl, Kim. "What's the Back Story of the 'Deck the Halls 'Song?" *LiveAbout*, 21 Apr. 2019, https://www.liveabout.com/deck-the-halls-traditional-1322574.

UP ON THE HOUSETOP

"About Christmas Carol 'Up on the Housetop 'by Benjamin Hanby." *Galaxy Music Notes*, https://galaxymusicnotes.com/pages/learn-about-up-on-the-housetop-by-benjamin-hanby. Accessed 17 July 2021.

"Gene Autry Celebrates Santa's Arrival On Christmas Eve By Singing 'Up On The Housetop.'" *Country Rebel*, https://countryrebel.com/blogs/videos/gene-autry-celebrates-santas-arrival-on-christmas-eve-by-singing-up-on-the-housetop/. Accessed 17 July 2021.

O LITTLE TOWN OF BETHLEHEM

"O Little Town of Bethlehem - Lyrics & Story Behind Popular Christmas Carol." *Salem Web Network*, https://www.crosswalk.com/special-coverage/christmas-and-advent/o-little-town-of-bethlehem-1457973.html. Accessed 17 July 2021.

BIBLIOGRAPHY

AWAY IN A MANGER

"History of Hymns: 'Away in a Manger.'" *Discipleship Ministries*, 18 July 2021, https://www.umcdiscipleship.org/resources/history-of-hymns-away-in-a-manger.

GO TELL IT ON THE MOUNTAIN

"Go, Tell It on the Mountain" — *The Story Behind the Song.* 20 Dec. 2012, https://gaither.com/go-tell-it-on-the-mountain-the-story-behind-the-song/.

CAROL OF THE BELLS

"'Carol of the Bells 'Wasn't Originally a Christmas Song." *Rice University News & Media*, 13 Dec. 2021, https://news.rice.edu/2004/12/13/carol-of-the-bells-wasnt-originally-a-christmas-song/.

SANTA CLAUS IS COMIN TO TOWN

Westover, Jeff. "The History of Santa Claus Is Coming to Town | My Merry Christmas." *My Merry Christmas*, 17 July 2021, https://mymerrychristmas.com/the-history-of-santa-claus-is-coming-to-town/.

WINTER WONDERLAND

Micucci, Matt. "A Short History of ... 'Winter Wonderland '- JAZZIZ Magazine." *JAZZIZ Magazine*, 21 Dec. 2018, https://www.jazziz.com/a-short-history-of-winter-wonderland/.

"The Story Behind 'Winter Wonderland '| FamilyTree.Com." *Family Tree*, 25 Dec. 2016, https://www.familytree.com/blog/the-story-behind-winter-wonderland/.

WHITE CHRISTMAS

"Best-Selling Single." *Guinness World Records*, https://www.guinnessworldrecords.com/world-records/best-selling-single. Accessed 17 July 2021.

Eames, Tom. "The Story of... 'White Christmas 'by Bing Crosby." *Smooth*, 3 Dec. 2020, https://www.smoothradio.com/features/the-story-of/white-christmas-lyrics-meaning-facts/.

Murtaugh, Taysha. "The Story Behind the Song 'White Christmas 'Is Even Sadder Than Its Lyrics." *Country Living*, 16 Sept. 2020, https://www.countryliving.com/life/news/a45720/white-christmas-song-history/.

Sewall, Katy. "The Sad Story Behind 'White Christmas, 'America's Favorite Christmas Carol." *Apple App Store Download Icon*, 25 Oct. 2018, https://www.kuow.org/stories/sad-story-behind-white-christmas-america-s-favorite-christmas-carol.

LITTLE DRUMMER BOY

Estrella, Espie. "The Story Behind the 'Little Drummer Boy 'Christmas Carol." *LiveAbout*, 8 Feb. 2019, https://www.liveabout.com/little-drummer-boy-history-2456078.

Moore, Bobby. "'The Little Drummer Boy': The Story Behind the Christmas Standard." *Wide Open Country*, 24 Nov. 2020, https://www.wideopencountry.com/little-drummer-boy-lyrics/.

Sosnowski, Pamela. "Why David Bowie Didn't Want to Sing with Bing Crosby." *REBEAT*. http://www.rebeatmag.com/why-david-bowie-didnt-want-to-sing-with-bing-crosby/. Accessed 17 July 2021.

HAPPY HOLIDAY

Pruitt, Sarah. "The War of Words behind 'Happy Holidays.'" *HISTORY*, 1 Sept. 2018, https://www.history.com/news/the-war-of-words-behind-happy-holidays.

I'LL BE HOME FOR CHRISTMAS

Blazeski, Goran. "'I'll Be Home for Christmas 'Is One of America's Most Popular Holiday Songs." *The Vintage News*, 9 Dec. 2016, https://www.thevintagenews.com/2016/12/09/ill-be-home-for-christmas-is-one-of-americas-most-popular-holiday-songs/.

Nunn, Christina. "Why Bing Crosby's 'I'Ll Be Home for Christmas 'Was Banned by the BBC During World War II." *Showbiz Cheat Sheet*, 13 Dec. 2020, https://www.cheatsheet.com/entertainment/why-bing-crosbys-ill-be-home-for-christmas-was-banned-by-the-bbc-during-world-war-ii.html/.

O'Donnell, Dan. "The Forgotten History of 'I'Ll Be Home for Christmas '| News/Talk 1130 WISN | Dan O'Donnell." *Dan O'Donnell*, 21 Dec. 2017, https://newstalk1130.iheart.com/featured/common-sense-central/content/2017-12-21-the-forgotten-history-of-ill-be-home-for-christmas/.

BABY IT'S COLD OUTSIDE

Eyman, Scott. "'Baby, It's Cold Outside': The Real Story of the Song." *The Palm Beach Post*, 8 Dec. 2010, https://www.palmbeachpost.com/article/20101208/ENTERTAINMENT/812039111.

Mamo, Heran. "Comparing Original 'Baby, It's Cold Outside 'Lyrics With John Legend's 2019 Remake: What's Changed?" *Billboard*, 1 Aug. 2019, https://www.billboard.com/articles/news/holiday/8543129/baby-its-cold-outside-2019-lyrical-transformation.

McDonell-Parry, Amelia. "'Baby, It's Cold Outside': A Brief History of the Holiday Song Controversy." *Rolling Stone*, 11 Dec. 2020, https://www.rollingstone.com/feature/baby-its-cold-outside-controversy-holiday-song-history-768183/.

THE CHRISTMAS SONG

Harrell, Phil. "The Story Behind 'The Christmas Song.'" *NPR*, 25 Dec. 2017, https://www.npr.org/2017/12/25/572408088/the-story-behind-the-christmas-song.

LET IT SNOW!

Debczak, Michele. "8 Surprising Facts About 'Let It Snow.'" *Mental Floss*. 19 Dec. 2019, https://www.mentalfloss.com/article/610499/let-it-snow-song-facts.

MERRY CHRISTMAS BABY

Browning, William. "Who Really Wrote 'Merry Christmas, Baby.'" *Smithsonian Magazine*, 1 Aug. 2021, https://www.smithsonianmag.com/arts-culture/who-wrote-merry-christmas-baby-180965207/.

HERE COMES SANTA CLAUS

Bmoore. "'Here Comes Santa Claus': The Singing Cowboy Origins of the Holiday Standard." *The Boot*, 23 Dec. 2020, https://theboot.com/here-comes-santa-claus-gene-autry-original/.

GeneAutry.Com: Clubhouse - Christmas Song History. https://www.geneautry.com/clubhouse/christmas/christmassongs.html. Accessed 17 July 2021.

BLUE CHRISTMAS

Fox, Courtney. "'Blue Christmas': The Story Behind The Classic Holiday Heartbreaker." *Wide Open Country*, 30 Nov. 2020, https://www.wideopencountry.com/blue-christmas-lyrics/.

SLEIGH RIDE

"It's Time To Recognize The Ronettes As Rock And Roll Pioneers." *NPR*, 12 Mar. 2018, https://www.npr.org/2018/03/12/590891692/its-time-to-recognize-the-ronettes-as-rock-and-roll-pioneers.

Mathias, Shari. "8 Cool Facts About Sleigh Ride | Parker Symphony Orchestra." *Parker Symphony Orchestra | Your Local Community Orchestra*, 25 Nov. 2018, https://parkersymphony.org/facts-about-sleigh-ride.

RUDOLPH

Kennedy, Lesley. "How 25 Christmas Traditions Got Their Start." *HISTORY*, 18 Dec. 2020, https://www.history.com/news/christmas-traditions-history.

Pupovac, Jessica. "The History Of Rudolph The Red-Nosed Reindeer." *NPR*, 25 Dec. 2015, https://www.npr.org/2015/12/25/461005670/the-history-of-rudolph-the-red-nosed-reindeer.

"'Rudolph the Red-Nosed Reindeer 'Is the #1 Song on the U.S. Pop Charts." *HISTORY*, 1 May 2021, https://www.history.com/this-day-in-history/rudolph-the-red-nosed-reindeer-is-the-1-song-on-the-u-s-pop-charts.

THE MAN WITH THE BAG

Vacher, Peter. "Kay Starr Obituary." *The Guardian*, 6 Nov. 2016, http://www.theguardian.com/music/2016/nov/06/kay-starr-obituary.

"Hal Stanley." *Discogs*, https://www.discogs.com/artist/1535122-Hal-Stanley. Accessed 17 July 2021.

SILVER BELLS

Coppens, Teresa. "History of Christmas Carols: 'Silver Bells.'" *Holidappy*, 10 Sept. 2019, https://holidappy.com/holidays/History-of-Christmas-Carols-Silver-Bells.

FROSTY

Gerzenstang, Peter. "The Origins of Frosty the Snowman." *Westchester Magazine*, 18 Nov. 2013, https://westchestermagazine.com/things-to-do/arts-culture/the-origins-of-frosty-the-snowman/.

Kovalchik, Kara. "8 Jolly Happy Facts About 'Frosty the Snowman.'" *Mental Floss*, 22 Dec. 2017, https://www.mentalfloss.com/article/72865/8-jolly-happy-facts-about-frosty-snowman.

I SAW MOMMY

Johnson, Kim. "Did You Know 'I Saw Mommy Kissing Santa Claus 'Was Sung by Riverside-Area Teen?" *Press Enterprise*, 20 Dec. 2018, https://www.pe.com/did-you-know-i-saw-mommy-kissing-santa-claus-was-sung-by-riverside-area-teen.

COOL YULE

http://www.steveallen.com/music/composer.htm. Accessed 17 July 2021.

SANTA BABY

Tarby, Russ. "Santa Baby: How Eartha Kitt's Sexy 1953 Novelty Became a Holiday..." *The Syncopated Times*, 1 Dec. 2016, https://syncopatedtimes.com/santa-baby-at-65-eartha-kitts-sexy-1953-novelty-is-now-a-holiday-standard/.

THE CHRISTMAS WALTZ

Gershman, Dave. "Frank Sinatra: 'The Christmas Waltz.'" *RESELECT.Com*, 21 Dec. 2015, https://www.reselect.com/2015/12/frank-sinatra-the-christmas-waltz/.

JINGLE BELL ROCK

Chilton, Martin. "Jingle Bell Rock: Bobby Helms 'Rockin 'Christmas Classic | UDiscover." *UDiscover Music*, 5 Dec. 2020, https://www.udiscovermusic.com/stories/bobby-helms-jingle-bell-rock-christmas-song/.

Fox, Courtney. "Reba McEntire Singing 'Jingle Bell Rock 'Puts Us in a Festive Mood." *Wide Open Country*, 1 Dec. 2020, https://www.wideopencountry.com/jingle-bell-rock-lyrics/.

SANTA CLAUS IS BACK IN TOWN

Songfacts. "Santa Claus Is Back in Town by Elvis Presley - Songfacts." *Songfacts*, https://www.songfacts.com/facts/elvis-presley/santa-claus-is-back-in-town. Accessed 17 July 2021.

RUN RUDOLPH RUN

Minogue, Jane. "Chuck Berry Run Rudolph Run." *Daily Doo Wop*, 10 Dec. 2017, https://www.dailydoowop.com/chuck-berry-run-rudolph-run/.

ROCKIN' AROUND THE CHRISTMAS TREE

Bernstein, Jonathan. "Brenda Lee: Inside the Life of a Pop Heroine Next Door." *Rolling Stone*, 20 Feb. 2018, https://www.rollingstone.com/music/music-features/inside-the-life-of-brenda-lee-the-pop-heroine-next-door-205175/.

Chilton, Martin. "Rockin 'Around The Christmas Tree: Brenda Lee's Timeless Christmas Hit." *UDiscover Music*, 2 Dec. 2020, https://www.udiscovermusic.com/stories/brenda-lee-rockin-around-the-christmas-tree-song/.

PRETTY PAPER

Overdeep, Meghan. "The True Story Behind Willie Nelson's Moving Christmas Classic, 'Pretty Paper.'" *Southern Living*, https://www.southernliving.com/culture/music/willie-nelson-true-story-pretty-paper-fort-worth-texas. Accessed 17 July 2021.

Kennedy, Bud. "Willie Nelson's sad 'Pretty Paper 'is a real story. And it's set in downtown Fort Worth." 19 Dec. 2017, https://www.star-telegram.com/opinion/bud-kennedy/article190507394.html

LITTLE SAINT NICK

Berry, Zachary. "How The Beach Boys Classic 'Little Deuce Coupe 'Became 'Little Saint Nick.'" *The News Wheel*, 28 Dec. 2017, https://thenewswheel.com/how-the-beach-boys-classic-little-deuce-coupe-became-little-saint-nick/.

PURPLE SNOWFLAKES

Schwartz, Drew. "June 18th, 1965: Marvin Gaye Takes Potential Stevie Wonder Hit." *Gaslight Records*, 17 June 1965, http://gaslightrecords.com/reviews/tracks/marvin-gaye-takes-potential-stevie-wonder-hit.

HOLLY JOLLY CHRISTMAS

Coates, Brandon. "Holiday Song History: 'A Holly Jolly Christmas.'" *The Buzz Adams Morning Show*, 11 Dec. 2018, https://buzzadamsshow.com/holiday-song-history-a-holly-jolly-christmas/.

SOMEDAY AT CHRISTMAS

"Stevie Wonder ' –Someday At Christmas '| Classic Motown." *Classic Motown*, https://classic.motown.com/story/stevie-wonder-someday-christmas/. Accessed 17 July 2021.

GRINCH

Criscitiello, Alexa. "Anatomy Of A Showtune: Inside the Horrible, Horrendous Holiday History of 'You'Re A Mean One, Mr. Grinch.'" *BroadwayWorld.Com*, 25 Dec. 2018, https://www.broadwayworld.com/article/Anatomy-Of-A-Showtune-Inside-the-Horrible-Horrendous-Holiday-History-of-Youre-A-Mean-One-Mr-Grinch-20181225.

SANTA CLAUS GO STRAIGHT TO THE GHETTO

"The BMI Holiday Countdown: James Brown, 'Santa Claus Go Straight to the Ghetto.'" *BMI.Com*, 29 Nov. 2011, https://www.bmi.com/news/entry/the_bmi_holiday_countdown_james_brown_santa_claus_go_straight_to_the_ghetto.

RIVER

Freedom du Lac, J. "'River, 'the 'Thoroughly Depressing 'Joni Mitchell Song That Somehow Became a Christmas Classic." *The Washington Post*, 7 Dec. 2016, https://www.washingtonpost.com/news/arts-and-entertainment/wp/2015/12/17/how-a-thoroughly-depressing-joni-mitchell-song-became-a-christmas-classic/.

FELIZ NAVIDAD

Cruz, Lenika. "'Feliz Navidad': How Jose Feliciano Won America's Heart." *The Atlantic*, 16 Dec. 2015, https://www.theatlantic.com/entertainment/archive/2015/12/feliz-navidad-jose-feliciano-history/420201/.

Runnells, Charles. "50 Years of 'Feliz Navidad': Fun Facts about José Feliciano's Holiday Hit, Livestream Concert." *The News-Press*, https://www.news-press.com/story/entertainment/2020/12/17/feliz-navidad-jose-feliciano-celebrates-50th-anniversary-christmas-music-livestream-concert/3811385001/. Accessed 17 July 2021.

HAPPY CHRISTMAS (WAR IS OVER)

"'Happy Xmas (War Is Over)': The History Behind The Christmas Song." *Allvipp.Com*, 23 Dec. 2020, https://www.allvipp.com/music/happy-xmas-war-is-over-song-meaning-history.

Nevarez, Beth Bullock. "'So This Is Christmas: 'A Holiday Song as Protest." *Beth Nevarez Historical Consulting*, 29 Nov. 2020, https://bethnevarez.com/2020/11/29/happy-xmas-war-is-over-by-john-lennon-and-yoko-ono/.

MERRY XMAS EVERYBODY

Anniezaleski. "The Story of Slade's Festive Glam Smash 'Merry Xmas Everybody.'" *Ultimate Classic Rock*, 9 Dec. 2018, https://ultimateclassicrock.com/slade-merry-xmas-everybody-history/.

FATHER CHRISTMAS

Anniezaleski. "When the Kinks Got Deceptively Festive on 'Father Christmas.'" *Ultimate Classic Rock*, 25 Nov. 2017, https://ultimateclassicrock.com/kinks-father-christmas/.

"The Kinks 'Dave Davies Says Band's Classic Holiday Song 'Father Christmas 'Is 'Very Special to Me '- Music News - ABC News Radio." *ABC News Radio*, http://abcnewsradioonline.com. Accessed 17 July 2021.

CHRISTMAS RAPPIN'

Adler, Bill. "Every Year Just 'Bout This Time, Kurtis Blow Celebrates With a Rhyme." *Smithsonian Magazine*, 3 Aug. 2019, https://www.smithsonianmag.com/smithsonian-institution/every-year-just-bout-time-kurtis-blow-celebrates-rhyme-180973639/.

Serrano, Shea. *The Rap Year Book*. Harry N. Abrams, 2015.

CHRISTMAS WRAPPING

Crae, Ross. "Story behind the Christmas Song: The Waitresses 'Christmas Wrapping - The Sunday Post." *The Sunday Post*, 17 July 2021, https://www.sundaypost.com/fp/story-behind-the-christmas-song-the-waitresses-christmas-wrapping/.

2000 MILES

"The Story Of... '2000 Miles 'by The Pretenders." *Smooth*, 13 Dec. 2017, https://www.smoothradio.com/features/pretenders-2000-miles-meaning/.

DO THEY KNOW IT'S CHRISTMAS

Pagetta, Joe. "Is 'Do They Know It's Christmas? 'The Most Misunderstood Holiday Song?" *America Magazine*, 19 Dec. 2018, https://www.americamagazine.org/arts-culture/2018/12/19/do-they-know-its-christmas-most-misunderstood-holiday-song.

Rossen, Jake. "Band Aid: The Charitable—and Controversial—History of 'Do They Know It's Christmas?'" *Mental Floss*, 19 Dec. 2019, https://www.mentalfloss.com/article/610472/do-they-know-its-christmas-band-aid-song-history.

LAST CHRISTMAS

Aroesti, Rachel. "Still Saving Us from Tears: The inside Story of Wham!'s Last Christmas." *The Guardian*, 14 Dec. 2017, http://www.theguardian.com/music/2017/dec/14/still-saving-us-from-tears-story-george-michael-last-christmas.

MERRY CHRISTMAS (I DON'T WANT TO FIGHT TONIGHT)

Hann, Michael. "Old Music: Ramones – Merry Christmas (I Don't Want to Fight Tonight)." *The Guardian*, 20 Dec. 2011, http://www.theguardian.com/music/2011/dec/20/old-music-ramones-merry-christmas.

FAIRYTALE OF NEW YORK

Eames, Tom. "The Story of... 'Fairytale of New York 'by The Pogues and Kirsty MacColl." *Smooth*, 19 Nov. 2020, https://www.smoothradio.com/features/the-story-of/fairytale-of-new-york-lyrics-meaning-pogues-facts/.

Lynskey, Dorian. "Fairytale of New York: The Story behind the Pogues 'Classic Christmas Anthem." *The Guardian*, 6 Dec. 2012, http://www.theguardian.com/music/2012/dec/06/fairytale-new-york-pogues-christmas-anthem.

CHRISTMAS IN HOLLIS

Phull, Hardeep. "Why Run-DMC Didn't Want to Make 'Christmas in Hollis.'" *New York Post*, 14 Dec. 2017, https://nypost.com/2017/12/14/why-run-dmc-didnt-want-to-make-christmas-in-hollis/.

Rytlewski, Evan. "We Talk Run-DMC's 'Christmas In Hollis 'with DMC Himself." *The A.V. Club*, 10 Dec. 2013, https://www.avclub.com/we-talk-run-dmc-s-christmas-in-hollis-with-dmc-himsel-1798242786.

CHRISTMAS ALL OVER AGAIN

Rossen, Jake. "The Bittersweet Story Behind A Very Special Christmas</Em>." *Mental Floss*, 21 Dec. 2017, https://www.mentalfloss.com/article/72524/bittersweet-story-behind-very-special-christmas.

ALL I WANT FOR CHRISTMAS IS YOU

Beck, Laura. "21 Things You Definitely Didn't Know About Mariah Carey's Iconic 'All I Want for Christmas Is You.'" *Cosmopolitan*, 7 Dec. 2020, https://www.cosmopolitan.com/entertainment/music/a8534458/mariah-careys-all-i-want-for-christmas-is-you-facts/.

Heigl, Alex. "Everything You Ever Wanted to Know About Mariah Carey's 'All I Want for Christmas Is You.'" *PEOPLE.Com*, 14 Dec. 2020, https://people.com/music/all-i-want-for-christmas-is-you-history/.

CHRISTMAS TIME IS HERE

"A Look Back at Vince Guaraldi's A Charlie Brown Christmas." *SFJAZZ Logo*, 18 July 2021, https://www.sfjazz.org/onthecorner/look-back-vince-guaraldis-charlie-brown-christmas/.

"The Most Famous Music from 'A Charlie Brown Christmas' Was Originally Written for a Different Project | American Masters | PBS." *American Masters*, 3 Dec. 2020, https://www.pbs.org/wnet/americanmasters/the-most-famous-music-from-a-charlie-brown-christmas-was-originally-written-for-a-different-project/16357/.

CHRISTMAS TREAT

Caffrey, Dan. "'I Wish It Was Christmas Today' Has Grown from Novelty Song to Holiday Standard." *The A.V. Club*, 19 Dec. 2015, https://www.avclub.com/i-wish-it-was-christmas-today-has-grown-from-novelty-1798287593.

12 DAYS OF CHRISTMAS

"The 2020 PNC Christmas Price Index." *PNC*, https://www.pnc.com/en/about-pnc/topics/pnc-christmas-price-index.html. Accessed 16 July 2021.

"About Dairy Cows." *Compassion USA*, https://www.ciwf.com/farmed-animals/cows/dairy-cows/. Accessed 16 July 2021.

Gleeson, Jill. "Here's What to Know About the Meaning Behind the '12 Days of Christmas'." *Country Living*, 28 Sept. 2020, https://www.countryliving.com/entertaining/a29832797/12-days-of-christmas-meaning/.

Gagnon, Stephanie. "Swan Song: 5 Fun Facts about These Majestic Creatures • The National Wildlife Federation Blog." *The National Wildlife Federation Blog*, 25 Oct. 2019, https://blog.nwf.org/2019/10/swan-song-5-fun-facts-about-these-majestic-creatures/.

Indiviglio, Frank. "European Blackbirds as Pets - Captive Care and Natural History." *That Bird Blog*, 8 Dec. 2011, http://blogs.thatpetplace.com/thatbirdblog/2011/12/08/european-blackbirds-as-pets-captive-care-and-natural-history/.

Montgomerie, Bob. "Three French Hens - American Ornithological Society." *American Ornithological Society*, 24 Dec. 2018, https://americanornithology.org/three-french-hens/.

Pai, Tanya. "The 12 Days of Christmas: The Story behind the Holiday's Most Annoying Carol." *Vox*, 1 Dec. 2020, https://www.vox.com/21796404/12-days-of-christmas-explained.

StackPath. https://www.gardeningknowhow.com/edible/fruits/pear/growing-pear-trees.htm. Accessed 16 July 2021.

"What Is a Turtle Dove? - Operation Turtle Dove." *Operation Turtle Dove*, 1 Apr. 2021, https://operationturtledove.org/turtle-doves/what-is-a-turtle-dove/.

https://www.nrcs.usda.gov/Internet/FSE_DOCUMENTS/nrcs141p2_018050.pdf. Accessed 16 July 2021.

MOVIES

"Christmas Theme - Box Office Mojo." *Box Office Mojo*, https://www.boxofficemojo.com/genre/sg2782851329/. Accessed 17 July 2021.

BIBLIOGRAPHY

SANTA CLAUS

"Watch 'Santa Claus – 'the First Christmas Film Ever Made (1898)." *Film Doctor*, 25 Dec. 2016, http://filmdoctor.co.uk/2016/12/25/watch-santa-claus-the-first-christmas-film-ever-made-1898/.

IT'S A WONDERFUL LIFE

VanDerWerff, Emily. "It's a Wonderful Life Is One of the Best Movies America Has Ever Made about Itself." *Vox*, 20 Dec. 2016, https://www.vox.com/culture/2016/12/20/14013388/its-a-wonderful-life-review-anniversary-70.

Wood, Jennifer. "25 Wonderful Facts About 'It's a Wonderful Life</Em.'" *Mental Floss*, 17 Dec. 2018, https://www.mentalfloss.com/article/592472/25-wonderful-facts-about-its-wonderful-life.

A CHRISTMAS STORY

Kashner, Sam. "How A Christmas Story Went from Low-Budget Fluke to an American Tradition." *Vanity Fair*, 30 Nov. 2016, https://www.vanityfair.com/hollywood/2016/11/how-a-christmas-story-became-an-american-tradition.

SANTA CLAUS: THE MOVIE

Club, The. "Why Is Santa Claus: The Movie so Merrily Maligned?" *The A.V. Club*, 5 Dec. 2014, https://www.avclub.com/why-is-santa-claus-the-movie-so-merrily-maligned-1798274686.

SILENT NIGHT DEADLY NIGHT

Bailey, Jason. "How Silent Night, Deadly Night Inflamed a Nation." *Vulture*, 24 Dec. 2018, https://www.vulture.com/2018/12/how-silent-night-deadly-night-inflamed-a-nation.html.

CHRISTMAS VACATION

Sorren, Martha. "National Lampoon Christmas Vacation Facts." *CafeMom.Com*, https://cafemom.com/entertainment/222911-national-lampoon-christmas-vacation-facts/323172-the_directors_small_cameo. Accessed 17 July 2021.

Wood, Jennifer. "41 Festive Facts About Christmas Vacation</Em>." *Mental Floss*, 1 Dec. 2018, https://www.mentalfloss.com/article/60330/27-things-you-might-not-know-about-christmas-vacation.

HOME ALONE

Hansen, Lauren. "Diagnosing the Home Alone Burglars 'Injuries: A Professional Weighs In." *The Week*, 30 Nov. 2021, https://theweek.com/articles/469307/diagnosing-home-alone-burglars-injuries-professional-weighs.

Pai, Tanya. "Home Alone's Enduring Popularity, Explained." *Vox*, 16 Nov. 2015, https://www.vox.com/2015/11/16/9731584/home-alone-popular.

DIE HARD

Kemp, Ella. "'Die Hard 'Writer Explains Why It's a Better Christmas Film than 'White Christmas.'" *NME*, 22 Dec. 2020, https://www.nme.com/news/film/die-hard-writer-explains-christmas-film-white-christmas-2844452.

KINKADE

Glaister, Dan. "Thomas Kinkade: The Secret Life and Strange Death of Art's King of Twee." *The Guardian*, 9 May 2012, http://www.theguardian.com/artanddesign/2012/may/09/thomas-kinkade-dark-death-painter.

CHRISTMAS ADJACENT

SHANE BLACK

Guerra, Felipe. "'Jingle Bang!': The Christmas Action Films Written by Shane Black." *FanFare*, 28 Dec. 2020, https://medium.com/fan-fare/jingle-bang-the-christmas-action-films-written-by-shane-black-43def03bd166.

Lambie, Ryan. "Shane Black Interview: Iron Man 3, Last Action Hero, Writing - Den of Geek." *Den of Geek*, 18 Apr. 2013, https://www.denofgeek.com/movies/shane-black-interview-iron-man-3-screenwriting-christmas/.

LETHAL WEAPON

Reyes, Mike. "If Die Hard Is A Christmas Movie, That Means Lethal Weapon Is Too." *CINEMABLEND*, 7 Dec. 2019, https://www.cinemablend.com/news/2485966/if-die-hard-is-a-christmas-movie-that-means-lethal-weapon-is-too.

TELEVISION

RANKIN BASS

Delgado, Michelle. "The Magical Animation of 'Rudolph the Red-Nosed Reindeer.'" *Smithsonian Magazine*, 23 Aug. 2019, https://www.smithsonianmag.com/innovation/magical-animation-rudolph-red-nosed-reindeer-180973841/.

Gavin, Michael. "New on ShopDisney (12/21/17): 5 Disney Princess Tops That Will Have You Feeling Like RoyaltyFav Five: Top Holiday Experiences at Central Florida Theme Parks." *YouTube Inside the Magic*, 21 Dec. 2017, https://insidethemagic.net/2017/12/making-christmas-animated-history-rankin-bass-productions/.

Heffernan, Virginia. "Rudolph, Bard of the Can-Do Christmas." *Slate*, 23 Dec. 2002, https://slate.com/culture/2002/12/rudolph-bard-of-the-can-do-christmas.html.

MR. MAGOO

Robinson, Mark. "More On Magoo: An In-Depth Look at Mister Magoo's Christmas Carol — Mark Robinson Writes." *Mark Robinson Writes*, 18 Dec. 2016, http://www.markrobinsonwrites.com/the-music-that-makes-me-dance/2016/12/18/more-on-magoo-an-in-depth-look-at-mister-magoos-christmas-carol.

Wilson, Joanna. "Mr. Magoo's Christmas Carol (1962)." *Christmas TV History*, 8 Nov. 2012, http://www.christmastvhistory.com/2012/11/happy-50th-birthday-mr-magoos-christmas.html.

CHARLIE BROWN

Altman, Tory. "How Santa Brought Coca-Cola in from the Cold." *National Museum of American History*, 17 Dec. 2014, https://americanhistory.si.edu/blog/santa-coca-cola.

GRINCH

Wong, Andrew. "12 Spirited Facts About How the Grinch Stole Christmas</Em>." *Mental Floss*, 9 Nov. 2018, https://www.mentalfloss.com/article/72593/13-spirited-facts-about-how-grinch-stole-christmas.

CHIPMUNKS

Cox, Stephen. "'The Chipmunk Song 'Turns 60: Secrets of a Holiday Novelty Smash." *The Hollywood Reporter*, 21 Dec. 2018, https://www.hollywoodreporter.com/news/music-news/chipmunk-song-turns-60-secrets-a-holiday-classic-1169762/.

SMURFS

"55 Years of Belgian Blues - A History of The Smurfs." *SimplyMaya News*, 22 Aug. 2014, https://simplymaya.com/news/55-years-of-belgian-blues-a-history-of-the-smurfs/.

CLAYMATION

"I Heard It through the Grapevine {1986} | Full Official Chart History | Official Charts Company." *Official Charts*, https://www.officialcharts.com/search/singles/i-heard-it-through-the-grapevine-%7B1986%7D/. Accessed 17 July 2021.

VARIETY SHOWS

BING AND BOWIE

Andrea Warner · Posted: Dec 21, 2017. "David Bowie, Bing Crosby and the Story of the Strangest Christmas Duet Ever | CBC Music." *CBC*, 6 Feb. 2019, https://www.cbc.ca/music/read/david-bowie-bing-crosby-and-the-story-of-the-strangest-christmas-duet-ever-1.5008343.

ANDY GRIFFITH

"9 Little Details You Never Noticed in the Andy Griffith Show Episode "Christmas Story"." *Me-TV Network*, 26 Nov. 2019, https://www.metv.com/lists/9-little-details-you-never-noticed-in-the-andy-griffith-show-episode-christmas-story.

DICKENS

Allen, Michael. "Charles Dickens, Warren's Blacking and the Chancery Court | The National Archives." *Archives Media Player*, 1 Oct. 2010, https://media.nationalarchives.gov.uk/index.php/charles-dickens-warrens-blacking-and-the-chancery-court/.

Broich, John. "The Real Reason Charles Dickens Wrote 'A Christmas Carol.'" *Time*, 13 Dec. 2016, https://time.com/4597964/history-charles-dickens-christmas-carol/.

Hawksley, Lucinda. *How Did A Christmas Carol Come to Be?* https://www.bbc.com/culture/article/20171215-how-did-a-christmas-carol-come-to-be. Accessed 17 July 2021.

Norman, Miller. "The Original Scrooge." *The Telegraph*, 20 Sept. 2016, https://www.telegraph.co.uk/only-in-britain/man-who-inspired-ebenezer-scrooge/.

INDEX

101 Dalmatians: The Series 298
12 Men of Christmas 191
2000 Miles 147
30 Rock 273-274, 318, 319
8 Simple Rules 317
98° 107
Abbott, Bud 218
About a Boy 210
Adam-12 251, 314
The Addams Family 275, 318, 319
Advent calendars 25-26
The Adventures of Ozzie and Harriet 296, 317, 318
Afanasieff, Walter 150-151
Affleck, Ben 198
Aiken, Clay 137
The Alcoa Hour 297
Alcott, Louisa May 33, 95
Alexander, Jason 291
ALF 277, 318
Alfred Hitchcock Presents 263
Alice 298, 318
All Alone on Christmas 152
All I Want For Christmas Is My Two Front Teeth 158
All I Want For Christmas Is You 15, 106, 151-152, 153, 158, 220
All I Want Is Truth (For Christmas) 154
All in the Family 275, 318
Allen, Debbie 298
Allen, Steve 135
Allen, Tim 180, 182, 183
Allman, Gregg 222-223
Ally McBeal 255-256
Almost Christmas 185
Almqvist, Howlin' Pete 153
Alone on Christmas Day 155
Amazing Stories 263
American Dad 295
American Horror Story: Asylum 266
The Amos and Andy Show 318
Andersen, Hans Christian 95

Anderson, Pam 255
Anderson, Richard Dean 257
Andrews Sisters 118, 128
Andrews, Julie 218
The Andy Griffith Show 268-269, 317
Angels We Have Heard on High 113
Animaniacs 244, 292
Aniston, Jennifer 186
Ann-Margret 224
Anna and the Apocalypse 190
Annoying Orange 300
The Apartment 187
Apollo 21
Apple, Fiona 134
Applegate, Christina 198
Aqua Teen Hunger Force 291
Arkin, Alan 198
Armstrong, Louis 136, 151
Arrested Development 273
Arthur 175
Arthur Christmas 183
Arthur, Bea 223-224
Asner, Ed 180, 299
Astaire, Fred 203, 227, 233
Atari 77, 83
Atkinson, Rowan 292
Auld Lang Syne 112
Austen, Jane 283
Autry, Gene 130, 132, 134, 225, 230
Ave Maria 114-115
Away in a Manger 106, 120-121
Aykroyd, Dan 206, 278
Azaria, Hank 258
B.C.: A Special Christmas 234
Babes in Toyland 170
Baby It's Cold Outside 127-128, 281
Baby Talk (TV Show) 318
Back Door Santa 150, 151
Back to the Future Part II 177
Back to the Future: The Animated Series 290-291
A Bad Moms Christmas 174, 185

351

Bad Santa 180-181, 184
Bad Santa 2 174, 181
Bagdasarian, Ross 237
Balanchine, George 168
Baldur 21-22
Baldwin, Alec 278
Bananarama 148
Banderas, Antonio 239
Baranski, Christine 185
Barbie 76, 80-81, 298
Barbie in A Christmas Carol 299
Barney 77
Barrymore, Lionel 171-172
Barrymore, Drew 239
Barton, Clara 302
Bass, Jules 224
Bassett, Angela 240
Bateman, Jason 186
Bates, Kathy 183
Batiste, Jon 112
Batman Returns 188
Battleship 76
Baum, L. Frank 97, 228, 233
Baywatch 255, 313
BBC/FX's A Christmas Carol 287-288
Be Cool, Scooby-Doo! 290
The Beach Boys 140, 155
Beanie Babies 76, 85
The Bear Who Slept Through Christmas 233
The Beatles 57, 140, 306
Beauty and the Beast 264
Beavis and Butt-Head 247, 288-289
Beckinsale, Kate 209
Behind Enemy Lines 209
Bell, Jillian 185
Bell, Kristen 185
The Bells of St. Mary's 204
Benson 275, 317
Beowulf 32
Berenstain Bears 234
Berlin, Irving 15, 124, 125-126, 134, 173, 310
Berry, Chuck 130, 138
The Best Man Holiday 174, 184-185
Better Off Dead 206
Betty Boop 136, 177
Beverly Hills, 90210 259-260, 261, 315
Bewitched 269, 289-290, 318
Biel, Jessica 197
The Big Bang Theory 317
Big Bird 2, 85, 249
Big Bulbs 155
Billingsley, Peter 175

The Bishop's Wife 172, 179
BJ and the Bear 265
Blacc, Aloe 151, 157
Black, Shane 213
Black Christmas 174, 189
Black Mirror 264
Black-ish 319
Blackadder 291
Blanchett, Cate 212
Blast of Silence 204
Blow, Kurtis 146, 147
Blue Christmas 130-131, 312
Bob B. Soxx & The Blue Jeans 131
The Bob Newhart Show 270
Bogart, Humphrey 204, 302
BoJack Horseman 248
Bon Jovi, Jon 150
Bond, James 205
Bono 148
Bono, Sonny 218, 222-223
The Boondocks 248
Boone, Pat 108, 279
Bosley, Tom 231, 289
Boston Pops 117, 131
Bowie, David 125, 219, 220, 222
Boy George 148
Boy Meets World 319
Boyd, Jimmy 135
The Brady Bunch 108, 111, 116, 317
Bradford, William 13
Branded (TV Show) 313
Brant, Sebastian 18
Bratz 76, 81
The Brian Setzer Orchestra 260
Bridget Jones's Diary 89, 210
Briggs, Raymond 238, 240
Bright Eyes 202
Broad City 276
Broderick, Matthew 182
Brooklyn Nine-Nine 274, 317, 318, 319
Brooklyn Tabernacle Choir 122
Brown, Chris 183
Brown, James 143-144, 303
Bryant, Aidy 186
Bryant, Anita 114, 117
Bryant, Kobe 307
Bublé, Michael 105, 135
Buck, Pearl S. 100-101
Buffett, Jimmy 118, 302
Buffy the Vampire Slayer 316
Bugs Bunny 234, 236, 288
Bugs Bunny's Christmas Carol 236, 288

INDEX

Bugs Bunny's Looney Christmas Tales 236-237
Bullock, Sandra 208
Burke, Solomon 151
Burns, George 217, 224, 298
Burns, Robert 112
Burton, Tim 189, 207
Caan, James 180
Cabbage Patch Kids 76, 84, 86, 179, 242
Cabbage Patch Kids: Vernon's Christmas 242
Caesar, Julius 7
Caesar Augustus 9
Caganer 55
Cage, Nicholas 294
Cagney & Lacey 314
Cahn, Sammy 129, 137
Cain 32
Caine, Michael 287
Calhoun, Monica 184
Caligula 8
Callow, Simon 294
Calloway, Cab 302
Cameron, Kirk 199
Camp Candy 293-294
candy canes 69-70
Candy, John 293-294
Capote, Truman 100
Capra, Frank 171
Captain and Tennille 218
Captain Kangaroo 222-223
Car 54, Where Are You? 317
Care Bears 77
Carey, Mariah 106, 113, 116, 150-151, 154, 157, 221
Carney, Art 225, 234, 265
Carol 212
A Carol Christmas 299
A Carol for Another Christmas 291-292
Carol of the Bells 122
The Carpenters 218
Carrey, Jim 179, 287
Carroll, Diahann 223
Carter, Clarence 151, 152
Carvey, Dana 278
Casablancas, Julian 153
Cash, Johnny 102, 218
Cassidy, David 134
Cast Away 209
Castellaneta, Dan 263
Castle-Hughes, Keisha 182
Catch Me If You Can 210, 308
Ceausescu, Nicolae 304

Chabert, Lacey 192
Chaplin, Charlie 303
Chappelle's Show 280
Charlemagne 304
Charles I 12-13
Charles II 13
Charles, Ray 111, 128, 129, 139, 152
Charles in Charge 318
A Charlie Brown Christmas 109, 111, 125, 209, 234, 235, 279
Charmed (TV Show) 316
Charo 220
Chase, Chevy 177
Chateau Christmas 193
Chatty Cathy 76
Cheech and Chong 184
Cheers 271, 318
Chenoweth, Kristin 192
Cher 218, 222-223, 252
Chestnut, Morris 186
chestnuts 66-67
Chewbacca 82, 83, 223
Chicago Hope 257, 315
The Chipmunks 159, 237, 295
A Chipmunk Christmas 237
The Chipmunk Song 158-159, 237
CHiPs 254
Christie, Agatha 101
Christmas All Over Again 150
Christmas and You 156-157
Christmas at Pee-Wee's Playhouse 220
Christmas Butt 157
Christmas cards 23-25
A Christmas Carol 14, 66, 68, 71, 94-95, 101, 107, 174, 231, 234-235, 237, 246, 247, 263, 280, 283-300
The Christmas Chronicles 193
Christmas Comes to Pac-Land 240-241
Christmas cookies 70
A Christmas Duel 152-153
Christmas Eve on Sesame Street 249
The Christmas Gift 196
Christmas in Connecticut 170
Christmas In Harlem 153
Christmas In Hollis 149-150
A Christmas Prince 193
The Christmas Shoes (song) 160
The Christmas Shoes (movie) 197-198
The Christmas Song 66, 128, 221
A Christmas Story 102, 174-175, 190
Christmas Rappin' 146
The Christmas That Almost Wasn't 196

353

Christmas Time Is Here 141-142, 209
Christmas Treat 153
Christmas trees 17-20
Christmas Vacation 89, 152, 174, 175, 176-177
Christmas with the Kranks 182
The Christmas Waltz 137
Christmas Wrapping 146-147
Chuck (TV Show) 314
Church, Francis P. 96-97
Clark, Bob 175, 189
Clarkson, Kelly 128, 154, 221
A Claymation Christmas Celebration 241-242, 247
Cleveland, Grover 20
Clooney, George 193
Clooney, Rosemary 173-174
Cobra Kai 261
Coca-Cola 31, 142, 235
Colbert, Stephen 112, 220-221
A Colbert Christmas: The Greatest Gift of All 220-221
Cole, Henry 23
Cole, Nat King 107, 109, 111, 113, 119, 128, 280
Coleman, Gary 299
Collette, Toni 185
Collins, Bootsy 118
Collins, Phil 148
Columbus, Chris (director) 177
Columbus, Christopher (explorer) 29
Community 274, 319
Como, Perry 123, 134, 146, 161, 218, 219
Connect Four 76
Cool Yule 135-136
Coolidge, Calvin 20
Cooper, Bradley 211
Cosby, Bill 128, 236
Costello, Elvis 149, 221
Costello, Lou 218
Cover Up 204
Cox, Tony 181
Craig, Daniel 211
Cranston, Bryan 252-253
Crayola Crayons 76
Cricket on the Hearth 226
Cromwell, Oliver 11-12
Cronos 207
Crosby, Bing 106, 118, 124, 125, 126, 130, 132, 133, 137, 151, 173, 203, 204, 218-219, 222, 249
Crowe, Russell 208
The Crown 266-267
Crown for Christmas 192

Cruz, Penélope 198
The Crystals 132
Csonka, Larry 302
Culkin, Macaulay 177
Cumberbatch, Benedict 187
Curb Your Enthusiasm 272
Currier and Ives 131-132
Curry, Tim 299
Curtis, Jamie Lee 182
Cusack, John 206, 209
Cyrus, Miley 193
D.C. Follies 250
Daddy's Home 2 174, 186
Dale, Dick 220
Dance of the Sugar Plum Fairy 168
Dangerfield, Rodney 219
Daniel Boone (TV show) 313
Danson, Ted 267
David, Larry 272
Davis Jr., Sammy 197
Davis, Judy 188
Dawson's Creek 261-262
De La Soul 152
De Niro, Robert 211
de Souza, Steven 188
de Wolfe, Billy 227
Deck the Halls (song) 106, 119
Deck the Halls (movie) 182
Deck the Halls with Wacky Walls 241
Deep Sea Diver 154
del Toro, Guillermo 208
DeLuise, Dom 219
Dennis the Menace 276, 296
A Dennis the Menace Christmas 297
Denver, John 108, 159, 161, 196, 218, 249
Deschanel, Zooey 128, 180
Desperate Housewives 262
Devine, Loretta 182
DeVito, Danny 182, 270, 288, 289
Dexter 254
Diagnosis Murder 315
Diamond, Neil 112
Diaz, Cameron 211, 239
DiCaprio, Leonardo 210, 308
The Dick Van Dyke Show 317
Dickens, Charles 15, 68, 72, 91, 94-95, 107, 226, 228, 281, 283-301
Dickinson, Angie 252
Dido 303
Die Hard 155-156, 187-188, 213, 274, 311
Die Hard 2 206-207
A Different World 295, 318

Diff'rent Strokes 317
Diggs, Taye 184
Dillon, Melinda 175
Diner 205
Disney's A Christmas Carol 287
Django Unchained 307
Do They Know It's Christmas? 36, 147-148
Dogg, Snoop 136
Dolly Parton's Christmas on the Square 297
Doogie Howser, M.D. 258, 315
Dora the Explorer 298
Douglas, Michael 287
Downton Abbey 267
Doyle, Arthur Conan 96
Doyle-Murray, Brian 242
Dr. Quinn, Medicine Woman 294
Dr. Teeth 139
Doctor Who 296
Dr. Kildare 315
Dragnet 254, 255
Dratch, Rachel 278
Drexell's Class 318
Drunk History 280
DuckTales 294
The Dukes 296
The Dukes of Hazard 295
Dumas, Alexandre 167
Dunaway, Faye 205
Durante, Jimmy 227
Duvall, Robert 184
Dylan, Bob 111
Dynasty 315
E.T. 178
EastEnders 300
Easy Bake Oven 76
Ebbie 291
Ebert, Roger 175, 190
Edison, Thomas 19-20, 116, 291
Edward Scissorhands 207
eggnog 25, 43, 61, 68-69, 159
El Chapo 303
Elba, Idris 182, 211
Electra, Carmen 220
Elf 33, 175, 180, 194, 201, 224
Elf on the Shelf 33
Elliott, Sam 176
Elmo 77, 85, 179
Elwes, John 285
Emmet Otter's Jug-Band Christmas 248
ER 257, 314, 315
Ernest Saves Christmas 174, 176
Estefan, Gloria 129

Etch-A-Sketch 76
Everybody Loves Raymond 276
(Everybody's Waitin' For) The Man with the Bag 132-133
The Equalizer 252
Extras 276
Eyes Wide Shut 209
F is for Family 248
The Facts of Life 185, 192, 317
Fairytale of New York 149, 303
Fallon, Jimmy 153
Fame 297
A Family Circus Christmas 234
Family Guy 247-248, 290
Family Matters 319
The Family Stone 188-189
Family Ties 289, 317, 318
Farley, Chris 278, 300
Fast Times at Ridgemont High 205-206
Fat Albert 233, 234, 236
The Fat Albert Christmas Special 236
Father Christmas (song) 145-146
Father Knows Best 267
Favreau, Jon 180, 224
Feast of the Seven Fishes 52
Feast of the Seven Fishes (movie) 195
Feig, Paul 186
Feliciano, José 118, 144
Feliz Navidad 144
Ferrell, Will 33, 180, 186, 211, 279
Festival of Family Classics: A Christmas Tree 228
Fields, W.C. 303
figgy pudding 65, 70-71
Finney, Albert 290
The First Noel 113-114
Fishburne, Laurence 240
Fisher-Price 76, 80
Fisher, Carrie 295
Fitzgerald, Ella 121
Flaherty, Joe 220
The Flash 316
The Flintstones 234, 243, 245, 291
A Flintstone Christmas Carol 291
Foley, Dave 220
Fonda, Jane 296
Fonzie 271, 296
Ford Model T 77, 79
Four Christmases 183
Fox, Michael J. 272, 289
Fox, Nellie 302
Foxx, Jamie 276, 307

Foxx, Redd 289
Franklin, Ben 14, 230
Frasier 271-272, 319
Fred Claus 183
Freeman, Morgan 186
The French Connection 205
Fresh Off the Boat 319
The Fresh Prince of Bel-Air 319
Friday Night Lights 266
Friends 275, 319
Frigg 21-22
Frosty Returns 242
Frosty the Snowman (song) 134
Frosty the Snowman (TV special) 225, 227, 234, 242
Frosty's Winter Wonderland 229
Frozen 86
fruitcake 56, 71-72, 100, 240, 278
Full House (TV Show) 318
Furby 77, 85-86
G.I. Joe 76, 81-82
G.I. Joe: The Real American Hero 245
Gabriel 9
Gandolfini, James 198
A Garfield Christmas 238
Garland, Judy 126-127, 203, 218, 221-222
Gaye, Marvin 141, 143, 153, 241
Gaynor, Mitzi 218
Gazzara, Ben 292
Geldof, Bob 148, 149
General Hospital 293
George III 19
Gervais, Ricky 272
Ghostface Killah 152
Ghostface X-mas 152
Giamatti, Paul 183
Gibson, Mel 186, 213, 290
Gifford, Kathie Lee 220
The Gift of the Magi 98, 232, 249
Gilligan's Island 140, 204, 317
Gimme a Break! 317
gingerbread houses 53, 72-73
The Girl with the Dragon Tattoo 211
Gleason, Jackie 131
Gloria 113
Glover, Danny 185, 213
Go 209
Go Tell It on the Mountain 121
God Rest Ye Merry Gentlemen 107-108
The Godfather 204, 205
Godmothered 212
Goldberg, Whoopi 299

The Golden Girls 275
The Goldbergs 317
Golding, Henry 186
Good Cheer 170
Good King Wenceslas 117
The Good, the Bad and the Ugly 196, 211
Good Times 270, 317
GoodFellas 202, 207
Goodman, John 211, 242
The Goonies 178
goose 67, 68
Gorbachev, Mikhail 304
Gordon-Levitt, Joseph 185
Gossip Girl 316
Grammer, Kelsey 291, 300
Grandma Got Run Over By a Reindeer (song) 2, 159-160
Grandma Got Run Over By a Reindeer (special) 242
Grant, Cary 172, 178, 202
Grant, Hugh 210
Grant, Richard 288
Grant, Ulysses S. 15
Green, Al 113
The Green Knight 212
Greene, Lorne 108
Gremlins 188
Grey, Joel 158
Grey's Anatomy 258-259, 315
Griffith, Andy 253, 269, 317
The Grinch 66, 101, 142-143, 174, 179, 186, 234, 236, 247, 288, 293
Grisham, John 182
Groening, Matt 239
Grounded for Life 319
Grumpy Old Men 207
Gryla 51
Guest, Nicholas 177
Gumby 78, 299
Gunsmoke 313
Gwenn, Edmund 172
Haakon the Good 11
Hackman, Gene 205
Hackett, Buddy 231
Hahn, Kathryn 185
Hall, Regina 184
ham 67
Hamm, Jon 263-264
Hammon, Jupiter 305
Hangin' with Mr. Cooper 318
Hanks, Tom 182, 207, 209, 210, 307
Hanna-Barbera's A Christmas Story 233

INDEX

Hannah, Daryl 207
Hanson 122
Happiest Season 194
Happy Christmas (War Is Over) 145
Happy Days 270, 318
Happy Holiday (song) 125-126
Harden, Marcia Gay 200
Hardy, Oliver 170, 298
Hark! The Herald Angels Sing 111-112
Harry Potter 170, 214-215
Hart to Hart 254
Hartman, Phil 179
Hasselhoff, David 255
Have Gun - Will Travel 313, 314
Have Yourself a Merry Little Christmas 127, 203, 298
Hawaii Five-0 314
Hayden, Sterling 292
He-Man and She-Ra: A Christmas Special 241
Head of the Class 318
Hearts Afire 319
Heat Miser 229
Helms, Bobby 138
Henderson, Ricky 303
Henry II 205
Henry III 304
Henry, Thierry 307
Hercules: The Legendary Journeys 265, 316
Here Comes Santa Claus 130-131
Herman, Pee-wee 220
Hicks, Seymour 288
Highway Patrol 313
Highway to Heaven 296, 316
Hill Street Blues 254
Hill, George Roy 307
Hill, Rowland 22-23
Hines, Cheryl 185
Hines, Gregory 233
Hirohito 304
The Hives 152-153
Hoffmann, E.T.A. 167
Hogan, Hulk 197
The Hogan Family 318
Holiday 202
The Holiday 210-211
Holiday Affair 172-173
Holiday Inn 124, 173, 201, 203
A Holly, Jolly Christmas 140, 142
Holmes, Katie 209
Home Alone 42, 174, 177-178, 189
Home Alone 2: Lost in New York 84, 174, 178
Home Improvement 198, 317, 318

Homicide: Life on the Street 254, 313, 314
The Honeymooners 275
Hope, Bob 133, 173, 218-219
Hopkins, Anthony 205
Horne, Lena 124
Horsley, J.C. 23-24
Hot Wheels 76
House (TV show) 258, 315
Houston, Whitney 178
How I Met Your Mother 276
How the Grinch Stole Christmas (book) 101, 237
How the Grinch Stole Christmas (movie) 174, 179
How the Grinch Stole Christmas (special) 66, 236
Huddleston, David 176
Huff 258
Hughes, John 172, 177
Hula hoop 76
Hussey, Olivia 189
Hynde, Chrissie 127, 147
I Love Lucy 267, 275, 317, 318
I Saw Mommy Kissing Santa Claus 135, 161
I Saw Three Ships 109-110
I Think You Should Leave 280, 289
I Want a Dog for Christmas, Charlie Brown 235
I'll Be Home for Christmas (movie) 197
I'll Be Home for Christmas (song) 126
The Ice Harvest 210
In Bruges 189
In Living Color 280
The Inbetweeners 276
Indiana Jones 178
Iovine, Jimmy 151
iPod 77, 86, 274
Iron Man 3 214
Isaac, Oscar 182
It Came Upon A Midnight Clear 116
It Happened on 5th Avenue 204
It's a SpongeBob Christmas 240
It's a Wonderful Life 99, 170-172, 175, 187, 194, 204, 260, 261, 263, 271, 278
It's Always Sunny in Philadelphia 274, 288
It's Beginning to Look a Lot Like Christmas 105, 134-135
It's Christmas Time (and I'm still alive) 154
It's Christmastime Again, Charlie Brown 235
It's Garry Shandling's Show 275
It's the Most Wonderful Time of the Year 139-140

357

Ives, Burl 141, 161
Jack Frost (snowman movie) 179
Jack Frost (horror movie) 190
Jack Frost (TV special) 231
Jackson, Janet 270
Jackson, Mahalia 121
Jackson, Shirley 99
The Jackson Five 120
JAG 313, 314
Jake and the Fatman 314
Jake and the Neverland Pirates 295
The Jamie Foxx Show 276
Jaws 178
Jefferson Starship 223-224
The Jeffersons 275, 317
Jenga 76
Jesus (birth of) 8-11
A Jetson Christmas Carol 297
Jingle All the Way 179
Jingle Bell Rock (song) 138, 210, 249, 277
Jingle Bell Rock (special) 234
Jingle Bells 15, 117-118, 138, 144, 244, 245
Jingle Jangle: A Christmas Journey 194
Jinnah, Mohammed Ali 43, 302
John Denver and the Muppets: A Christmas Together 249
John the Baptist 11
John, Elton 159
Johnson, Edward H. 19-20
Johnson, Magic 220
Jones, Chuck 236
Jones, Grace 220
Jones, K.C. 303
Jones, Norah 128, 158
Jones, Rashida 193
Joseph 9, 55, 64, 226
Joy to the World 110
Joyeux Noel 195
Just Friends 210
Just Shoot Me! 275-276, 319
Juvenalia 8
Kattan, Chris 154
Kaye, Danny 173
Keaton, Diane 211
Keaton, Michael 179, 212
Keats, Ezra Jack 240
Kendrick, Anna 194
Stabler, Kenny 303
Kenan & Kel 319
Kentucky Fried Chicken 43
Key & Peele 280
Key, Keegan-Michael 186, 194

Kidder, Margot 189
The Kid Who Loved Christmas 197
Kidz Bop 108
Kilmister, Lemmy 139
King of the Hill 248
King, Albert 151, 193
King, Bernard 306
King, Regina 182, 240
Kinkade, Thomas 199-200
The Kinks 145-146
Kiss Kiss Bang Bang 214
Kitt, Eartha 233, 303
Klaus 193-194
Knight Rider 255, 313
Knight, Steven 288
Knightley, Keira 186
Kojak 251
Kool & The Gang 148
Korman, Harvey 223
Krampus 46-47
Krampus (movie) 185
Kung Fu Panda Holiday 239
Kung Fu: The Legend Continues 314
Kunis, Mila 185, 197
L.A. Confidential 208
L.A. Law 313, 314
LaBelle, Patti 233
Lady Gaga 220
Landon, Michael 296
Lane, Charles 290
Lang, Gerhard 26
Lansbury, Angela 229
Larry the Cable Guy 185
Las Vegas (TV show) 295
Last Action Hero 214
The Last Boy Scout 213
Last Christmas (movie) 186
Last Christmas (song) 148, 186
Late Night with Conan O'Brien 280
Late Night with David Letterman 279
Lauper, Cyndi 152-153
Laurel, Stan 170, 298
Laverne & Shirley 276, 317
Lawrence, Jennifer 211
Leachman, Cloris 176
Leary, Denis 188, 220
Lee, Brenda 139
Lee, Harper 100, 307
Legend, John 128, 221
The Legends of Tomorrow 316
LEGO 26, 76, 81
Leigh, Janet 173

Lemmon, Jack 187, 207
The Lemon Drop Kid 133, 173
Lennon, John 106, 145
Lennox, Annie 303
The Leprechaun's Christmas Gold 232
Let It Snow! Let It Snow! Let It Snow! 129
Lethal Weapon 177, 213
Letterman, David 280
Levine, Ted 254
Levinson, Barry 206
Lewis, Leona 154
Liebert, Omar 119
The Life and Adventures of Santa Claus (book) 97-98
The Life and Adventures of Santa Claus (special) 233
Lincoln, Andrew 181
Lindo, Delroy 182
The Lion in Winter 205
Lionel Trains 76
Lite-Brite 76
Lithgow, John 176, 186
Little Drummer Boy (song) 124-125, 220, 222
The Little Drummer Boy (TV special) 227
The Little Drummer Boy, Book II 229
Little House on the Prairie 265, 267
Little Rascals 170
Little Richard 220
Little Saint Nick 140
Little Women (book) 32, 95
Little Women (1994 movie) 208
Little Women (2019 movie) 212
Little, Rich 298
Livingston Jr., Henry 92-94
Lois & Clark: The New Adventures of Superman 264-265, 316
Loki 21
Lombardo, Guy 112, 123
Long, Nia 184
The Long Kiss Goodnight 213
Look Who's Talking Now 207
The Looney Tunes Show 292
Los Lobos 156-157
Lost 264
Love Actually 181
Love the Coopers 211-212
Love, Darlene 123, 137, 152, 156, 279
Lovitz, Jon 278, 279
Lowe, Rob 197-198
Lucas, George 82, 223-224
Lucci, Susan 291
Lucky Soul 151

The Lumineers 131
Luther, Martin 18, 121
Lynde, Paul 218
M*A*S*H 256-257
MacColl, Kirsty 149
MacGowan, Shane 149, 303
MacGyver 255
Mackie, Anthony 185, 212
MacLaine, Shirley 187
MacMurray, Fred 187, 202
Mad Men 266
A Madea Christmas 174, 184
Madonna 136, 161
MadTV 280
Magic 8-Ball 78
Magnum, P.I. 254
Mama's Family 318
The Man from U.N.C.L.E. 314
The Man Who Invented Christmas 286
Mandrell, Barbara 302
Mannheim Steamroller 118, 311
Mara, Rooney 211, 212
March of the Wooden Soldiers 170
Marks, Johnny 132, 138-139, 141, 225
Married…with Children 271, 318
Marshmallow World 137
Martin 293, 319
Martin, Andrea 190
Martin, Billy 303
Martin, Dean 106, 123, 128, 129, 218, 219, 303
Martin, Jesse 291
Martin, Steve 188, 279
The Mary Tyler Moore Show 269
Mase 136
Matchbox Cars 76
Matlock 252, 313
Matthau, Walter 207, 231, 289, 297
May, Robert L. 98-99, 132, 225
McCarthy, Joseph 268
McCartney, Paul 160
McCloud 314
McDowall, Roddy 226
McDowell, Ephraim 305
McGavin, Darren 175
McKellar, Danica 192-193
McKinnon, Kate 186
McNichol, Kristy 251
Mean Girls 210
Meet John Doe 203
Meet Me in St. Louis 126, 203
Meggot, John 285
Melrose Place 260, 293, 316

Mendelson, Lee 142, 235
Mendelssohn, Felix 111
Merchant, Stephen 272
Merman, Ethel 231
Merry Christmas (I Don't Want to Fight Tonight) 148
Merry Christmas Baby 129-130
Merry Madagascar 239
Merry Xmas Everybody 145
Metamorphoses 21
Michael, George 147, 148, 186, 303
Mickey Mouse 77, 290, 294
Mickey's Christmas Carol 289
Mike & Molly 319
Mike Tyson Mysteries 248
Miller, T.J. 186
The Mindy Project 276
Miracle on 34th Street 172, 174, 175, 264
Mirren, Helen 186
Mister Magoo's Christmas Carol 234-235, 288, 294
mistletoe 2, 21-23, 189, 215, 251, 310
Mitchell, Joni 144
Mitchum, Robert 174
Mithra 8
Mixed Nuts 189
The Mod Squad 313
Modern Family 274
Money Train 208
Monk 253
The Monkees 113
Monopoly 76
Montalban, Ricardo 128
Montgomery, Elizabeth 269
The Moonglows 137
Moonlighting 252
Moore, Clement Clarke 93-94
Moore, Dudley 175-176
Moore, Michael 300
Moral Orel 248
Moranis, Rick 163
Morgan, Tracy 154
Moss, Elisabeth 242
Most, Donny 133
Mottola, Tommy 151
Mr. Belvedere 295
Mr. Ed 275
Mr. Potato Head 77, 80
Mr. Willowby's Christmas Tree 250
Mulroney, Dermot 188
Munn, Olivia 186
Muppets 108, 162, 174, 248, 249, 287

The Muppet Christmas Carol 287
A Muppet Christmas: Letters to Santa 249
A Muppet Family Christmas 249
Murder, She Wrote 314
Murphy, Charlie 220
Murphy, Eddie 206, 239, 278
Murray, Bill 155, 192-193, 287
Murray, Keith 136
Musgraves, Kacey 156, 221
My Two Dads 318
Myers, Mike 220, 239
The Mynabirds 154
Mystery Science Theater 3000 280
Nabors, Jim 115
Nast, Thomas 30-31, 96
Nathan For You 280
National Lampoon's Christmas Vacation 89, 152, 174, 175, 176-177
The Nativity Story (movie) 174, 182
Nazis 18, 50, 80
NCIS: Los Angeles 313, 314
Nelson, Willie 108, 120, 121, 128, 130, 140, 220-221
NERF 77, 82
Nero 8
Nestor, the Long-Eared Christmas Donkey 230
New Girl 319
The New Scooby-Doo Mysteries 299
The New York Times 50, 182
Newhart 275
Newhart, Bob 219, 270, 275
Newman, Paul 208, 307
Newton, Isaac 302
NewsRadio 275, 317
Newton-John, Olivia 119
The Nice Guys 214
The Night Before 185
Night Court 275
Nintendo 77, 106
The Night the Animals Talked 233
The Nightmare Before Christmas 201, 208
Niven, David 172, 179
Nobody's Fool 208
Noel 198
Noelle 194
Northern Exposure 257, 293
The Nutcracker (ballet) 166-167
The Nutcracker and the Four Realms 174, 186
NYPD Blue 253, 313, 314
The O.C. 260, 316
O Holy Night 115-116

INDEX

O Little Town of Bethlehem 120
O Tannenbaum 109, 142
O. Henry 98
O' Come All Ye Faithful 110-111
O'Hanlon, Virginia 97
O'Hara, Catherine 198
O'Hara, Maureen 172
O'Neal, Shaquille 307
O'Reilly, Bill 300
O'Toole, Peter 200
The Odd Couple 292, 317
Odin 6, 29
The Office (BBC) 272-273
The Office (US) 186, 273, 319
Office Christmas Party 185
Old Man Winter 6
Olive the Other Reindeer 239
Olyphant, Timothy 209
On Her Majesty's Secret Service 205
One Life to Live 299
One Magic Christmas 196
One More Sleep 154
Ono, Yoko 145
Onyx 136
Operation 76
Orange is the New Black 261, 316
Orbison, Roy 140
Oscar the Grouch 2, 249, 292
Osmond, Donny 111, 218
Osmond, Marie 121, 218
Our House 265
Ovid 21
Owen, Reginald 289
pajamas 89-90
Palance, Jack 293
Palminteri, Chazz 198
Pantoliano, Joe 195
Parenthood 267
Parker, Sarah Jessica 188
Parks and Recreation 276, 319
Parson Brown 123
Parton, Dolly 151, 218, 250, 297
The Partridge Family 134
Payne, John 172
Pearce, Guy 287
Peck, Gregory 307
Pentatonix 110
Perry, Tyler 185
Pesci, Joe 177-178
Pet Rock 78
Peter Pan and the Pirates 292
Petty, Tom 150

Peyo 237
Pez 77
Phifer, Mekhi 182
Phoenix (band) 155
Pilgrims 13
Pink Panther 236
Pinocchio's Christmas 234
Pintard, John 29
The PJs 247
Play-Doh 76
Playmobil 77
Playstation 77
Plummer, Christopher 186, 286
PNC Bank 163
Poehler, Amy 193
The Pogues 149-150, 304
Poirot, Hercule 102
Pokémon 78
The Polar Express (book) 103
The Polar Express (movie) 181-182, 183
Police Woman 251-252, 314
Polish Club 151
Pong 77
Pope Julius I 11, 68
Popeye the Sailor 243, 244
Potter, Beatrix 97-98
Pottersville 212
Prancer 176
Prang, Louis 24
Prep and Landing 239
The Preacher's Wife 172, 174, 178
Presley, Elvis 111, 124, 130, 131, 138, 139
Preston, Kelly 179
The Pretenders 127, 147
Pretty Paper 140
Price, Vincent 299
Priestley, Jason 220
Prince Albert 19
The Princess Switch 194
Private Practice 315
Prometheus 211
Providence 315
Psych 254
Psycho 190
Punky Brewster 318
Purple Snowflakes 141
Pushing Daisies 264
Puss N Boots 157
Quantum Leap 289
Queen (band) 152
Queen Elizabeth I 74
Queen Victoria 19

Radio Flyer wagon 77
Raffi 108
Raggedy Ann 76, 234
Raising Hope 319
Rambo 243, 245
The Ramones 148
Rankin, Arthur 225
Rankin/Bass 33, 180, 224-233, 239, 242, 275, 289
Rare Exports: A Christmas Tale 190
Rathbone, Basil 298
Ravenscroft, Thurl 142-143, 236
Rawhide 314
Rawls, Lou 238
Ray, Aldo 204
Razor scooters 77
The Real Ghostbusters 290
Rear Window 173, 237
Red Ryder BB Gun 76, 102, 175
Redbone, Leon 128
Redding, Otis 124, 130
Redford, Robert 205, 307
The Ref 188
Reilly, John C. 211
Remember the Night 202
Remington Steele 314
Reynolds, Ryan 210
Ribbons and Bows 156
Richter, Andy 220, 273
Rick and Morty 248
Henderson, Ricky 304
River 144
Robin and the 7 Hoods 204
Robot Chicken 248, 293
Rock 'Em Sock 'Em Robots 77
Rock, Chris 193
Rockefeller Center 20, 180, 204
Rockin' Around the Christmas Tree 139
Rockwell, Norman 15, 33
Rocky IV 206
Rogan, Seth 185
Romeo and Juliet 189, 283
Roosevelt, Eleanor 50
The Ronettes 131, 134, 135
Roseanne 318
Roswell 316
A Royal Christmas 192
The Royal Tenenbaums 208
Rubik's Cube 76, 84
Rubenstein, Helena 302
Rudolph the Red-Nosed Reindeer (book) 98-99, 132

Rudolph the Red-Nosed Reindeer (song) 43, 132-133, 134, 139, 140. 142
Rudolph the Red-Nosed Reindeer (special) 33, 225-226, 227, 230, 231, 232, 234, 235, 240, 293
Rudolph, Maya 193
Rudolph's Shiny New Year 230
Run-DMC 149-150
Run Rudolph Run 138-139
Russell, Kurt 193
Russell, Nipsey 219
Ryan, Meg 209
S.W.A.T. 254
Sabrina: The Animated Series 296
Sabrina the Teenage Witch 192, 319
Sadat, Anwar 302
Sahloff, Willard 225
Saint Francis of Assisi 52, 108
Saint, Eva Marie 292
Salt-N-Pepa 136
Sanders, Colonel 43
Sandler, Adam 115, 279
Sanford and Son 289
Santa and the Three Bears 233
Santa Baby 160
Santa Claus (silent film) 169-170
Santa Claus Conquers the Martians 195, 280
Santa Claus Go Straight to the Ghetto 143-144
Santa Claus is Back in Town 138
Santa Claus is Comin' to Town (song) 122-123
Santa Claus is Coming to Town (special) 225, 227-228, 233
Santa Claus Wants Some Lovin' 151, 193
Santa Claus: The Movie 175-176
The Santa Clause 178, 183
The Santa Clause 2 174, 179
The Santa Clause 3: The Escape Clause 182
Santa With Muscles 197
Santa, Baby! 233
Sanz, Horatio 153
Saperstein, Henry 235
Sarandon, Susan 185, 198
Saturday Night Live 115, 153, 180, 278-279, 289, 290, 292
Saturn 6-7, 29
Saturnalia 6-7
Savalas, Telly 251
Saved by the Bell 317, 318
Saving Christmas 199
Schitt's Creek 276
Schubert, Franz 114
Schulz, Charles 142, 235

INDEX

Schwartzman, Jason 193
Schwarzenegger, Arnold 170, 179
Scott, Adam 185
Scott, George C. 288
Scrabble 76
Scrooged 174, 287
Scrubs 276
SCTV 163, 190
Sea Monkeys 78, 80
Sealab 2021 248
Sedaris, David 103
Seibold, J. Otto 239
Seinfeld 272, 319
Sellers, Peter 292
Seneca the Younger 7
Serendipity 209
Serling, Rod 291, 302
Sesame Street 85, 248, 249, 292
A Sesame Street Carol 292
Seuss, Dr. 101, 142-143, 179, 186, 186, 236
Seymour, Jane 294
Shakespeare, William 32, 283
Shalhoub, Tony 253-254
Shannon, Michael 185, 212
Sharon Jones & the Dap-Kings 107, 133, 156
Shatner, William 220, 299
Shaw, Robert 292
Shepherd, Cybill 252
Shepherd, Jean 101-102, 174-175
Sherlock 256
Sherlock Holmes 96, 258, 298, 300
Shields, Brooke 218
The Shop Around the Corner 202, 209
Short, Martin 182
Shrek the Halls 239
Sia 156
Sigillaria 8
Silent Night 42, 112-113
Silent Night, Deadly Night 190-191
Silly Putty 78
Silver Bells 133, 173
Silver Linings Playbook 211
Silver Spoons 276-277, 317, 318
Silverstein, Shel 102
Sim, Alastair 286-287, 294
Simon (game) 77, 83
Simon, Carly 111
The Simpsons 239, 245-246, 288
Sinatra, Frank 106, 114, 116, 123, 126, 137, 151
Siskel, Gene 190
Six Feet Under 266

The Six Million Dollar Man 291, 316
Skid Row 118
Slade 145
Sleepless in Seattle 207
Sleigh Ride 131-132
Slinky 78, 79, 241
Smallville 264, 299, 316
Smigel, Robert 279
Smurfs 77, 237-238, 241, 294
The Smurfs' Christmas Special 237-238
The Smurfs: A Christmas Carol 295
Snow Miser 229
Snowman (song) 156
The Snowman (animated special) 238
The Snowy Day 240
Solo, Han 223
Someday at Christmas 115, 142, 143
The Sonics 151
The Sopranos 265-266
South Park 247
Space Ghost Coast to Coast 248
Spacek, Sissy 303
Spacey, Kevin 183, 188
Spall, Rafe 263-264
Spandau Ballet 148
Spector, Phil 130, 131, 132, 134, 135, 151, 207
Spelling, Tori 299
The Spice Girls 57, 131
Spielberg, Steven 263, 307
Spin City 273, 319
The Spirit of Christmas 152
SpongeBob Squarepants 89, 239-240, 244
The Spooktacular Adventures of Casper 296
Spotlight 212
Square Pegs 318
St. Elsewhere 315
St. Nicholas 27-31
St. Paul & The Broken Bones 137
Stabler, Kenny 302
Stanton, Harry Dean 196
Stanwyck, Barbara 170
Staples, Mavis 152
The Star 174, 186
Star Trek Generations 208
Star Trek: The Next Generation 297
Star Wars figures 77, 82-83
The Star Wars Holiday Special 223-224
Starr, Kay 133
Starr, Ringo 123, 305
Starsky and Hutch 251, 313, 314
Steenburgen, Mary 183, 196
Step Brothers 211

363

Step Into Christmas 159
Stepmom 209
Stern, Daniel 177
Stevens, Dan 286
Stevens, Sufjan 113
Stewart, Jimmy 172-173, 204
Stewart, Jon 222
Stewart, Kristin 194
Stewart, Patrick 288
Sting (singer) 148
The Sting (movie) 307
The Stingiest Man in Town 231, 289, 297
Straight No Chaser 120
Styne, Jule 129, 137, 235
sugarplums 73
The Suite Life on Deck 299
Sullivan, Margaret 202
Sundblom, Haddon H. 31
Supergirl 316
Supernatural 316
Superstore 319
The Sure Thing 206
Surviving Christmas 198
Swaggart, Jimmy 116, 120, 121
Swank, Hilary 260
Swayze, Patrick 291
sweaters, ugly 88-89
Swingers (movie) 180
T.J. Hooker 254, 314
Tales from the Crypt 263
Tales from the Darkside 264
Tangerine 211
Tarantino, Quentin 209, 307
Tarloff, Frank 268
Taxi 270-271
Tchaikovsky, Pyotr Ilyich 166-167, 186
Ted Lasso 275
teddy bear 76, 78
Teddy Ruxpin 77, 84
Teenage Mutant Ninja Turtles 77, 243
Tell Your Mama 157
Temple, Shirley 76, 79, 202
Tesh, John 122
That '70s Show 319
That Girl 270
The Thin Man 202
Thirtysomething 265
This Christmas 182-183
Thomas, Dylan 100
Thomas and Friends 299
Thomas Kinkade's Christmas Cottage 198-199
Thomas, Danny 226

Thomas, Dave 162, 220
Thomas, Jonathan Taylor 197
Thompson, Emma 181, 186
Thor: The Dark World 185
Thornton, Billy Bob 181
Three Days of the Condor 205
Three Kings 9-10, 229
Three's Company 275
Tim and Eric Awesome Show, Great Job! 221, 281
Tiny Tim (singer) 125
To Kill a Mockingbird 307
Tokyo Godfathers 194
Tolkien, J.R.R. 102-103
Tomei, Marisa 211
Tonka truck 76
Topham, Edward 285
Torme, Mel 129, 221-222
Toy Story That Time Forgot 239
The Tracey Ullman Show 246
Trading Places 206
Transformers 77
Trapper John, M.D. 315
Travolta, John 119
Tubb, Ernest 131
turkey 41, 43, 58, 61, 66, 67, 68
Turner, Ike 130
Turner, Ted 175
Turner, Tina 130
Twain, Mark 95-96, 206, 309
'Twas the Night Before Christmas (poem) 15, 30, 93, 244, 250
Twas the Night Before Christmas (special) 228
Twelve Days of Christmas 161-165
The Twilight Zone 263, 302
Twisted Sister 127
Twister 76, 82
Tyler, the Creator 143
Tyson, Cicely 292
Unaccompanied Minors 189
Underneath the Tree 154
Uno 76, 82
Up on the Housetop (song) 119-120
Up on the Housetop (special) 234
Ustinov, Peter 204
V: The Series 316
The Vampire Diaries 316
Van Allsburg, Chris 103, 181-182
Vance, Courtney B. 179
Vandross, Luther 218
Varney, Jim 176
Vaughn, Vince 183

Vega$ 313
Veep 274-275
VeggieTales 186, 242-243
The Velveteen Rabbit 98
The Venture Bros. 293
Vera-Ellen 173
Vernon, Jackie 226-227, 229
A Very Harold & Kumar Christmas 174, 184
A Very Merry Cricket 233
A Very Murray Christmas 155, 192-193
Vigoda, Abe 176
Vince Guaraldi Trio 109, 125, 142
Voight, Jon 300
Voyagers! 264
Wahlberg, Mark 186
The Waitresses 147
Walker, Paul 198
Walker, Texas Ranger 314
Wallach, Eli 211
Walsh, Vivian 239
The Waltons 265
Waltz, Christoph 307
Waltz of the Flowers 168
Washington, Denzel 179
Washington, George 68, 304
Wayans, Damon 280
We Got It Made 317
We Three Kings 118
We Wish You A Merry Christmas 71, 108-109
We're No Angels 204
Webster 318
Weezer 111
Weisz, Rachel 183
Welcome Back, Kotter 275, 317
Welk, Lawrence 218
West, Kanye 153
The West Wing 267
What Christmas Means to Me 143
What's Happening!! 275
What's New, Scooby-Doo? 244
Whiffle Ball 76
While You Were Sleeping 208
White, Gleeson 23
White Christmas (movie) 173, 188
White Christmas (song) 15, 43, 58, 124-125, 127, 131, 137, 151, 203, 229
Whitaker, Forest 194
Wiig, Kristen 278
William the Conqueror 304
Williams, Andy 88, 126, 140, 218, 219
Williams, Esther 128
Williams, John 178

Williams, Margery 98
Williams, Robin 198
Williams, Vanessa 233
Willis, Bruce 214, 252
Willy Wonka 172
Wilson, Owen 209
Window on Main Street 267
Winehouse, Amy 135
Winfrey, Oprah 220
Wings 271, 319
Winkler, Henry 294
Winnie the Pooh and Christmas Too 238-239
Winslet, Kate 210-211, 294
Winter Wonderland 123
Winters, Jonathan 218, 242
The Wire 253, 313
A Wish for Wings That Work 234
A Wish That Changed Christmas 234
Witherspoon, Reese 183
WKRP in Cincinnati 275, 290
Wonder, Stevie 114-115, 135, 141, 142, 143, 151
Wonder Woman 212, 265, 297, 316
The Wonder Years 259, 315
Wonderful Christmastime 160
Wood, Natalie 172
Woods, James 300
Woodward, Edward 252
wreaths 20-21
Wu Tang Clan 89, 153
WW84 212
The X-Files 264, 316
Xbox 77
Xena: Warrior Princess 296, 316
The Year Without a Santa Claus 229
Yes, Virginia, There Is a Santa Claus 97
yo-yo 76, 78-79
Yogi Bear 234, 237
Yogi's First Christmas 237
York, Michael 299
You're a Mean One, Mr. Grinch 142-143
You've Got Mail 209
Young, Paul 148
The Young and the Restless 299
Yuen, Steven 186
Yukon Cornelius 141, 226
Yule 4-6
Yule Log 281
Zat You, Santa Claus 136
Zemeckis, Robert 181-182, 287
Ziggy's Gift 234
Zucker, David 300
Zwarte Piet 46, 47-48

Made in the USA
Coppell, TX
21 December 2021

69784424R00203